Teso in Transformation

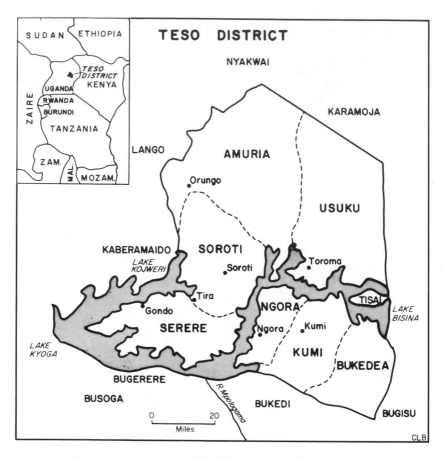

Teso District

Teso in Transformation

The Political Economy of Peasant and
Class in Eastern Africa

Joan Vincent

University of California Press

Berkeley / Los Angeles / London

University of California Press
Berkeley and Los Angeles, California

University of California Press, Ltd.
London, England

Printed in the United States of America

1 2 3 4 5 6 7 8 9

Library of Congress Cataloging in Publication Data

Vincent, Joan.
　　Teso in transformation.

　　Bibliography: p.
　　Includes index.
　　1. Teso, Uganda—Economic conditions.　2. Peasantry—
Uganda—Teso—History.　3. Social classes—Uganda—
Teso—History.　4. Great Britain—Colonies—Africa—
History.　I. Title.
HC870.Z7T478　　330.9676'1　　80-28813
ISBN 0-520-04163-1

Contents

Figures and Tables

Figures

Tables

Acknowledgments

Between 1966 and 1970 archival research was carried out at District Headquarters in Soroti; among the Secretariat Archives in Entebbe; at Kawanda Research Station (Department of Agriculture) in Kampala; at Serere Experimental Research Station in Teso; and at the East African Institute of Social and Economic Research in Kampala. Manuscript sources in the Africana section of Makerere University College and the University of Nairobi were also used. Between 1976 and 1978 further archival research was carried out in England at the Colonial Record Office; Rhodes House, Oxford; the Cambridge University Library; the Royal Commonwealth Society; the Royal Geographical Society; the Church Missionary Society; and St. Joseph's College, Mill Hill, London. I thank the librarians and archivists at all these institutions for their assistance.

At Makerere University College and the East African Institute of Social and Economic Research, where my fellowship was funded by a grant from the Ministry of Overseas Development of the United Kingdom, I received advice and help, as well as stimulation, from many colleagues in several departments. I would especially like to thank Lois Anderson (who first introduced me to Teso), Raymond Apthorpe, Anne Sharman Bader, Edward Brett, Beverley Brock Gartrell, James S. Coleman, Martin Doornbos, Joseph Gugler, N. Q. King, Brian Langlands, Colin Leys and M. Crawford Young.

In Teso, I am in considerable debt to Washington Ekwaru, who acted as my research assistant in Serere County and who, as a friend, introduced me to the people of Ogera. To them and to the people of Gondo, who were my neighbors in 1966–67, I wish to dedicate this study in small repayment for their kindness. Mr. Joseph Wabwire, of Serere, was indefatigable in traveling with me throughout the district; and along with Frederick C. Odaet and Vincent Mu-

viii *Acknowledgments*

sana, he did much to further my research. I must acknowledge, too, the assistance of F. Bijurenda, district commissioner of Teso during much of my stay; of the several district officers and members of the district council with whom I worked; and of the many eminent leaders of Teso affairs, past and present, who, in their homes, provided both hospitality and enlightenment.

The manuscript for this book traveled with me to the three continents whose interdependencies underpin its thesis. Begun at the Institute of Development Studies at Sussex University in England during a sabbatical leave from Barnard College in 1976 and continued in the Department of Anthropology at the University of Cape Town in South Africa in 1979, it was completed at Barnard College in New York in May 1980. Secretarial and library staff at all these institutions were most helpful and colleagues most supportive. Above all, however, I must express appreciation of the work of Elizabeth Collins (of the English Department at Barnard College), who has suffered with me for three years through several library searches, deciphering my handwriting and providing seemingly endless typewritten drafts. Christopher Brest, of the Geography Department of Columbia University, drew the maps.

To friends, students, colleagues at Columbia University—many of whom are responsible for this work having taken so long to complete—I would express my appreciation for the excitement of their ideas and my enjoyment of the rich diversions, intellectual and other, that they have provided over the years. To mention a few is to neglect many; but may the names of those who read the manuscript in an earlier draft—George Bond, Shirley Charles, Ashraf Ghani, Clive Kessler, Gerry Sider, Brian Sheehan, Ida Susser, and Sharifa Zawawi—stand for many. I should also like to thank David Parkin and E. A. Brett, as well as the anonymous readers of the University of California Press, for their comments. I am grateful to Meryl Lanning for her careful copy editing of the manuscript. Several of the ideas in this book were triggered by exchanges with members of what has become, in my eyes, a historic City University of New York Graduate Seminar on Western Europe in 1977–78. To Jane Schneider, its organizer, and to its members I wish to express gratitude.

Finally, but not minimally, I gratefully acknowledge financial assistance from the trustees and administration of Barnard College of Columbia University.

A Note on Orthography

In the writing of proper names I have aimed at consistency in the use of modern orthography. This means, e.g., that the Luganda names Bunyoro, Buganda, Busoga etc. are used rather than the Swahili Unyoro, Uganda, Usoga of the nineteenth century, except when original sources are quoted. The turn of the century region of Bukeddi is distinguished from the modern district of Bukedi. Prior to 1912, I write of "the Teso region" and after that date of Teso district. The people of Teso were first called Bakeddi; they are now called Iteso. Their language is Ateso. I have adopted the spelling Kakungulu rather than the Kakunguru of some authors simply because this is how he himself signed letters now in the Teso district archives. On the other hand, the modern Soroti is used, not Soloti.

Introduction

There is nothing in the present but the past.
Bergson

It might seem an outrageous demand to make on any reader that he be interested in a somewhat obscure sector of a small Third World country at the opening of this century. Both historians and anthropologists must be strange breeds to think anyone should wish to hear of events that occurred eighty years ago, or of social structures that exist in backward, out-of-the-way corners of the world. And they would be strange breeds indeed, if that were all such studies set out to be.

Anyone who carries out research into past or alien cultures must, in some odd way, believe that what he is doing is important, even worthwhile. Today, it is, perhaps, less idiosyncratic than it used to be to express a conviction that the more obscure portions of the world are anything but remote from the heartland of Europe and North America. The world of the imperial frontier has in its turn begun to impinge upon the daily economies of Western households, and grand theory in the social sciences now explicitly addresses itself to world economic systems.

Although the man in the street would not then have heard of Teso in eastern Uganda, it was between the years 1898 and 1963 an integral part of the political economy of the United Kingdom. Before that, American commerce—along with that of Portugal, Oman, India, Britain, France, and Brazil—brought East Africa into the modern world system. New England merchants, especially those of Salem, Massachusetts, held a virtual monopoly of the trade of the Zanzibar sultanate by the mid-ninteenth century. Ivory, hides, cloves, cowries, sesame, pepper, coconut oil, and gum copal were traded for muskets, gunpowder, hardware, cotton goods, brandy, beads, English cottons, brass wire, and china. The manufacturing industry of New England grew on its African trade. So important was the supply of East African ivory to the United States—ivory used for billiard balls, piano keys, fans, and ornaments—that, when warfare in Africa interrupted its supply, Connecticut factories were closed down and people thrown out of work.[1]

Although the American flag was never hoisted over African soil as a symbol of sovereignty, New England's trade in Africa created capital that contributed in the nineteenth century to the opening up and development of the United States.[2] And in Great Britain and Ireland the establishment of protectorates and colonial territories in East Africa was a very real response to the industrial, social and labor problems of the British economic situation following upon the

1. Ernest D. Moore, *Ivory, Scourge of Africa* (1931), pp. 116–117; for an account of the operations of one Connecticut ivory-working company in East Africa, see esp. pp. 50, 172, 234–235. The connections between the ivory trade and the import of European arms is made explicit, and anecdotes of elephant hunters relate to, among others, Capt. Frederick Lugard and W. D. M. Bell in Uganda. Moore notes: "The Yankee ivory-cutters of Deep River and Ivoryton, Connecticut, and a third American company located in Buffalo together manufacture the keyboards for practically all the pianos made in this country, Canada, and Australia, and are the largest individual users of ivory in the world. The demand of these three factories influences almost to a dominating degree the price of ivory even in the remotest depths of Africa." For an attempt to view such international trade from the African perspective, see Edward A. Alpers, *Ivory and Slaves* (1975b), pp. xvi–xvii, 31, 201–203, 247, 252–253, 264–267. See also R. W. Beachey, "The Arms Trade in East Africa in the Late Nineteenth Century" (1962) and "The East African Ivory Trade in the Nineteenth Century" (1967a).

2. Clarence Clendenen, Robert O. Collins and Peter J. Duignan, *Americans in Africa, 1865–1900* (1966), p. 21.

American Civil War.[3] Uganda, then, and Teso within it, numbers among those regions of the world that helped make the European and American industrial systems work.

Structurally, the pattern of Third World development is remarkably homogeneous. The universe grows smaller as international airports scattered throughout the globe become more and more indistinguishable from one another, while the men and women who represent their people in the assembly halls of the United Nations and the international congress halls grow less and less like those they represent. In Third World nations, as in the West, the emergence of class comes to dominate history.

As scholars—historians, political scientists, and economists among them—come to share an interest in peasant economies, feudalism, and the emergence of capitalism they recognize that the time has come to treat African and European experience alike in categories derived from world history, "rather than to squeeze world history into Western European categories."[4] Anthropologists have a particular part to play; there are several reasons for this, but two are outstanding. First, an anthropologist, like a Marxist, abhors intellectual compartmentalization. He is concerned with the unwinding veil of social fabric within which are interwoven the life trajectories of innumerable individuals. Second, unique to the anthropologist in the interdisciplinary (or unidisciplinary) endeavor, is the fieldwork experience; living among the people with whom one works, learning their language, staying around long enough to learn why they might at first have lied to the stranger who entered their midst from academia. And the ultimate credo of the historical anthropologist is that "the bulk of what I have eventually seen (or thought I have seen) in the broad sweep of social history I have seen (or thought I have seen) first in the narrow confines of country towns and peasant villages."[5] Anthropologists have long asserted that their parochial analyses have more than parochial significance,

3. See, e.g., Gareth S. Jones, *Outcast London* (1971), pp. 10–16, and Bernard Semmel, *Imperialism and Social Reform, 1895–1914* (1960), esp. pp. 13–52.

4. J. F. Ade Ajayi, "The Continuity of African Institutions under Colonialism," in Terence O. Ranger (ed.), *Aspects of Central African History* (London, 1968), p. 197.

5. Clifford Geertz, *Islam Observed* (1968), p. x.

and statements of the world system in operation are of long standing in the anthropological study of Africa. Reaching their apogee, perhaps, in the 1930s, Godfrey Wilson gave them expression when describing the inhabitants of an African territory as

> members of a huge worldwide community . . . their lives . . . bound up at every point with the events of its history . . . Their standard of living now depends on economic conditions in Europe, Asia and America to which continents their labour has become essential. Their political development is largely decided in the Colonial Office and on the battlefields of Europe, while hundreds of their one-time separate tribes now share a single destiny. They have entered a heterogeneous world stratified into classes and divided into states, and so find themselves suddenly transformed into the peasants and unskilled workers of a nascent nation state.[6]

In the 1940s and 1950s, attention, for the most part, turned away away from world issues, but the development decade of the sixties brought, in harness, a renewed concern with economic anthropology and social change. At the same time, historians began to enter Africa in considerable numbers. Today Edward Alpers may with confidence assert the necessity of placing African history within the context of the historical roots of underdevelopment in Africa, "an argument which is beginning to gain a foothold among students of Africa and does not bear repeating here, except as it becomes possible to do so within the context of the evidence presented in the study that follows."[7]

The argument that not colonialism but international capitalism (or, as others would call it, economic imperialism) provides the framework for a local study goes back a long way. With East Africa specifically in mind, Leonard Woolf and Sydney A. Haldane (Lord Olivier) argued the case most forcibly in the 1920s. This Teso study study could then be seen as further documentation of a case well made. It is, indeed, in part concerned with the dynamics of a particular situation, but it is also of generic interest to those who are concerned with how conditions came to be as they are today in the Third World. The study attempts to go further, first in delineating

6. Godfrey Wilson, *An Essay on the Economics of Detribalisation in Northern Rhodesia* (1941), p. 12.
7. Alpers (1975b), pp. xvi–xvii.

how a viable political and economic unit was crafted out of the East
African landscape to form a colonial district—the making of Teso
District—and second in tracing the formation of conflicting interests and social groups within the new political dependency: the
making of a peasantry, a rural proletariat, a nascent bourgeois class.

The Framework of the Study

The study clearly has theoretical underpinnings that must be
identified at the outset. Three bodies of writing contribute to this
analysis of eastern Uganda between 1890 and 1927. The first relates
specifically to the agrarian nature of Teso society; the second to its
incorporation within the British empire; and the third to its encap-
sulation within a global capitalist economy. The study attempts to
spell out the interconnectedness of these three interests, arguing that
the nineteenth century development of modern Europe rests upon
the productive forces of tropical countries.

An anthropological view of the modern world system requires
that it be placed, even in its earliest formative stage, within the context of production and exchange in other than European societies,
specifically those in Africa and colonial South America (whose gold
and silver flooded the Spanish market), the Islamic world (whose
agriculture transformed European commodity production), and the
Orient (whose trade in spices made possible the navigational feats
of the sixteenth century). Production in all these areas was generated in state systems a considerable time before the emergence of the
state in Europe itself.

Given then the consolidation of the modern world system in the
long sixteenth century, it is critical to note, as does Immanuel Wallerstein, that it is not the European states that provide its dynamism,
but commercial, financial, and industrial interests that overflow the
boundaries of states. By the time one is viewing the advent of
capitalist interests in Uganda, as elsewhere in Africa, it is clear that
joint stock companies on the one hand and missionary interests on
the other precede Britain's imperial entry on the scene. Indeed, as in
the case study that follows, the three interests are seen to be at
various times in conflict with one another. When coherence occurs
it often involves only fractions within each. That coherence occurs
at all can be attributed to the bedrock conflict between capitalism

and the mercantile (here, Islamic) system that historically preceded it. The development of capitalism in Teso was a phenomenon born of a relationship between a tropical region and competing economic systems.

A bias toward studying production and conflict is derived from a reading of eighteenth-century political economy—especially in its Scottish and English varieties—and the subsequent nineteenth-century contributions of Marx, Engels, Luxemburg, and Lenin. It emerges as partially derivative of, and partially antagonistic toward the twentieth-century studies of the Annales school in France; the North and Latin American writings of Paul A. Baran, Andre Gunder Frank, and Fernando H. Cardoso; the European dimension of Immanuel Wallerstein and his critics (particularly Robert Brenner, Sidney Mintz, and Jane Schneider); and, finally, the African perspective of Samir Amin. As the world economy itself has developed, so each generation of scholarship has added its particular veneer; and so, within this framework, this case study of Teso addresses the transformation of an African savanna region as it is encapsulated within the global economy.

The particulars of Teso's incorporation involved the creation of a colonial dependency: the Uganda Protectorate. It is anachronistic to label, as others have done, the period between 1890 and 1966 (the date of Uganda's independence) as a period of state formation. One of the contentions of this study only partly documented is that the development of capitalism in colonial Uganda can only be analyzed within the context of imperial possessions elsewhere and, especially, within the context of Britain's relationship with Kenya. The creation of a peasantry in Uganda was structured upon the establishment of viable capitalist farming in the Kenya highlands.

This view of imperialism and the management of colonial estates in Africa derives primarily from the writings of Leonard Woolf, Sydney Olivier, and Ida Greaves. The theoretical models of their contemporaries, Hobson and Lenin, critically underlie the writings of our contemporaries; and here, with specific reference to Africa, I have drawn upon the analyses of Terence Ranger, Harold Wolpe, John Saul, Edward A. Brett, and Colin Leys, as well as upon the recent work of African historians of the "development of underdevelopment" in colonial territories. This book documents the destructuring of indigenous production systems, the realigning of market systems, and the deleterious results of compulsory monocrop cultivation (in this case, cotton) for a metropolitan market. Particular interest can be derived from the Teso case in that this systemic analysis is related to the question of the emergence of class interests.

Beyond, however, a concern with the capitalist cosmopolitical economy and imperialism, this study is addressed to an analysis of the agrarian question in savanna Africa. The years between 1890 and 1927 witnessed the transformation of a society (or societies) of pastoralists and (largely) subsistence agriculturalists into a society of peasant small-holders and wage laborers. They witnessed the growth of towns, the building of roads, the introduction of corvée labor, military conscription, famine, and the spread of a universal religion. Though I do not wish to suggest timeless comparisons—the concomitant analysis of monopoly capitalism and colonial conquest should put such fears at rest—the theoretical underpinnings for the analysis of agrarian change in Teso rest in European social and economic history and in European ethnography. The work of Bernard H. Slicher van Bath, Lenin, A. Chayanov, Teodor Shanin, Eric Wolf, Eric Hobsbawm, and Edward Thompson—along with experience of research into the nineteenth-century history of an Irish county—led me to examine the Teso data for wandering men, the presence of enclosures, the changing position of women, artisans, the role of epidemics, and related phenomena.

Within anthropology, an approach such as this to field data reflects a trend. It also throws down a gauntlet. The trend is apparent in a passage beyond the methodological and theoretical concern with anthropology and history—a concern that has been most marked since the development decade of the 1960s when anthropologists began to confront the "problem" of social change. This study contends, following Lucy Mair, that continuity (reproduction), not change, requires explanation. Further, however (and, I suspect, unlike Lucy Mair), this study contends that the divorce of anthropology from history is both unreal and deleterious. In this respect, the gauntlet is flung down—not at the feet of social anthropologists (for have not Isaac Schapera, Sir Edward E. Evans-Pritchard, Ioan Lewis, and Victor Turner been writing history all the time?) but at the feet of those cultural anthropologists who attach no theoretical or substantive importance to the development of capitalism, and who trace the roots of their contemporary societies back into the archaeological past. Hobsbawm says it best in his denial of "the crude and non-historical dichotomy between 'traditional' and 'modern' society. History," he observes,

> does not consist of a single step. Traditional societies are not static and unchanging, exempt from historical change and evolution, nor is there a single model of "modernisation" which determines their transformation. But to reject the crudities of some social sciences should not lead us to underestimate the profundity, and the qualitative difference from earlier developments, of the transformation which, for most countries, resulted from the triumph of industrial capitalism.[8]

At issue is a choice between a conservative, gradualistic, model of adaptive change and one that delineates thresholds and recognizes revolutions and, inevitably, the reality of conflict without resolution. Within anthropology, explanations of response to change have taken three forms. In the first (and within the present study this nineteenth-century view is well reflected in the attitudes of the British to the African, and the Baganda to the Iteso), racial characteristics were believed to have explanatory value. In the second (and this is still the dominant mode in anthropology), cultural explanations are proffered. An emphasis on cultures places a value on customs, fosters a heuristic bias toward the isolation of systems and the static, and tends to be conservative.

A third mode of explanation is process-theory. The clearest statement of its premises has been made, perhaps, by Victor Turner: "as between societies, and often in different situations in a single society . . . components are varyingly clustered and separated. Clues to their clusterings and segregations may be found if societies are analyzed in terms of process-theory."[9] Thus one might perceive, in the world around us, more similarities between an urban center in Uganda and one in, say, Brazil, than between urban Soroti or Kampala and the rural settlements of Teso or Buganda. Or to take a more general case, there are more similarities between fishing communities in Labrador, Brazil, and Portugal than there are between those communities and upcountry villages even within the same cultures within the same societies. What, then, *are* the components? What process are we addressing? Clearly, that of Karl Polanyi's

8. Eric J. Hobsbawm, "Peasants and Politics" (1973), p. 4.
9. Victor W. Turner, "Witchcraft and Sorcery" (1964), p. 324.

Great Transformation, the development of capitalism and the global system. This is not new within anthropology: the Puerto Rico research project of the 1950s and (especially) the work of Eric Wolf and Sidney Mintz then and now was about this very thing.

The Argument

Britain's involvement in a second wave of imperial ventures followed upon the American Civil War and, particularly, upon her loss of Southern cotton, upon which her industrial strength depended. After a generation in which interests in Europe funded geographical and missionary expeditions into the African interior, a joint stock company—the Imperial British East Africa Company—entered the kingdom of Buganda on the northern shores of Lake Victoria close to the source of the Nile. The Uganda Protectorate that evolved was shaped by the military weakness of the initial British forces; their dependence upon the Buganda state or, more particularly, upon war lords and factions within it; and, subsequently, by the converging presence of other European powers—French, Belgian, and German —in the region (see Chapter One).

The Protectorate's expansion from the western lacustrine kingdoms across the Nile to the east was apparently due to a desire to tap the food resources of that region, since the caravans entering from the south, epidemics, and three decades of war had depleted the resources of the capital and its environs. The moving economic frontier thus extended to Bukeddi, the "land of the naked ones" or "the east"—capitalizing upon the freebooting of Semei Kakungulu, a Muganda warlord who had been instrumental in colonial conquest. By this time it had become apparent that the Buganda kingdom with its entrenched aristocracy was not proving the most fruitful ground for the controlled production of cotton.

The Teso region at this time lay within an economic sphere that linked Bunyoro in the west to the ivory and arms trade of the coastal caravans. Largely producing for local markets, Teso's cultivators and pastoralists variously participated in three distinctive political economies. In the southwest, peninsular Serere lay within the Lake Kyoga trade orbit on the periphery of the so-called Bantu kingdoms. The northern Teso region—north of Lake Bisina—was involved in the ivory trade, while the three southern counties evolved around the breadbasket of Bukedea. Political and military leadership throughout the region was highly amorphous, although, as the end of the nineteenth century and colonial domination approached, larger military confederacies arose in the north and south. The pacification of the region was achieved between 1907 and 1915, first by Kakungulu in the south and finally by the British administration in the north (Chapters Two to Four).

Teso district was created in 1912, after five years in which Iteso and missionary enterprise negotiated working arrangements to their mutual benefit. The extent to which mission Christianity provided the ideology of capitalism permits the characterization of this period as one of hegemony and secondary pacification (Chapter Five).

The establishment of colonial rule in Teso saw the introduction of taxes; the growth of an ethnically heterogeneous and racially administered population; the creation of a hierarchy of civil service chiefs (partly out of the structure of indigenous leadership and Baganda overrule); mission education; and the growth of a small middle sector in the economy. Most strikingly, however, the censuses that colonial bureaucracy required of its cotton-producing society revealed that over 20 percent of the society was made up of laboring men—a rural proletariat, apparently, *not* a peasantry in the making (Chapter Six).

The policies and practices of British administration in Teso largely revolved around the production of cotton for the imperial market. The indigenous economy was destructured, and preexisting regional variations took on the form of uneven development within the new, closely administered district—to the great advantage of its southern counties. As the development decade (1908–1917) proceeded, the growth of small towns and mission stations expanded into other regions, taxes were collected effectively, and canals and roads were constructed on a massive scale to provide an infrastructure for a district whose cotton export economy was critical for the Protectorate. The intensity of cotton production was matched only by the severity of the famine, accompanied by plague and epidemics, with which the development decade ended (Chapter Seven).

The so-called peasant cultivation of Uganda can be reanalyzed as one in which small-holders were workers in an agricultural system controlled by urban and commercial interests. Although there was during this period some alienation of land, for the most part household production continued to be the main feature of the Teso economy. New land was available for colonization, and pastoral activities remained unintegrated into the cotton economy. The most drastic change for the Teso cultivator was the inculcation of his immobility and what might be termed the production of passivity. Excluded from the marketing process through an insistence on technical controls of the quality of the product, the Iteso peasant remained poor. "The statistical correlation between cotton growing and poverty is startling"[10] (Chapter Eight).

It was, therefore, not the introduction of a cash crop that brought Teso into the cosmopolitical economy of the twentieth century, but the articulation of its labor. The process required the creation of a rural proletariat, and this was realized through forced labor for the government, the mass mobilization required for the construction industry, porterage, and military service, as well as through voluntary labor for private enterprises, ginneries, mission stations, and growing commercial centers. The labor movement was clearly in conflict with the need to maintain a stable cotton-producing peasantry, and the costs of the contradiction were borne by other than laboring men—women, children, and the aged. The population declined (Chapter Nine).

The question of whether nascent class had appeared in Teso by 1927 is addressed in the concluding chapter. The changed material condition of the salariat (mainly the chiefly class), its aggressiveness in defense of its privileges and power, and its self-consciousness had to be set beside the lack of self-consciousness of the mass of the people. Such conflicts as occurred took an individualistic or a religious form. What emerged, rather, during this period, was a confrontation between the administration and the chiefs over what appeared to be the control and marketing of the cotton crop. What was more critically at issue, however, was the command of labor, the commodity upon which rested both class aggrandizement and colonial efficiency. The conflict was resolved by a purging of the chiefs. The state of no-classness that Hobsbawm sees as a precapitalist societal condition is here viewed as a global, nonstate, colonial condition—that of transnational capitalism (Chapter Ten).

10. Erich W. Zimmerman, *World Resources and Industries* (1972), p. 326.

The Teso model is of widespread applicability to that portion of the Third World where capitalist and colonial penetration did not encounter indigenous political economies honed on class.

Field Research

Research in the field was carried out in 1966–67 and again in 1970 in two adjacent parishes of Serere County in Teso district, Uganda.[11] My purpose initially was to study a small country town, and I chose to work in Gondo, a small trading center on Lake Kyoga, because of its long history (by recorded Teso standards) and its heterogeneous population. In the days of water communication that preceded the building of the railway in Uganda, cattle and cotton were exported from this backwater of the Nile to the fertile crescent of colonial Buganda. Men and materiel were shipped eastward through the port to furbish the Protectorate's moving frontier. While I was engaged in day-by-day research among the men and women of this particular locality, two sectors of intensive field research in Gondo and Serere carried me further afield. For several weeks I worked closely on the career histories of all the men who had ever held the office of chief in Bugondo, the subcounty of Serere within which Gondo lay. A few were dead, and I had to reconstruct their lives with the help of relatives and records. The remainder I visited, wherever they might be in Teso and the wider region. Through long interviews relating past to present, and through viewing their homes and social environments (as well as those of other prominent men in the district), I gained a familiarity with that landscape of mobility—social and geographical—which they all shared.

The second field experience that carried me throughout Teso opened up, as it were, the underside of the district's life. A particular research interest in Bakenyi led me to work closely with members of

11. Research in 1966–67 was financed by a grant from the Ministry of Overseas Development of the United Kingdom and was carried out as a research fellow of the East African Institute of Social Research. Research in 1970 was financed by a Faculty Research Grant from Barnard College. I would also like to thank Barnard College for a grant towards the cost of preparing this manuscript.

this minority group at a time when an effort was being made to mobilize it for political action within the district. Here I came to know the lives and political views of men and women engaged not in agriculture and cattle-rearing—the pursuits that formed the principal sector of the Teso economy, even as the Iteso formed the dominant stratum within the district's political system—but in trade and fishing. Many Bakenyi were adherents of Islam and Roman Catholicism, rather than members of the Native Anglican Church (formerly the Church Missionary Society), and had emerged in recent years as a political opposition to the predominantly Iteso and predominantly Protestant Teso District Council. This unofficial hidden world of the Bakenyi provided a counterpoint to my research among chiefs and notables, most of whom were Iteso. Ultimately, these two aspects of my fieldwork nudged this study into being.

My goal in writing was to lay bare the transitions in Teso society that underlay the condition of the people among whom I worked between 1966 and 1970. Some of the cruel fatalities of the Idi Amin regime and its overthrow have been, for the people of Teso, loss of their cattle, destruction of the cotton industry, near ruin of the district's roads and public works, lack of clothing, and return to subsistence farming under conditions of near famine. Links between the region and the global economic system are but tenuously maintained through the *magendo* (black market), a liberating but foreign army, and a struggling government bureaucracy. Current advice from development agencies would appear to involve restructuring the cotton economy and establishing within it handicraft and domestic industry. The elements of discontinuity and change are essentially the same now, in 1981, as they were between 1912 and 1927, the formative period discussed in this book. Critically different is the place of impoverished Uganda in our contemporary global economy and the political and social ideologies and technologies that now exist—to be brought into play or not, as only tomorrow's history can tell.

1. The Uganda Protectorate

Imperialism is no word for scholars.

William Hancock

Quibbles about imperialism are best resolved by reference to concrete facts.

John Hobson

On Sunday April 9, 1865, Robert E. Lee of the Army of North Virginia surrendered to General Grant at the courthouse in Appomattox, marking the end of the American Civil War. Over half a million men lay dead on the battlefields of the South. The impact of the war on Europe and, in the long run, on the colonial possessions that fed her global economy brought about a mortality perhaps no smaller.

In 1860, the southern states of America furnished five-sixths of all Europe's cotton.[1] The cotton industry of Great Britain alone employed one-fifth of the entire British population and imported 80 percent of its cotton from the South. By 1862 the industry—the capstone of the British industrial economy—was severely dislocated. Mills closed. "Only 121,129 of the 533,959 operatives were working full time . . . while 247,230 were entirely out of work with no prospect of employment."[2] By the end of the year about two million people were without support of any kind, as the "cotton famine" reached its peak and soup kitchens were set up in

1. For further documentation, see George McHenry, *The Cotton Trade* (1863), pp. 116–131, and James A. B. Scherer, *Cotton as a World Power* (1916), pp. 257–269.

2. Scherer, p. 267. The extent to which the cotton industry lay at the heart of Britain's nineteenth-century economy is discussed in Stanley D. Chapman, *The Cotton Industry in the Industrial Revolution* (1972), pp. 62–72, and in Walt W. Rostow, *The Stages of Economic Growth* (1960), pp. 21–24. But see also Alfred P. Wadsworth and Julia de Lacy Mann, *The Cotton Trade and Industrial Lancashire* (1931), esp. pp. 211–310, and H. J. Habakkuk and P. Deane, "The Take-off in Britain" (1965), pp. 13–14, 71–75.

the streets of Liverpool and Manchester. Meanwhile, the manufacturers adapted. They produced thinner fabrics; mixed cotton
with wool or linen; even added flour to the cotton yarn to increase
its weight.[3] Scarcity, as David Landes has it, "is the greatest alchem-
ist of all. In the seventh decade of the nineteenth century, a long
anticipated yet wishfully unexpected civil war in America erased at
one stroke most of the world's supply of cotton, ravaged the greatest of manufacturing industries, and turned fuzzy white fibres into
gold."[4]

Short-term measures were not enough. Although cotton production in the South actually increased after the war, not Britain but
the eastern seaboard of the United States stood to gain. A wave of
social reforms swept England in the face of prolonged unemployment and the imminent danger of political unrest.

By 1875 London faced a development crisis in industry and social
planning, and the central place in that crisis was occupied by the
problem of unemployment and casual labor.[5] To an upsurge of
social and economic imperialism Cecil Rhodes gave its charter, lion
rampant, in 1895. "To save the forty million inhabitants of the
United Kingdom from bloody civil war, we . . . must acquire new
lands to settle the surplus population, to provide new markets . . . If
you want to avoid civil war, you must become imperialists."[6]

High on the imperial agenda was the search for new sources of
cotton. India, Egypt, and Brazil came first to mind, but even Spain,
Australia, and the Fiji Islands were considered.

In this global context must be placed British and French explorations of the Nile, the scramble for Africa, and, ultimately, the
creation of the Uganda Protectorate and within it Teso.

This is a study of society and economy in early modern Uganda.
Long dominated by research into the development of Buganda and
its neighboring kingdoms, historical scholarship has more recently
turned its eyes northward and eastward to the peoples of the plain
that stretches east of the Victoria Nile. The Nile dominates Ugan-

3. David S. Landes, *Bankers and Pashas* (1958), p. 71.
4. Ibid., p. 69.
5. Gareth Jones (1971), pp. 1–15; Semmel (1960), esp. pp. 15–23.
6. Quoted in Semmel, p. 16.

da's history, and the geographical divide between north and south (or, more accurately, between north and east, south and west) is a very real one. As the Nile moves sluggishly from Lake Victoria in the southeast to the north, it divides African peoples of distinctive cultures, distinctive histories. The Nile moves slowly, its waters over the centuries eroding the silted shores and weaving their way between tall papyrus swamps to penetrate far into the interior.

Unlike mountain ranges or dense jungle, stretches of water bring peoples together as much as they divide. The development of Europe's economy as it expanded across oceanic frontiers to transform islands of distinctive and separate economies into one world system, passed through two phases. The first occurred in the long sixteenth century, and its repercussions along the coasts of eastern Africa reached the region that became Uganda as Indian Ocean trade was encapsulated within the developing capitalist economic system. The second occurred in the nineteenth century, when mercantilism gave way to industrialism in Europe, transoceanic communication became fast and profitable, and a new age of empire began. It was during this second era that the Nile, like the Rhine in Europe, began to carry its backwater regions into the developing world system. With the Nile frontier crossed, pockets of distinctive and separate economies were rendered accountable to one another; their societies were transformed and their peoples subjected to imperial rule, itself a manifestation of the larger forces at work.

To write of Teso and to mean by this, roughly, four and a half thousand square miles of swamp and dry land that came to lie within a Ugandan district of that name from 1912 until modern times would be anachronistic. For the greater part of its history, a vaster backcloth must be painted that, at its widest, would include imperial India, Egypt, the Sudan, Ethiopia, Oman, southern Africa, Italy and the Roman Catholic Church, the United Kingdom of Great Britain and Ireland, France, and Germany, as well as the United States. At its narrowest, the canvas might stretch at least from Ethiopia to the Ruwenzori Mountains and from the swamp-bound lands of the Shilluk in the southern Sudan to the arid Masai grassland of the Rift.

From east to west, north to south, across this region tracked a score of peoples out of whose passing was generated the Teso district of modern Uganda. Teso at the end of the nineteenth century was a region yet to be carved out, given a name and, with that name, an identity. It would be not simply an anachronism but an injustice to African realities to survey the landscape of eastern Uganda in isolation from the world about it. The year 1912, the year in which Teso district was crystallized within a colonial territory still in the making, represents no more than an instant when the movements of countless peoples over five hundred years were peremptorily halted, to be embedded in colonial history. The peoples of Teso and their societal forms, as well as those features of the terrain that enter into the accounts of traders, missionaries, soldiers, and administrators and the recollections of Africans recounting their histories, are, indeed, but the epiphenomena of preceding centuries. Those of the migrating population that eventually gave a name to the colonial district took that name and their body out of movement. Ethnic distinctions emerged between peoples as they responded to ecological change. Over time, as "peoples" were created and the district given shape, an imbricated social map became a political reality. To derive the landscape and peoples of Teso district from all else that it might have been, one is led initially to a much larger arena. That the arena shrinks is what politics is all about.

Perspective From the West

As far as we know, the peoples east of the Nile in the nineteenth century were enmeshed in the political affairs, not of the lands to the north and east from whence they came, but of expansive states to the west. The proviso is critical, for it is a feature of African historiography that a knowledge of the political histories of societies that are not states is arrived at through those that are. Thus, while almost nothing is known of the relations of the peoples of Teso with those to their north and east in Labwor, Nyakwai, and Karamoja, and little is known of relations with the petty fiefdoms of Busoga in the south, yet a little more is known of relations with centralized or centralizing states west of the Nile in Bunyoro and Buganda. It is through the windows of these two kingdoms, as it were, that the colonial powers at the end of the century viewed the prospects of Teso or Bukeddi, as it was then called. Thus, although trade routes from Mumias and Masaba were of tangential interest at least to southern Teso, it was only through Iteso raiding and trading into

Busoga when Basoga chiefs were tributary to Buganda that connections began to emerge; in 1893 it was reported that to enforce
tribute from Busoga "on the original scale" only resulted in "the
Wasoga chiefs selling women to Wakeddi and other tribes to purchase ivory."[7] The moment at which it can be said that the Teso
region was brought into the modern world economy is, indeed,
unclear; but certainly world forces can be recognized working
themselves out in the area long before the formal advent of the
Imperial British East Africa Company in 1888.

European thinking at the middle of the nineteenth century was
dominated by "the challenge of the age-old quest for the equatorial
sources of the Nile."[8] The explorations of John Hanning Speke and
his "discovery" of Lake Victoria have been seen as setting the stage
for British entry into Buganda in 1862 and the rise of the curtain on
Uganda's imperial drama. Such romanticism can be set alongside
the effect of the American Civil War on European industrial and
financial interests.[9] "Klondike on the Nile" is one historian's characterization of the boom in Egypt's cotton economy after 1865; and
the years that followed were dominated by Khedive Ismail's political ambition to build an African empire. One of the goals of the
Egyptian Commercial and Trading Company (originally the Sudan
Company) was the creation of new commercial ties with the region
to the south, thus securing the economic solidarity of the Nile basin.
The explorations of the Nile were underwritten by Henry Op-
penheim and the bankers of Alexandria, Paris, and London.[10] Ardor

7. Capt. Macdonald to Sir G. Portal, Despatch III (1894), Inclosure 1,
Oct. 21, 1893 (PRO FO/403/193).

8. Harold B. Thomas and Robert Scott, *Uganda* (1935), p. 7.

9. See, e.g., Leonard S. Woolf, *Empire and Commerce in Africa* (1920),
esp. pp. 21–47.

10. Landes (1958), esp. pp. 69–101. Speke's expedition was funded by
the Royal Geographical Society of London. Applying to the British government for a grant of £2,500, the Society suggested the advantages that might
accrue to "commerce and civilization" (R. C. Bridges, "John Hanning
Speke," 1970, pp. 133–135). Nor were the advantages for Britain's heavy
industry negligible. "The appearance of great lakes upon the hitherto recent
vacant spaces of the map of Africa had a special fascination for a generation
that was just experiencing the new power afforded by steam navigation"
(Roland A. Oliver, *The Missionary Factor in East Africa*, 1952, p. 27).

fanned by the Royal Geographical Society led to the gradual filling in of the blank spaces on the map between Gondokoro, by this time a veritable Marseilles for travelers from the northern latitudes, and the Victoria Nyanza, pronounced by Speke the source of the Nile.[11] East of the Nile at the point where it flowed into Lake Kyoga lay the Teso region.

Speke's map of 1862 sets the scene: a perspective from the west (see Figure 1).[12] Speke, accompanied by J. A. Grant, entered the region from the south following a well-established caravan route to the west of Lake Victoria. Familiarity with the lake shore is as apparent from the map as unfamiliarity with the course of the Nile and with its lakes. The region to the west of the river bears three names: Chopi, Unyoro, and Uganda. Speke's limited knowledge of Unyoro is evident from the clustering of campsites and place names along the Nile. His perception of its size is significant, capturing a

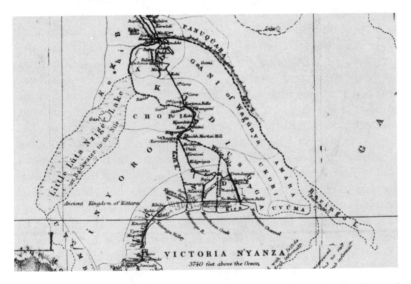

Figure 1. Speke's Map of 1862 (detail). Source: John H. Speke, *Journal of the Discovery of the Source of the Nile* (1863).

11. John H. Speke, *Journal of the Discovery of the Source of the Nile* (1863). See also Leonard Woolf (1920), pp. 187–201.

12. Woolf (1920). See also John Beattie, *The Nyoro State* (1971), esp. pp. 26–32.

moment of balance in a power struggle between that kingdom and Buganda. To the east of the Nile, from a point north of Urondogani in Busoga (clearly shown in 1863 as tributary to Buganda) lies an expanse of territory called, simply, Kidi–East. Beyond Kidi (later to enter the colonial record as Bukeddi), reaching to the Asna River, are the Gani of Wagunya—the El Gunyi or Elgumi of later records—at the foot of Mount Masaba. Far in the distant east lies an unnamed lake that can be taken to represent Lake Rudolf. Beyond this is Ethiopia. Somewhere between these two—the White Nile and Lake Rudolf—was to be carved out the district that became Teso.

In 1862, Mukama Kamurasi of Bunyoro exercised suzerainty of a sort over an area that included much of modern Buganda, Nkole, and parts of the Teso region. Bunyoro overlordship was acknowledged on the further shores of Lake Albert, and influence extended both east and north of the Nile. At the time Speke and Grant visited Kamurasi, Bunyoro (contrary to the impression conveyed by its magnitude on Speke's map) was on the edge of decline, and control of the northern marches was being severely challenged by a cousin, Ruyonga. In welcoming the Englishmen to his court, Kamurasi hoped for their armed assistance in crushing the incipient rebellion.

Whether at this time the eastern reaches of Teso lay within the Mukama's sphere of influence is not clear. Nothing could be more confusing than the history of Lake Kyoga's shores at this period, largely because the legacies of history relate to metropolitan seats of government and not to their lake shore peripheries. Local chronicles convey the triumphs and tribulations only of culture heroes among the peoples fringing Lake Kyoga, whereas later scholarly analyses of political structures tend to disregard the marginal peoples: the Banyala and Bachopi of Bunyoro and the Bagerere and Balamogi of Buganda. Yet these are the very peoples with whom the Teso population interacted most closely. It is not a straightforward matter to disentangle the historical record.[13]

In the fourteenth and fifteenth centuries, according to traditions of the Bunyoro-Kitara court, kings of its Babito dynasty presided

13. For efforts in this direction, see David W. Cohen, *The Historical Tradition of Busoga, Mukama, and Kintu* (1972), esp. pp. 70–82, and John Tosh, *Clan Leaders and Colonial Chiefs in Lango* (1978a), esp. pp. 17–63.

over periodic tribunals in which the affairs of subject peoples were settled. At one of these tribunals, Orukurato rwa Bemeanagaho (Court of the eastern peoples), the Mukama was said to have received Baganda, Basoga, Bagisu, and Iteso, as well as other peoples from the east.[14] Nothing is known of the connections between the Mukama and the "Iteso" peoples who appeared at his court, but certainly it is an anachronism to describe them as Iteso. By the early nineteenth century, there is no doubt that the inhabitants of Teso's Serere peninsula (Iseera) were in some form of political relationship with Bunyoro. Certain individuals—Osodo of Madoch was one—were invested with the insignia of Bunyoro political office: a drum, stool and spear.[15] Bunyoro overrule might have been similar to that in Bugwere, Bulamogi, and Bukono, where princelings established not only thrones and fortunes but virtual independence. Their relations with the parent house in Bunyoro-Kitara were tenuous, and numerous alliances were made outside the family circle.[16] More likely, however, links between Bunyoro and Serere were even less formal than this, consisting, for the most part, of trade rather than tribute.[17] Offshore islands provided bases from which trade could be conducted in the interior; Kawere (Awere) to the north and Namuliba at Serere's southern tip served as way stations in the passage of cattle and iron hoes.

In this manner, a trading territory was developed that reached south to the Mpologoma Lakes region and north to Lake Bisina. Within it, there was a degree of self-sufficiency about the local

14. A. R. Dunbar, *A History of Bunyoro-Kitara* (1965), p. 41.

15. M. Louise Pirouet, "The Expansion of the Church of Uganda (NAC) from Buganda into Northern and Western Uganda between 1891 and 1914" (Ph.D. thesis, 1968), p. 326. Field notes, Serere, 1966.

16. See, e.g., Dunbar (1965), esp. pp. 41–44, and M. S. M. Semakula Kiwanuka, *Empire of Bunyoro-Kitara* (1968a).

17. On the nature of tribute as social contrast, see Lars Sundström, *The Exchange Economy of Pre-Colonial Tropical Africa* (1974), and the many ethnographic references he cites. For the importance of the tributary mode of production in the emergence of the state, see Samir Amin, *Unequal Development: An Essay on the Social Formation of Peripheral Capitalism* (1976). There is nothing in the evidence to suggest the existence of other than what Amin would call the primitive-communal mode in the Teso region in the nineteenth century.

economy—the homestead clusters of related big men forming a regional trade system—that made any form of political allegiance or subservience both difficult to establish and unnecessary. Whether, indeed, client or tributary ties of any kind extended further inland, east of Serere, is not clear. It may well have been in the interest of some men to have attempted to control trade at the expense of others, and the price asked for cooperation by the Banyoro might have been token recognition of Babito supremacy. On the other hand, there is no evidence of the growth inland of market places (as opposed to markets); and since the traders were not superior in arms to the local people, they were not in a position to offer either protection or alliance. A largely egalitarian relationship appears to have been maintained both among the people themselves and with the foreign traders.

The eastern end of Lake Kyoga was the meeting ground for Banyoro and Baganda. Kalwala, Bugerere, and Buruli, as well as Serere, were well studded with Banyoro settlements. By the end of the nineteenth century over a thousand Banyoro had settled on the Serere mainland, holding land at Kagwara opposite Namuliba Island. Residents in Gondo insisted that, prior to the coming of the Baganda and British, they had been, as they put it, "ruled" by the Banyoro.[18] Bunyala, in the north of Bugerere, was similarly affiliated with Bunyoro, while Bulondoganyi in the south was tributary to Buganda. Inhabited by fishermen and herders, Bunyala was ruled by Mukonga, who was said to have come with some of his people "from around Bugondo" in Serere.[19] Control of northern Bugerere was vitally significant for the course of events in Teso, since it lay as a buffer between the war-ravaged states of the south and the lands of Bukeddi.

Banyoro influence reached Teso from the north as well as from the south. From the north, Banyoro movement formed part of extensive Lwoo migrations over several centuries.[20] Along the western

18. Field notes, Serere, 1966. "Removal of Banyoro" (TDA XNAF/3,135/13). See also Joan Vincent, *African Elite: The Big Men of a Small Town* (1971), esp. pp. 166–168.

19. A. O. Jenkins, "A Note on the Saza of Bugerere, Buganda Kingdom" (1939), p. 204.

20. Bethwell A. Ogot, *History of the Southern Luo* (1967), esp. pp. 40–62.

banks of the Nile, the Lwoo settled and intermarried with local
people to become known as the Jo-pa-Lwoo of Pa-wiir or, to adopt
the Bantu form in place of the Nilotic, the Bachopi.[21] Their territory,
Chopi, is marked on Speke's map. Speaking a Nilotic language, and
closely related to the Acholi across the Nile, the Bachopi occupied
Bunyoro's undulating northern savanna.

For reasons not clear from early accounts, but probably related to
slave and ivory raiding, the Bachopi began to move across the Nile
and along the northern littoral of Lake Kyoga. The words of Egweu
Opio in Kaberamaido suggest the embroglio of kin connections that
had come into being at the eastern end of Lake Kyoga by the turn
of the century. Opio was able to go back four generations in his
genealogy to an ancestor who lived in Bunyoro, on the banks of the
River Kafu. (This can be dated approximately to 1790.)

> Looking for good hunting grounds they came to Bululu, which the
> Banyala had abandoned migrating to Bugerere. From Bululu, the Jo-pa-
> wiiri . . . crossed Lake Kyoga to Kaberamaido and Kumam country,
> which latter was mainly a hunting ground [a *grenzwildnisse* or no-man's
> land]. It was in Bululu that they changed their traditional hide clothing
> for bark cloth which they obtained from the Banyala in return for chick-
> ens. Upon the arrival of the Kumam in Kalaki and Kaberamaido . . . and
> the further arrival of the Lango-Omiru from the north, the Jo-pawiiri
> had to retire towards the lake . . . In the course of time the Jo-pawiiri fell
> under the domination of the Banyala (of Namionjo of Bugerere).[22]

If responsibility for this Bachopi diaspora is to be attributed to
any one individual, it must be to the English explorer Samuel Baker.
The Bakers, husband and wife, were Bunyoro's second English visitors in the mid-nineteenth century, and, unlike Speke and Grant,
they entered Bunyoro not by way of Buganda but from the north.
Worse, they entered with an armed escort of Sudanese. A party of
Sudanese such as these had, after the departure of the earlier explorers, entered Kamurasi's court on the pretext of being friends of
the Englishmen. In collusion with the rebellious Ruyonga, the Sudanese had massacred about a hundred of their Banyoro hosts.
Notorious throughout the region for allying themselves with one

21. J. Pasquale Crazzolara, *The Lwoo* (1950–54), pp. 6, 73, 76. These
people were also called Ipagero in Serere county (see Vincent, 1971), esp.
pp. 143–147.

22. Crazzolara, pp. 79–80.

local ruler against another, then turning on their allies, the Sudanese were hardly the most trusted company in which the Bakers could have traveled.[23]

Necessity may have bred Baker's initial contact with Bunyoro; opportunism led him to capitalize on it when need arose. When Kamurasi refused to go along with some of his wishes, Baker threatened him with reprisals from the Sudanese. That Baker and his wife left the country unharmed in 1864 says much for the restraint of the Bunyoro ruler; but it was upon Baker's violent antipathy to Kamurasi, nevertheless, that British views of Bunyoro were subsequently based. John Beattie, Bunyoro's political enthnographer, attaches considerable significance to the implanting of this early and formative colonial bias.

> A typical comment is that of a Victorian author, the Revd. J. G. Wood, who in 1868 described the Banyoro (whom he had never seen) as "forming a very unpleasant contrast to the people of Buganda, being dirty, mean-looking and badly dressed." He went on to describe their character as being "quite on a par with their appearance, for they are a mean, selfish, grasping set of people, sadly lacking the savage virtue of hospitality, and always on the look-out for opportunities to procure by unfair means the property of others." The reverend author airily sums up, from the depths of his Victorian armchair: "They seem, indeed, to be about as unpleasant a nation as can well be imagined."[24]

Clearly derived from Baker's writings, comments such as this set the tone for the British view of the Bunyoro state and, by extension, of early colonial Bukeddi.

Perspective from the South

British views of Bukkedi and the Bakeddi were shaped not only by a negative assessment of Bunyoro, but also by a positive appraisal of Buganda.[25]

23. See Beattie (1971), pp. 68–71.

24. J. G. Wood, *The Natural History of Man* (1868), quoted in Beattie, pp. 30–31.

25. Thus Rowe noted how Sir Samuel White Baker's *Ismailia* (1874) "began the long-lived myth of treacherous Kabarega, King of Bunyoro, contrasted to friendly and helpful Mutesa of Buganda" (Rowe, "Revolution in Buganda, 1856–1900," Ph.D. thesis, 1966, p. 230). Per-

In the 1770s France had established sugar and tobacco plantations on the Indian Ocean islands of Bourbon and Mauritius. This projection of Europe into the "world" economy of the Indian Ocean transformed the political economy of Africa from the Nile to the Zambezi. A mercantile system in which slaves had been relatively insignificant was transformed almost overnight with the establishment of a plantation economy. Clove plantations were introduced on the islands of Zanzibar and Pemba, and in 1840 Seyyid Said bin Sultan transferred his capital from Oman to Zanzibar City. At the northern periphery of this transoceanic mercantile system, the kingdom of Buganda evolved.

Until the eighteenth century, Buganda had been an indeterminate territory founded by a dissident Bunyoro princeling; from that time on, it expanded significantly. Its success has been variously attributed to extensive banana groves, cultivated by women, which freed the men for war and leisure; to lack of a royal clan and a hereditary aristocracy; to the growth of a centralized and despotic government; to success as a military state; and to "the Baganda genius."[26] Throughout, however, Buganda continued to maintain diplomatic and commercial relations with Bunyoro.

In 1862, when Speke visited the court of Kabaka Mutesa, the Buganda capital served as the conduit for European goods brought from the coast by Nyamwezi and Zanzibari traders to Karagwe, which either traded with or paid them in tribute to Buganda.[27] At this time the kabaka's capital had a population of around forty thousand, and special quarters were allotted to foreign traders and envoys from other states. Among the side effects of contact were the introduction to Buganda of venereal disease and firearms. The traders were of various "nationalities," among them Arab, Baluchi, Indian, Zanzibari, and Malagassy. An estimated fifteen thousand Zanzibari Muslim traders resided in the capital in 1875, and this

---

sonal relations between the two rulers were in fact good; Mutesa recognized the value of a strong Bunyoro between himself and the advancing, annexing troops of the Khedive of Egypt.

26. See, e.g., Conrad P. Kottack, "Ecological Variables in the Origin and Evolution of African States: The Buganda Example" (1972); C. C. Wrigley, "Buganda: An Outline Economic History" (1957); and E. A. Alpers, "Eastern Africa" (1975a).

27. Rowe (Ph.D., 1966), p. 46.

foreign community was supplemented periodically by deserters from passing caravans. These expatriates, all Muslim, were highly valued and often given political office. Five years after Speke's departure from Mutesa's capital, the the influence of the Zanzibari traders was clearly evident, not only in new trade goods and crafts, but also in the practice of Islam. Mutesa spoke Arabic, wore the *kanzu* (Muslim robe), fasted, and attended mosque. In spite of later assertions by Christian missionaries, it was not slaves but ivory that interested the Muslim traders.[28] It was arms, as well as Islam, that interested Mutesa.

According to Henry Morton Stanley, Mutesa in 1875 had only five hundred guns, many of them obsolete muzzle loaders, and much of the tension that developed between Bunyoro and Buganda at this time revolved around access to the arms trade. Bunyoro's needs increased with the southern advance of the Egyptian imperial frontier—especially after Baker, by then in the employ of the Egyptian government, ran up the khedive's flag to announce the annexation of northern Bunyoro. In Buganda, internal strife escalated. Four factions developed: English Protestants, French Catholics (the first Anglican missionaries reached Buganda in 1877, the first Roman Catholic priests in 1879), Zanzibari Muslims, and Baganda traditionalists. Revolution, civil war, and famine followed. The events of these years provided both prologue and rationale for British incorporation of the Bukeddi region within a protectorate centered upon Buganda, in spite of its historical connections with Bunyoro. Such a reorientation of precolonial political economies seems almost a necessary attribute of imperialism.

In January 1885 the Conference of Berlin marked out for Britain, as for other European powers, a sphere of influence in Africa. Uganda was acquired, it has been suggested, as one of a complex series

---

28. Ibid., p. 51. In *Politics and Class Formation in Uganda* (1976), p. 19n., Mahmood Mamdani refers to Abdul M. H. Sheriff's "The Rise of a Commercial Empire: An Aspect of the Economic History of Zanzibar, 1770–1873" (Ph.D. thesis, 1971) thus: "Reasoning that slave trade figures were grossly exaggerated by Livingstone and the British navy as part of the ideology of colonialism, and that these have formed the basis for the estimates used [in recent works], Sheriff estimates the annual export of slaves at 40,000 on the basis of an examination of customs records."

of moves to protect the Nile and Britain's route to India, her most valuable possession. British Africa thus appears as a gigantic footnote to the Indian Empire.[29] Yet, as one critic has pointed out, an explanation of the partition of Africa that fails to explain why there was, at the same time, a "partition of the Pacific, almost a partition of China and, at a later date, a partition of Persia" could not but be inadequate.[30] Alternative explanations are sought, not in the development of nineteenth-century colonialism, but in the development of industrial capitalism.

Interests in the commerce of the Indian Ocean shared by Britain with France and the United States, and expressed in the ivory and slave trades (and opposition to them), had given way, after 1865, to to the demands of Britain's emerging industries, cotton manufacture and the building of ships and railways. Even as the United States began to expand westward, and French enterprise laced with railways the countryside of Eastern Europe, so British financial interests envisaged the opening of the Dark Continent. In Europe, a new economic institution emerged, the joint stock company, which began to challenge the supremacy of the long-established merchant banks.[31] It was bolstered by the new doctrine of Social Imperialism.[32] The economic history of early modern Uganda, and within it Teso, is linked to the development of two such companies: first the Imperial British East Africa Company (IBEA Co.) and, later, the Uganda Company.

29. Ronald Hyam, "Review of Africa and the Victorians" (1964), p. 155, quoting Ronald E. Robinson and John Gallagher, with Alice Denny, *Africa and the Victorians* (1961), p. 616. See also G. N. Sanderson, *England, Europe, and the Upper Nile, 1882–1899* (1965). "No African people possessed the technological skill to interfere with the northward flow of the Nile waters. The European powers did. Thus, to protect Suez, that lifeline of empire, the British . . . had to defend the Nile waters wherever they might be—Khartoum, Lake Tana, Fashoda, Uganda" (Robert O. Collins, *Problems in African History* [1968]).

30. Hyam (1964), pp. 157–158. For a further critique of geopolitical explanations, see Richard D. Wolff, *The Economics of Colonialism: Britain and Kenya, 1870–1939* (1974), pp. 2–28.

31. Landes (1958), esp. pp. 3–40, 47–68.

32. Compare Lewis H. Gann and Peter J. Duignan (eds.), *Colonialism in Africa 1870–1960* (1970), vol. I, pp. 5–11, 100–129, and Leonard Woolf (1920) pp. 3–46.

Formerly the British East Africa Association, the IBEA Co. was formed in 1885 with a capital of £250,000. Its director, until his death in 1893, was Mr. (later Sir) William Mackinnon, who in 1872 had opened a regular mail service, the British India Steam Navigation Company, between Europe, Zanzibar, and India. His codirectors included members of the aristocracy; men who had recently held high administrative posts in East Africa (Sir Charles Euan-Smith and Sir John Kirk); one field marshal; three generals; Sir Thomas Fowell Buxton, vice-president and treasurer of the Church Missionary Society (CMS); and several leading bankers and financiers.[33] The long-term goals of the IBEA Co. were to open a safe route from the coast to Uganda and to build a railway along it. The company received a royal charter in September 1888, and shortly afterward its employee Frederick Jackson set out with a caravan from Mombasa.[34] His instructions were to explore the territory behind the ten-mile strip around Mombasa in preparation for Mackinnon's scheme to take over the administration of the territory, and to be prepared to go to the rescue of Emin Pasha—fleeing Mahdist forces in Equatoria—should Stanley's earlier expedition prove unsuccessful. Commercial interests underlay both projects. Jackson had acquired a reputation as a big game hunter; and the acquisition of ivory was important to England and the United States at this time, as was the sale of arms and ammunition.

The second of Jackson's objectives—had it been approached—would have taken him through Masailand and thence by way of Kavirondo to either Labwor or Litem, two of Emin's outposts in Karamoja. The company's route would thus have ringed, and perhaps impinged upon, the Teso region. As it was, on December 10, 1889, Jackson diverged from his planned route, traveling instead toward Lake Rudolf in search of ivory. In the course of his safari he climbed, along with three European companions and several unnamed Africans, Mount Masaba—an achievement that led to the so-called discovery of Lake Salisbury [Bisina]. On Jackson's return

33. Leonard Woolf, p. 243. See also Marie De Kiewet, "The Imperial British East Africa Company, 1875–1895" (Ph.D. thesis, 1955) and Edward R. Vere-Hodge, *Imperial British East Africa Company* (1960).

34. The account that follows is taken from Sir Frederick Jackson, *Early Days in East Africa* (1930), pp. 221–253.

to his base camp at a resting place called Mumia's in early March, he found that Dr. Karl Peters, a German explorer in the service of the Kaiser, had not only entered his camp, "crossing into the British sphere," but had *"opened my letters and read them."*[35] Jackson records the incident with indignation.

Disregarding the specific instructions of the IBEA Co. *not* to enter Uganda, since civil war was known to be raging there after a Muslim coup d'etat, Jackson set out posthaste after Peters. Arriving on April 14, he entered a field of contending forces: Protestant against Catholic Baganda factions within the Buganda court; Muslim and traditionalist forces countering both; Baganda armies warring against Bunyoro; the kingdom in flux as Mwanga, Mutesa's successor, tried to maintain ascendancy in an arena filled with new combatants, new alignments, new doubts and hopes. The Anglo-German Agreement of 1890 put an end to British fears of German intervention, and Capt. Frederick Lugard headed an expedition to Uganda the following month. His objective was to offer Mwanga the company's "protection and powerful assistance." As Woolf puts it, "Mwanga, it is true, showed considerable reluctance to receive the Company's 'protection and powerful assistance,' but, after a civil war in which Captain Lugard's Maxim gun and armed forces were employed with great effect against the king and his supporters, and after the king and his armies, who had fled to an island, found themselves bombarded by the expedition which had come to protect and assist them, Mwanga was induced to reconsider his position and to accept the Company's protection."[36]

Company Perspective: Gandaphilia

Important as Buganda was in catapulting Muslim and Christian, African and European contestants into the Teso arena, we turn aside temporarily from this cauldron of political action for a reconstruction of the company's view of the territory it was entering. Company officials divided the African world they encountered into

35. Ibid., pp. 256–257.
36. Leonard Woolf, p. 280. For Sir Frederick Lugard's own account of his mission, see his *The Rise of Our East African Empire* (1893), vol. 2, pp. 33–472.

three parts: the densely populated Kavirondo and Busoga plains through which their caravans passed; the Buganda kingdom; and, as yet remote, the Muslim north. The division mirrored the company's economic interests during its three-year existence in Uganda (from April 1880 to April 1883) and prevailed to shape the British government's political interests there during the next decade.

Even as Speke's map of 1862 can be studied to recapture the European view of Bukeddi from the West, so can be used Seymour Vandeleur's to recreate the company's view of it from the south at the end of the nineteenth century (see Figure 2).[37] Intricate detail again distinguishes the area west of the Nile, but added now is the caravan route through north Kavirondo to Fort Kampala and Mengo. The resting places along it are named after local chiefs— Mumia's, Wakoli's, Lubwa's—and become prominent in the wars that precede the Uganda Agreement of 1900. To the north still lies, as in 1863, a vast unexplored territory east of the Nile, although, to be sure, Lake Salisbury now appears on the map, as do other sketchy (and, it turns out, imaginary) watery expanses. Here are to be found, in north, east, and south, peoples called at this time Wakeddi, Kamima, and Elgumi.

From the outset, all hopes of civilization and commerce were seen to lie in the south. Jackson's description of the lavish hospitality of Chief Wakoli leaves no doubt as to the fertility and productivity of Busoga, for example. His IBEA Co. caravan of around four hundred "were practically his guests" during its stay.

> Never before or since have I seen so much food brought into camp—all gratis: cows for milk, a bullock almost daily, sheep, fowls, basketsful of eggs, sweet-potatoes, and bunches of banana galore, too many, in fact, as there was a very considerable waste. The men had the time of their lives, and some of them filled out so quickly after their hardships on the Turkwel and Mount Elgon, that I failed, at first glance, to recognise two of them I knew quite well.[38]

The rich country had attracted the attention of the Baganda in the eighteenth century, when Kyaggwe (much of it tributary to Bun-

37. Seymour Vandeleur, *Campaigning on the Upper Nile and Niger* (1898).
38. Jackson, pp. 256–257.

Figure 2. Vandeleur's Map of 1895 (detail). Source: Seymour Vandeleur, *Campaigning on the Upper Nile and Niger* (1898).

yoro) had been incorporated into Mwanga's kingdom. From eastern Kyaggwe, Baganda forces frequently crossed into the rich but
warring Basoga states. For caravans from the coast, Busoga and
Kavirondo comprised the promised land, the home of "forty thousand agriculturalists in a magnificent food-supplying country."[39]

From the first moments of encounter, Gandaphilia[40] was blatant
in official despatches. "The kingdom of Uganda," wrote Lugard in
1892, "is probably the most civilised of any native state in Africa,"[41]
an evaluation echoed by missionary, soldier and administrator alike.
The imperial coinage that had the Mukamo of Bunyoro on its base
side bore the "loyal Muganda" on its face. For the missionaries, the
Baganda were the chosen people: a designation of strategic import.
Discussing the tactics of conversion, Bishop John J. Willis, of the
CMS, advocated that initially every effort be concentrated on the
dominant tribe in any region.

> Large numbers, a widely diffuse language, a strategic geographical posi-
> tion, and above all a marked personality, will indicate one tribe as the
> natural point on which to concentrate the first efforts; because, humanly
> speaking, that is the tribe most likely to influence the surrounding peo-
> ples. God chose the Jews . . . Hardly less clearly did the hand of God
> point to the peoples of Uganda [Buganda] as His instruments in the
> evangelisation of Central Africa."[42]

The bishop went on to quote with approval the notorious Karl
Peters: "if native races may be divided into two classes, those who
are destined to rule, and those who are compelled to obey, the
Waganda [Baganda] belong unquestioningly to the former class."[43]

---

39. John Ford, *The Role of Trypanosomiases in African Ecology* (1971),
p. 238.

40. Compare Ali Mazrui, "Tanzaphilia" (1967), p. 20: "A political
phenomenon . . . the romantic spell which Tanzania casts on so many of
those who have been closely associated with her."

41. Capt. Lugard to IBEA Co., Sept. 5, 1892 (PRO FO/403/260).

42. John J. Willis, *An African Church in the Building* (1925), p. 54.

43. Ibid. Note, however, that the bishop goes on to say, "No one tribe,
however, no one centre, no one class must be allowed to monopolise
attention. The aim of the missionary is the widest possible *diffusion*," first
by itineration and second "by training and supervising native agents, until
the entire tribe has heard the message of the Gospel, each of his own village,
in his own language, from his own people."

The gentility of the Baganda appealed most strongly to early colonial administrators. Not only did the Baganda have straight roads, and spotless gowns of imported calico, but their chiefs "already excelled in the art of making tea, and of providing it, charmingly served, for the weary European traveller at the thirstiest points along the road."[44] Many—like Harry Johnston, sent out as Her Majesty's special commissioner to report on conditions in Uganda and to advise upon the country's future—must have

> felt at home with the densely-settled, smiling Bantu peasants of the Lake Victoria basin, so different from the graceful but reserved Nilo-Hamitic pastoralists of the Kavirondo highlands. Unlike many, perhaps most Englishmen, [Johnston] was a consistent evolutionist. The true savage might be noble, at least in appearance, but he preferred those who were in economic and social development a stage nearer to himself . . . the people of Buganda . . . topped all Johnston's expectations. He crossed the Nile near its outlet from Lake Victoria, and sensed himself immediately in another country, where the principle of authority, recognised by all classes in the community, offered, no matter how it had been abused in the past by bad and bloody tyrants, the first and surest foundation for future progress.[45]

Encapsulated in impressions such as these, conveyed by Lugard and Johnston to their masters in London and to the reading public in England, is the unholy trinity of social Darwinism, the Protestant ethic and the natural supremacy of a ruling class. With respect to all three, Buganda acquires the status of a favored nation.

Three Englishmen alone appear to have emerged critical of the Buganda experience: Frederick Jackson, son of a Yorkshire farmer, drop-out from Cambridge, big game hunter, and naturalist of professional repute; Frederick Spire, a valet to Colonel Colville, later to become commissioner of the Eastern Province of Uganda; and William Crabtree, a West countryman and CMS missionary.[46] Possibly

44. Roland A. Oliver, *Sir Harry Johnston and the Scramble for Africa* (1957), p. 298.

45. Ibid., pp. 296–297.

46. For a sensitive appreciation of Jackson's career, see the introduction by Harold B. Thomas to a 1969 reprint of Jackson's autobiography, pp. v–xi. A. T. Matson, "A Note on F. Spire" (1966). See also Oliver (1957), p. 310, and E. P. Thiel, "Frederick Spire, S. M. B." (1962). A microfilm copy of Crabtree's diary is to be found in the Makerere University College

there was something in the social backgrounds of these men to account for their nonestablishment predilections. Whatever the case, they remained exceptions. For the vast majority of Britishers who served the Protectorate, the interest of Uganda was best served if the interest of Buganda was in the forefront of their attentions. Once Buganda was established as the heart of the colonial enterprise—the center of government, mission endeavor, communication, and commerce—Gandaphilia characterized successive generations of colonial officials, and a Gandacentric administration proved blind to any understanding of the amorphous regions beyond the pale. Even so, for Teso, as we shall see, more important than the deliberate preferences and rational actions of specific individuals were the interdependencies that were unconsciously established.

Because Uganda history has so long been viewed through southern, Gandacentric eyes, the incorporation of the periphery—those countries north and east of the Nile—has been perceived as part of one grand imperial design. Yet it would be wrong to accept the establishment view of steady and upward progress. From its initial phases, contact with the IBEA Co. brought deprivation. The regions bordering the caravan route were subject to considerable harrassment: "incessant thefts by passers-by, whether government caravans, mail-runners, private individuals, or, worst of all, parties of Sudanese women passing to and fro between Jinja and Mumia's."[47] By the end of the century, much of Busoga was impoverished, and it was partly on this account that the eyes of imperialism turned northward toward Bukeddi.

Religion, Commerce, and Arms

Christian missionaries both preceded and outnumbered company and Protectorate officials in Uganda at the end of the nineteenth century. To a large extent, Uganda's incorporation into the modern

---

library, according to Rowe (Ph.D. 1966), p. 225. I have not been able to locate the biography of Crabtree written by his daughter, referred to by Vincent Battle, "Education in Uganda" (Ph.D. thesis, 1974).

47. Jackson (1930), p. 257.

world economy was brought about with Protestant zeal. Yet Protestants were not alone in the field: the warring nations of Christ contested both the Islam of the merchant traders and indigenous African beliefs that coexisted with it.

The mission interests that made the Protectorate Christian did not make it harmonious. When Buganda fell within the British sphere of influence, the kingdom already housed missionaries from France and Germany. An association in the Baganda lay mind of Catholic missionaries with France and Protestant missionaries with England was no primitive misunderstanding. Official correspondence with the Foreign Office and with Church House in London indicated that international rivalry was recognized by officials and missionaries too. African converts were called Wa-Ingleza and Wa-Fransa. Jackson reported the "fanatical demeanour of the French priests from the date of their first arrival in the country";[48] equally fanatical, it would appear, were the Anglicans. John Roscoe of the CMS wrote during the civil war that it was a "wonderful thing to see the whole country in a blaze with the Roman Catholic houses which were fired by the Protestants."[49] Missionaries of the CMS labeled their religious confreres Romanists and Papists, as well as Catholics.[50] Protestant fear of treachery and papist plots was expressed no more clearly than in the Reverend Robert Ashe's escalation of rumors that a French bishop was plotting with German officials to smuggle a thousand breech-loading rifles into Buganda.[51] There is, indeed, always an elusive connection between religious

48. Ernest L. Bentley, Ag. Sec. IBEA Co., July 14, 1892; encl. copies of letters from Capt. Williams and Capt. Lugard, respectively (PRO FO/403/172 [52]).

49. Mr. Portal to Marquis of Salisbury, June 22, 1892; transmits two letters from missionaries, Mr. Roscoe and Mr. Boustead, regarding Uganda disturbances; Roscoe's letter is dated Jan. 24, 1892 (PRO FO/403/172 [66]).

50. Mr. Portal to Marquis of Salisbury, July 17, 1892; encl.: Précis of report by Captain Lugard, Feb. 4, 1892 (PRO FO/403/172.132). The missionaries were W. Collins, George A. Pilkington, and George K. Baskeville.

51. Mr. Portal to Marquis of Salisbury, July 28, 1892; contains extracts from letters respecting affairs in Uganda (PRO FO/403/181.47). Compare Robert F. Ashe, *Chronicles of Uganda* (1895), esp. pp. 203–208.

militancy and the international arms trade throughout this period.[52] Lugard's military intervention in 1892 (defeating Baganda Catholics at the Battle of Rubaga) was aimed at undermining the organization and unity of those Baganda feudal lords whose military strength was a threat to British interests. As Johnston observed: "If there is any country forming part of the Uganda Protectorate which could do us any real harm it is Uganda itself—the Kingdom of Uganda. Here we have something like a million fairly intelligent, slightly civilised negroes of warlike tendencies, and possessing about 10,000 to 12,000 guns." Not foreseeing the mutiny in their own ranks, Johnston believed the Baganda to be "the only people for a long time to come who can deal a serious blow to British rule."[53]

Given Gandaphilia—and reliance on Baganda arms—the divisiveness of religion was carried into the outlying regions of the Protectorate. Baganda forces conquered parts of Bukeddi, establishing military garrisons with catechists in residence. Baganda agents were later posted there, salaried officials who emerged as an important reference group for a local nascent bourgeoisie. Many Baganda entrepreneurs entered the country on their own account. Inevitably questions arise. Did the conquerors win religious converts through their military power? Did local chiefs align with Baganda protectors in matters of religion? Did Baganda agents carry religious factionalism into new territories? Was the power structure of Buganda religious discrimination reflected in the Teso scene? Were Buganda-bred hostilities perpetuated in the local setting, and if so, what effect did this have upon the administration of the new territories? As Protestant and Roman Catholic missionaries—

52. Perhaps at any period; on the European arms trade in Africa, and on papal strategies to counter what are considered Islamic arms blockades, see Sundström (1974), pp. 197–200. The significance of arms will be a matter of constant reference in the pages that follow.

53. Mr. H. Johnston to Marquis of Salisbury, Mar. 17, 1900. Quoted in Mamdani (1976), p. 42. Note the twentyfold increase since Stanley's report of 1875. Although Johnston's figures may be illusory, there is strong evidence of the increased flow of arms in the southern savanna and in eastern Africa, especially following upon American and European wars. See, for example, R. A. Caulk, "Firearms and Princely Power in Ethiopia in the Nineteenth Century" (1972) and J. P. Smalldone, "Firearms in the Central Sudan: A Revaluation" (1972).

English, Irish and Belgian, for the most part—entered Bukeddi, were European national interests served in the local political arena?

Before all these questions, however, comes the large central issue of Islam. In the particular configuration of Islam, much comes together. This chapter began with an account of British activities along the Nile in the middle of the nineteenth century. Arab slave raiding in that region contributed to the Bachopi diaspora, which strengthened Bukeddi's links with the Bunyoro kingdom. The advent of the Bakers from the north and the interventions of the Sudanese planted the Egyptian flag in northern Bunyoro. Little wonder, then, that a conflict of interest between Buganda and Bunyoro was seen, through European eyes, as a battleground of the Cross and the Crescent. As early as 1877, the CMS submitted a memorial to the British foreign secretary urging that the khedive of Egypt be dissuaded from his imperial enterprises. Anglican anxiety was expressed in a request that the kabaka's independence be guaranteed and that "the neutrality of, and free trade on, Lake Victoria" be secured.[54] British business enterprise linked Christianity with commerce "backing philanthropy by hard cash."[55] The "dangers of Islamic expansion" reflected, essentially, a fear of mercantile competition, albeit couched in ideological terms. Jackson, for example, wrote home of "combined Banyoro and Mohammedan hordes" to the north: the implicit analogy is instructive.[56] To the north of the fertile, settled states of Busoga and Buganda lay barbarians intent on plunder and destruction; even so had the civilizations of Europe been sacked by the restless, nomadic peoples of the northern plains.

The clash of Indian Ocean mercantile and European capitalist systems came to a head in the 1880s, expressing itself in requests for official intervention in East Africa. In 1892, the IBEA Co. directors, tors, "somewhat appalled at the vast responsibility . . . forced upon them,"[57] issued a financial statement. Their capital, now of

54. Oliver (1952), p. 87.

55. Charles Pelham Groves, "Missionary and Humanitarian Aspects of Imperialism from 1870 to 1914" (1970), p. 465.

56. Memorandum, July 19, 1892, by Mr. H. Jackson, late leader IBEA Co. caravan, 1888–1890, on probable results of evacuation of Uganda (PRO FO/403/172.54).

57. Sir Frederick Jackson (1930), p. 265. Sir John Scott Keltie calculated that the IBEA Co. could only call on about 10 shs. of capital for every

£500,000, could not maintain an expanding administration. Because they could not obtain government permission to raise taxes, or raise a subsidy to build a railway from the coast, they announced that they were compelled to withdraw from East Africa. A special campaign was initiated under dramatic circumstances. Bishop Alfred Tucker of the CMS was guest at a country house in the Scottish highlands when Sir William Mackinnon, chairman of the IBEA Co., unexpectedly arrived. Mackinnon, it would appear, challenged the bishop, who deplored the company's imminent departure from Uganda, to raise £10,000, declaring that he would match this sum with a further £5,000 raised among his own friends. In two weeks the transaction was effected, and the government, yielding to public opinion, agreed that the company could continue in business.[58]

"Not unnaturally," one commentator observes, "this unusual episcopal operation, together with the society's action, has since been, and was even at the time, the subject of critical comment."[59] Missionary outcry, and this intriguing success in raising funds at the last minute, postponed the company's departure. Lugard urged that access to "the greatest ivory preserve of the world" was reason enough for government intervention,[60] but by now this was becoming an obsolete interest; different forces were at work in the British economy.

At the Foreign Office, the earl of Rosebery pondered whether Buganda could be placed in the care of the sultan of Zanzibar—an extension, as it were, of Britain's protective interest in East Africa. This might have appeared a logical course, since trade routes had carried both the slaver and the commercially minded antislaver from Zanzibar to Mengo in the first place. But, like Lugard's thinking, it was outmoded. Mercantilism and laissez-faire Christianity

---

square mile it was supposed to administer and develop (Keltie, *The Partition of Africa* (1893), pp. 326–328).

58. For his own account of this incident, see Alfred R. Tucker, *Eighteen Years in Uganda and East Africa* (1908), p. 64.

59. Groves (1970), p. 474. For an account of the confusion surrounding the matter, see Leonard Woolf (1920), pp. 295–297.

60. Mr. Portal to Marquis of Salisbury, July 17, 1892, transmits précis of Capt. Lugard's report on Uganda. (PRO FO/403/172.118–119).

had given way to industrial capitalism and the aggressive onslaught of Christianity against Islam. Rosebery set the scheme aside. Better for the inland territory to become a Protectorate in its own right: Christian and open to commerce.[61]

In 1893 a military administration was established, superseding that of the IBEA Co., which had held the country through the efforts of Capt. F. D. Lugard and Capt. W. H. Williams. Sir G. H. Portal was appointed commissioner; he was followed by Capt. J. R. L. Macdonald and Col. the Hon. H. E. Colville, also military men. From the moment of their entry onto the Uganda scene, British officials could not but be aware of their military weakness. Lugard had arrived in 1890 with two Englishmen (William Grant and De Winton), a Muslim Swahili interpreter, 50 Nubian soldiers, and 250 armed Swahili porters. Captain Williams of the Royal Engineers had arrived six weeks later with 50 Nubians and 100 armed Swahilis. As soon as he could, Lugard had traveled into Bunyoro to recruit the remnants of Emin Pasha's force, a further 600 men; and Sir Gerald Portal's first act after hauling down the company's flag was to recruit the remainder.[62] Colville's arrival in November 1893 had marked the beginning of the military campaign against Kabalega, who had succeeded to the throne of Bunyoro.

A provisional protectorate was proclaimed—its success entirely dependent upon the deployment of Baganda troops—and an assault was launched on Bunyoro. On June 18, 1894, Buganda formally became a dependency. By the end of the nineteenth century the "necessary" elimination of an Islamic threat to Christian and commercial interests in the area was all but complete.

Encapsulated in the ideology of religious conflict in Uganda—Christian against Muslim—was the structural conflict of two disparate political economies, the mercantilist Islamic world system of the Mediterranean and Indian Ocean and the modern world system of European (and American) industrial capitalism. The expression of this conflict united in late nineteenth-century Uganda the warring Christian factions (missionaries, converts, soldiers, company officials, government servants) against a common enemy: Islam. That

61. Memorandum by the Earl of Rosebery on the subject of Uganda and the policy to be followed with regard to it (PRO FO/403/173.148).
62. Sir Frederick Jackson, p. 268.

Bunyoro was a base for disaffected and rebellious Baganda Muslims was among the reasons for war against its ruler in 1893, the declaration of which was written in Arabic. The "Unyoro campaign" was "necessary" for the establishment and perpetuation of a strategic geographical position (to use Bishop Willis' phrase) from which military and commercial interests could operate. The strategic location of Bukeddi between the Christianizing Bantu-speaking south and the Islamicizing Nilotic-speaking north meant that "Christianity was first brought to Teso not by missionaries but by an army."[63] From that, much else followed.

63. A. M. Bishop and D. Ruffell, " A History of the Upper Nile Diocese" (MS., n.d.), p. 1.

2. Bukeddi: The Moving Frontier

Pioneering doesn't pay.
Andrew Carnegie

Show me the first capitalist.
Fernand Braudel

Intensification of conflict followed the establishment of the Protectorate in 1894, culminating in the decisive War of 1897–99, when longstanding opposition to the British takeover was finally crushed—thereafter only to take on more subtle forms than military confrontation. Dependent as the British were on local arms to maintain an existence in the region, it was to the Buganda court that they turned for support and to those Baganda who mobilized their followers that they, in consequence, owed recompense. The Baganda capital was at this time, as we have seen, the hub of thriving commerce and religious dispute; the material life of its people reflected their position on the frontier of the world economy. The next step for the kabaka and the British was to extend the power of the capital into the countryside.

Such an enterprise drew its strength inevitably from the competition around the throne. Cutting across the factions of the capital, subimperialism (as it has been termed) united those who saw new and greater opportunities further from home.

In a true spirit of adventure and service which had characterised their forefathers, the Baganda became the vanguard of western civilisation at the loss of important positions at home, settled lives and prestige among their own people . . . The impact they made, particularly their culture in its various forms, will need more violent methods to undo it.[1]

The outstanding cultural builder of the time was, without doubt, Semei Kwakirenzi Kakungulu. A "man of sterling qualities, he was a successful war leader, an administrator of genius, and a church-builder"; and to Kakungulu is attributed the conquest of Bukeddi and, within it, Teso. These territories he administered for the British "until such time as they had sufficient manpower to assume responsibility": such is the judgment of posterity.[2]

Yet accounts of Bukeddi's incorporation within the Uganda Protectorate in terms of Baganda subimperialism and the exploits of Kakungulu greatly magnify the man, on the one hand, and the nature of his political domain, on the other. Sir John Gray, who interviewed Kakungulu on at least two occasions, suggested that "the legendary Kakungulu was in no small measure the creation of Semei Kwakirenzi Kakungulu himself."[3] Kakungulu's Bukeddi fiefdom seems similarly to be in no small measure a creation of his biographers. Kakungulu's own reminiscences require collaboration from other sources, of course, and nowhere is this more true than of his assertions concerning his achievements in "Bukeddi." Divided as his contemporaries were over his goals and ambitions, this least well-documented period of Kakungulu's career was the most distorted for private and personal reasons. Whether from Kakungulu himself, his Baganda followers, Anglican missionaries, or colonial officials, much that others came to know of Kakungulu in Bukeddi furnished a political ideology that Gandaphilia glorified at the expense of Teso political reality. Yet, ideology notwithstanding, Kakungulu's career depicts in miniature the process by which Teso was

1. M. S. M. Semakula Kiwanuka, *A History of Buganda* (1972), pp. 152–153.

2. Ibid. See also Sir John M. Gray, "Kakungulu in Bukeddi" (1963); Harold B. Thomas, "Capax Imperii: The Story of Semei Kakungulu" (1939); Michael J. Twaddle, "Politics in Bukeddi, 1900–1939" (Ph.D. thesis, 1967).

3. Sir John M. Gray (1963), p. 31.

encapsulated within the colonial state. There was little that was imperial about it and much that now appears fortuitous.

Whether Kakungulu's exploits in Bukeddi should be regarded as subimperialism depends upon whether he is regarded as a Muganda chief with the command of levies that he placed at the disposal of the British military command, or as an actor, a spiralist perhaps, moving into a larger arena whose boundaries were delineated in a precolonial era. The question is not a slight one, since later hostility to the Baganda and subsequent political instability in Uganda has been attributed to recollections of these early years in Bukeddi.[4]

Semei Kakungulu was among the first of Uganda's New Men, member of an elite, Christianized group, newly marginal to the society into which they were born, opportunist and upwardly mobile. Both racialist identifications of the man and anachronistic perceptions of tribal society can be set aside in order that his spiralist activities can be perceived as instrumental to British capitalism per se rather than as an expression of Baganda subimperialism, so-called.[5] Kakungulu's actions as a fervent Protestant convert can-

---

4. Michael J. Twaddle, "'Tribalism' in Eastern Uganda" (1969), esp. p. 196.

5. See esp. A. D. Roberts, "The Sub-Imperialism of the Baganda" (1962). Terence O. Ranger, in "African Reactions to the Imposition of Colonial Rule in East and Central Africa" (1970), p. 302, notes that the struggle against such sub-imperialisms provides "one of the dominant themes" in the modern political history of East and Central Africa. It is, perhaps, necessary to suggest that just as it is useful to distinguish between Britain's national interest in colonialism and certain British financiers' and industrialists' interest in global capitalism, so it is surely necessary to distinguish between Buganda state interests and those of certain Baganda. Yet, e.g., C. C. Wrigley (1957), pp. 72–73, moves easily from one to the other, from nineteenth-century Buganda as a "brigand state" to "Ganda society [as] acquisitive and competitive to a degree unparalleled in east or central Africa":

> The Ganda were an ambition-ridden people, and though their ambition expressed itself almost solely in political intrigue, it could easily be diverted into other channels once these had been dug. Their acquisitiveness, moreover, was not oriented toward any particular form of property. Cattle were highly valued, but they were not, as for many African peoples, the sole measure of value. Any commodity having

not easily be disentangled from those he performed as commander of Baganda levies, as a servant of the IBEA Co., or from his own material interests. Even as Kakungulu's career presents a microcosm of the events leading to the invasion of Teso, so his character and ambitions seem not so very different from those of the soldiers, missionaries, and administrators he counted his friends. In those "early co-operative days," to use one missionary's phrase, Semei Kakungulu was one of a cohort.[6] Indeed, one of the problems Kakungulu encountered, as the nature of British overrule changed in its passage from military to civilian government during the years that followed the establishment of a Protectorate, was that he remained representative of the frontier generation to whom hunting for ivory and "sporting" wars were of the essence. As tensions developed within the British establishment between military and civilian officers and between company and Foreign Office officials, so Ka-

---

intrinsic utility could serve equally well as an object of cupidity and as a counter in the struggle for honour and power. Similarly, though war bulked large in the economy of the Ganda, it was not an essential part of their culture; there was no exaggerated cult of military virtues. They looked on warfare primarily as a business and were quite ready to turn their hands to any other form of business that might offer.

The concept of spiralism was introduced by William Watson, "Social Mobility and Social Class in Industrial Communities" (1964), p. 147, to refer to the progressive ascent of specialists of different skills through a series of higher positions in one or more hierarchical structures, and the concomitant residential mobility through a number of communities at one or more steps during the ascent forms a characteristic combination of social spatial mobility."

6. The phrase is taken from the obituary of Father Christopher J. Kirk, a member of the Mill Hill mission's third expedition to Uganda, by Joseph McGough, "The Late Father Christopher J. Kirk, O. B. E." (1956), p. 15. Although it refers to Kirk's maintaining close ties of friendship with colonial administrators who shared his early experiences, it seems not inappropriate to apply it to the leading Africans of his day as well. Yet, as will become apparent, Kakungulu's career is not without disparagement. In weighing contradictory statements, I have tended to follow Sir John Gray, who knew the man and whose manuscript notes indicate his own informed struggle to order the confusion surrounding Kakungulu.

Besides Gray's published work (1963), several unpublished papers were

kungulu, at first an asset and praised, became Kakungulu, an embarrassment and reviled.

Semei Kakungulu was born, not in Buganda, but in the south of Koki sometime between 1864 and 1870.[7] He belonged to the Mamba clan, the son of a Muganda father and a Koki mother. He first crossed the threshold of Mwanga's court by supplying him with ivory with which to make purchases from Arab traders, a characteristically entrepreneurial approach to the seat of power. Becoming a Protestant "reader" in Buddu at a time when most converts there were becoming Roman Catholics, he was among those who retreated to Ankole with Apolo Kagwa after the Muslim coup d'etat of 1888. Although his conversion enabled him to profit from the subsequent Christian victory, the kabaka's identification with the Catholic party, along with opposition from Apolo Kagwa, prevented his achieving any higher office than that of a chief in Kyaggwe. There he was well placed for private ivory trading with Busoga.[8] Already an outstanding notable in his mid-twenties, Kakungulu by his actions in the religious wars of 1892—now between the victorious Protestants and Roman Catholics—cemented his Protestant allegiances. It was mainly owing to him, apparently, that two Anglican missionaries, R. H. Walker and Robert Ashe, were rescued from danger in Buddu in 1892. Bishop Tucker was later to

---

used. Chief among them were Gray's "Report on the Claims of Semei B. Kakunguru . . . " (1924) and an uncatalogued box file of undated notes relating to Kakungulu in the Cambridge University library. See also A. T. Matson, "Bibliography of the Works of Sir John Gray" (1971). Michael Twaddle's Ph. D. thesis (1967) was also used, as well as his "The Founding of Mbale" (1966); "Tribalism in Eastern Uganda" (1969); "Segmentary Violence and Political Change in Early Colonial Uganda" (paper, University of East Africa, Nairobi, 1969); and "The Muslim Revolution in Buganda" (1972). For the significance of warlords, such as Kakungulu, in Ugandan history, see Donald A. Low, "Warbands and Ground-Level Imperialism in Uganda, 1870–1900" (1974–75).

7. William J. Ansorge, *Under the African Sun* (London, 1899), pp. 103–106; Gray, "Report" (1924), Appendix A.

8. John A. Rowe, "Land and Politics in Buganda, 1875–1955" (1964). Since there were no elephants in Busoga, Kakungulu's operations presumably involved middlemen trading with the Bakeddi of the northern savanna.

describe Kakungulu as "one of nature's gentlemen,"[9] and Hesketh Bell, governor of Uganda from 1905 to 1909, echoed and improved upon the sentiment when he wrote of Kakungulu as "evidently one of Nature's noblemen."[10] Such might not have been the view of Roman Catholic missionaries, since "less creditable" actions in Sesse, including attacks on the Catholic party, brought about a diplomatic incident between the British and the French governments.[11]

Despite these international repercussions, locally Kakungulu's troops were in demand by the British officers under Lugard, whose intervention in the civil war had decided the issue in favor of the Protestants. Later in 1892 Kakungulu and his levy accompanied Captain W. H. Williams to Busoga to reinstate Miru as an agent of the IBEA Co. On June 17 of that year Kakungulu was a signatory to two letters, one addressed to Queen Victoria and the other to the directors of the IBEA Co., asking that a protectorate be established in Uganda.[12] Not only in missionary and military, administrative and commercial spheres was Kakungulu's stature at its zenith, but in Uganda court circles, too. At the end of the year, in the annual redistribution of Buganda chieftainships, Kakungulu was created *kimbugwe*, the third highest office in the land. He also married into the kabaka's family. With two thousand guns and three thousand spears under his command, Kakungulu again served under Williams to suppress Bavuma islanders threatening to disrupt lake trade to Mengo. Four months later he was in action against Muslim rebels in Kampala, then commanded an expeditionary force in Toro, one of the western kingdoms.[13] When at the end of 1893 Colonel Henry Colville led his decisive expedition against Kabalega of Bunyoro,

9. Alfred Tucker (1908), p. 277.

10. Sir Henry Hesketh Bell, *Glimpses of a Governor's Life* (1946), p. 127.

11. Gray, "Report." For an account of this incident, see Hubert P. Gale, *Uganda and the Mill Hill Fathers* (1959), pp. 66–69.

12. Gray "Report."

13. Accounts of these early campaigns appear in Herbert H. Austin, *With Macdonald in Uganda* (1903), pp. 36–54; John R. L. Macdonald, *Soldiering and Surveying in British East Africa* (1897), pp. 307–322; Trevor P. B. Ternan, *Some Experiences of an Old Bromsgrovian* (1930), pp. 169–191; Arthur B. Thruston, *African Incidents* (1900), pp. 106–192; and Seymour Vandeleur, *Campaigning on the Upper Nile and Niger* (1898).

the leadership of the Baganda levies was entrusted to Kakungulu, who was counted one of the few men wholly above the factionalism of the Buganda court.

It has been suggested that Kakungulu was dependent upon CMS missionaries for his advancement.[14] The missionaries believed the opposite to be true, and their indebtedness to him for his intervention on their behalf in 1892[15] blinded them to his faults for a considerable period thereafter. Whatever the truth of the matter, with both the military and the Protestant missionaries behind him, Kakungulu was well on his way to achieving greater prominence. The Bunyoro campaign on which he was about to embark might well have made a Wellington or Eisenhower of him, and it will probably never be clear whether high political office within Buganda escaped him or whether he had the vision to see that his greatest opportunities for advancement lay in a world outside that realm.

The nature of Kakungulu's command in the Unyoro Campaign reveals the extent to which the colonial power was dependent, at that time, upon his contribution. Out of a total force of 14,603 men, men, 14,130 were Baganda chiefs, filemen, musketeers, and spearmen.[16] In this engagement the Baganda forces were an auxiliary battalion, irregulars, as it were, under British overall command, contracted for a specific task and for a limited time. It seems apt to label them mercenaries. Kakungulu himself, according to his own accounting, was paid in ivory, cowries, iron hoes, and copper to the value of £116,285.6.0. Everything received, he claimed, was later expended for arms and ammunition to equip his Bukeddi expeditions in the service of the Uganda government.[17]

Kakungulu's success in Bunyoro served as a springboard for his ambitions. His finest hour was possibly that on April 22, 1894, when, accompanying Grant and a body of Nubian troops, he led a "naval brigade" of 123 canoes from Bugosa in an assault on Ka-

---

14. Thomas (1939), pp. 125–128.

15. See, e.g., Bishop and Ruffell, p. 2.

16. Col. Colville to Mr. Cracknell, Jan. 2, 1894 (PRO FO/403/193.146). There were also Masai spearmen and Swahili headmen, askaris and armed porters, totaling a further 253 men.

17. Gray, "Report."

balega's stockaded position on the east bank of the Nile.[18] Their combined troops jointly pursued Kabalega's retreating forces into Bukeddi. "The operation lasted only three days [and] the party cannot have penetrated vary far, but it came back with five hundred head of cattle."[19]

Shortly afterward, Kakungulu broke with the Baganda court at Mengo—typically, over the legalities involved in the distribution of cattle captured on the Bukeddi expedition. Called upon to deliver the Baganda share to the court for distribution, Kakungulu declined to do so. An appeal to Major G. G. Cunningham failed,[20] and Kakungulu immediately resigned as kimbugwe. Bishop Tucker described Kakungulu's resignation as "due entirely to his strong conviction that as a Christian man it was impossible for him to live a life of continual contention with a fellow Christian" such as the traditional relation between the chieftainship of the kimbugwe and the *katikiro* (Prime Minister) in the royal household required. Kakungulu "abandoned his high office and large emoluments from conscientious motives" and retired into the "comparative obscurity" of Bugerere.[21] Given this scenario by their bishop, it is not surprising that CMS missionaries later portray Kakungulu's invasions of Bukeddi as pioneer efforts at evangelization.

What was "comparative obscurity" to the Anglican bishop housed in Kampala was a cockpit of action for the new protectorate during the next five years. In northern Bugerere (Bunyala), which at that date was still an appendage of Bunyoro, Kakungulu was to all intents and purposes working for his own ends. Nevertheless, "both the British and the Baganda governments tacitly acquiesced in his

---

18. "From the account of an eye-witness, it was a really magnificent spectacle; and one that will certainly never be seen again" (Sir Frederick Jackson, 1930, p. 272). Compare Lt. Col. Hubert Moyse-Bartlett's comment: "[Lugard's] troops marched in the centre of a vast throng of 25,000 Baganda levies, advancing across country in parallel columns, each with its chief at its head. It was an extraordinary spectacle, often to be repeated in succeeding years and one that frequently invoked the wonder of officers new to Uganda and unused to the cooperation of such strange allies" (Moyse-Bartlett, *The King's African Rifles*, 1956, p. 50).

19. Sir John M. Gray (1963), p. 32.

20. Ibid., p. 33; see also Thomas (1939), pp. 129–130.

21. Alfred Tucker, "Correspondence" (1896).

acts since they furthered their own interests."[22] Harold B. Thomas suggested that to be "a baron of the marches was peculiarly in tune with Kakungulu's temperament";[23] it allowed him full scope for maneuver.

It is not clear whether Kakungulu's accompanying a reconnaissance team on Lake Kyoga was part of any regular services that he was called upon by the Protectorate government to carry out in Bugerere[24] or whether it was simply opportune. The team's object was to survey the eastern end of the lake, and, as a member, Kakungulu, along with Captain R. T. Kirkpatrick and Surgeon-Captain G. S. McLoughlin visited Kawere Island, Bugondo, Madoch, Namusana, Kagwara, Namuliba Island, Sambwe, and Pingire. Whatever the circumstances of his participation, Kakungulu later claimed that his establishment in Bugerere was the beginning of his government service, independent of his role as a Buganda chief.[25]

Kakungulu's interest in Bukeddi almost certainly preceded that of the British in the region: his personal wealth, accumulated through ivory transactions, attests to this. But it was not the prospect of ivory alone that turned Kakungulu's eyes northward. The richness of food supplies northeast of the lake was apparent to a commander of troops accustomed to living off the land. Kakungulu may well have entertained a desire to carve out eastern estates like those wrested from the Bunyoro plains four or five years earlier. Or it may indeed have been that, as a fervent Christian convert in close contact with missionaries, he, like them, turned his eyes toward Ethiopia, the upper Nile, and the threat of the Muslim north. Whatever the immediate reason, or whatever the convergence of past experience that brought him to this point, in 1896 Kakungulu turned to exploit the land lying to the east rather than to the north of Lake Kyoga.

22. Gray, "Report" (1924), Appendix A.

23. Thomas (1939), p. 129.

24. The former is the impression conveyed by Thomas, p. 131; the latter by Simion Waswa, "Kakungulu" (MS., n.d.), par. 19.

25. Thus he claimed: "I, B. S. Kakungulu, in the year 1895, discovered Bukedi District. I came with 1,246 soldiers and they were with their personal servants 4,321. Altogether we were 5,567 men, and out of these 739 were killed in the war, and I spent £421,500 for feeding and helping them, and I had 1,246 rifles also, I spent £652,300 to buy ammunitions" (Gray, "Report").

The events of the Buganda court in that year may well have contributed to his decision. Many notables had been disappointed by
the kabaka's honors list of that year, which left several unpromoted
and ready to enter Kakungulu's service, with the possibility of acquiring estates in Bukeddi.[26]

In 1896, fifty armed men were sent across the lake from Bunyala
to capture and occupy the trading island of Kawere. Permanent
houses were built and twenty men garrisoned there, under the command of Paulo Kalulwe. Another force established a similar base on
Namuliba Island, where fifteen men were left, under Lasito Nubiru.
Trees were planted: sambya, palms, and plantains to be used in
building, thatching, and sustaining a permanent settlement.[27] Although several persons from Kaberamaido—Otagi, Omaswa, Amolo, and "about a hundred others"—sought "the aid of the Baganda" against their Langi neighbours,[28] others around the lake
joined to attack them, and it was necessary to despatch reinforcements (thirty men who stayed for two months until their military
presence was needed elsewhere). The need for this action suggests a
contrast between contact with the Banyoro and with Kakungulu's
force; whereas there was an element of mutual benefit in the former,
the latter smacked of plunder.

Whatever the local view of Kakungulu, as freebooter or Muganda
military commander in the field, he himself later claimed that he was
acting as an officer of the Protectorate government. In 1896, he
stated, he was given the task of "subduing (*kuwangula*) the people
of Bukeddi, who were very backward."[29] He was supplied with guns
(1,246 rifles) and ammunition by the Protectorate administration,
and it was to this end that he—along with over four thousand camp
followers—established a fort, which he named Galiraya (Galilee), at
the northern tip of Bugerere.

The only report of Kakungulu's engagement in Bukeddi in the
months that followed arose out of his need to account for the loss
of fifty men and twenty-seven guns when intervening to support one
party of Wakeddi against another: clear evidence, one would have

26. Gray, "Report," p. 46; Thomas (1939), p. 132.
27. Waswa (MS., n.d.), par. 16.
28. G. Emwanu, "The Reception of Alien Rule in Teso, 1896–1927"
(1967), p. 172.
29. Gray, "Report," p. 34.

thought, of his accountability to the British command. In this intervention, Kakungulu chose the losing side. Sir John Gray assumes the incident to have involved conflict between Iteso and Langi,[30] but there is no reason why it should not have been between one group of Iteso and another; perhaps it was one of the affrays narrated in the next chapter.

In September 1896 Kakungulu accompanied to the Mengo court a deputation of Kumam and Teso chiefs who wished to ask for protection against the Langi. Among them, according to Kakungulu, were five Kumam—Kyeunda I, Mulema, Tagi, Koladyani, and Nyamulange—and Masa of "Teso" and Kyeunda II of Musala, near Soroti.[31] The significance of this action bears some consideration. It seems likely that Kakungulu was acting upon Claude Sitwell's recommendation, even instruction. At that time the Protectorate government was not in a position to extend its activities into Bukeddi, and yet, clearly, it would not have wished such strategically placed collaborators to have gone unnoticed. For Kakungulu to have acted as their intermediary at Mengo would appear to have been yet another interim measure, and one that Kabaka Mwanga would not have opposed. How Kakungulu presented himself at the court cannot be known; the event is pristine in that it provided the occasion for the first reporting of Iteso names in the colonial record. Nothing is known of the outcome.

According to Kakungulu, he had by 1897 pushed his forts out as far as Kanyiriri, Bululu, Lale, Kisoga (near Serere), Wamasa, and Nyala in eastern Bukeddi. Any further moves he might have made into the interior of Teso were halted by the outbreak of a British army mutiny, which rapidly escalated into full-scale war.

The War of 1897–99: Resistance, Rebellion, and Mutiny

In 1897, that opposition to British colonial rule in Uganda crystallized which has been characterized as a configuration of Muslim interests: those of Kabalega of Bunyoro, who had been defeated in 1896; the rebellious Kabaka Mwanga and his Baganda followers; and Nubian mutineers from the Protectorate's standing army. The War of 1897–99 brought about the final and irrevocable declara-

30. Ibid. p. 35.
31. Ibid. Compare Gray (1963), p. 34.

tion of imperial intent in Uganda, the deployment of imperial troops from India marking Uganda's formal initiation into the world of monopoly capitalism.[32]

The army mutiny began among Nubian troops assigned to accompany Lt. Col. James R. L. Macdonald on an expedition whose nominal destination was the headwaters of the Juba River, north of the Protectorate.[33] A multitude of grievances had accumulated: the troops had just returned from long campaigns in Nandi country and Buddu and were loath to see service again so soon; they had suffered long periods of separation from their wives and families; their clothing and pay were often in arrears; their pay compared unfavorably with that of Swahili porters in nongovernment employ; they had recently learned of mutinies in the Congo and sought to improve their condition by the same means.[34] Quickly, however, the

32. When Mackinnon had earlier proposed the use in Uganda of military levies raised in India and the Sudan, the Foreign Office had objected; see Leonard Woolf (1920), p. 275.

33. Macdonald's secret orders have given birth to a growing historiography. See, e.g., A. T. Matson, "Macdonald's Expedition to the Nile" (1965); "Macdonald's Manuscript History of the Events of 1897 to 1899" (1968a); "A Further Note on the Macdonald Expedition, 1897–1899" (1969); and "Introduction" to H. H. Austin (1973 ed.). The manuscript of Macdonald's projected book on the Juba expedition and the Sudanese mutiny was banned by the Foreign Office. The publishers, Arnold, then brought out Major Austin's *With Macdonald in Uganda* in 1903. For local dimensions of the expedition, see James P. Barber, "The Macdonald Expedition to the Nile 1887–99" (1964) and *Imperial Frontier* (1968) pp. 6–18; R. W. Beachey, "Macdonald's Expedition and the Uganda Mutiny" (1967b); and Sir Frederick Jackson (1930), pp. 318–319. For global diplomatic dimensions, see Robinson and Gallagher (1961), pp. 359–366; Sanderson (1965), esp. pp. 256–258; and G. N. Uzoigwe, *Britain and the Conquest of Africa* (1974), pp. 201–202, 264.

34. The account that follows is a reconstruction from two series of Foreign Office dispatches (PRO FO/403/261.85,86,89,90 and PRO FO/403/262.41) and the memoirs of European contemporaries. As a rounded account this is clearly suspect. The narrow, reactionary focus on the army mutiny—here treated as part of a much larger attempt to overthrow the Protectorate (hence my coinage, "The War of 1897–99")—leaves unexamined the possibility of earlier and, perhaps, preliminary, contacts between Kabalega, Mwanga, and elements of the army.

affair took on major proportions, as the grievances of the Nubian troops fell into line with both the disaffection of Mwanga and the warring hostility of Kabalega. The campaigns of the previous five years against dissident elements in Buganda and on its frontiers came together all of a piece as the colonial power in Uganda reached a moment of disabling crisis. In the closing months of 1897 all three fields of military activity—Buddu (by then the Catholic-dominated stronghold of the rebellious Mwanga in southern Buganda), Kabalega's Bunyoro wasteland, and Busoga, where the Nubian rebels made their stand—south, west, and east, all coalesced as combatants from each rebellious zone converged upon the southern shores of Lake Kyoga. Whereas the first twenty years had seen British force moving progressively outward, westward and northward from their garrison state in Buganda, the events of 1897 brought the periphery to the center as the political interests of Mwanga, Kabalega, and Rehan Tobi's Nubian soldiers converged to challenge the colonial power.

In July 1897 Mwanga fled from Mengo, and disaffection spread to Busoga. Kakungulu, as the native governor of Bugerere, bullied the northern Busoga chiefs into throwing in their lot with the British, thus thwarting Kabalega's hopes for their support. Conflicting accounts tell of Kakungulu leaving the battle of Luba's Hill and being sent back by the government, with one hundred men, to reoccupy Kabagambe, a Lake Kyoga fort captured by the mutineers. With some foresight, Kakungulu's men had removed most of the canoes before leaving to take part in the southern campaign, and the mutineers had been obliged to look around for others. This action was considered fundamental to the victory of the government forces, since the delay that resulted allowed British troops to forestall the rebel force at Mruli. For the next two months the Bugerere garrison was harassed on all sides. Mutineers continued to be, as Macdonald reported, "active in the country of the Wakeddi," crossing the Nile to attack from the south. Their ally, the Musoga chief Gabula, launched an assault from the northeast. It was subsequently at Kabagambe that reinforcements (largely Sikhs, Swahili, Nubians, Indians, and recruits from the coast) defeated the main body of mutineers as they, in turn, were about to cross the lake. Some one hundred rebels fled, taking refuge in the swamps of Lake Kyoga.

After a visit to Kabagambe, the British military commander, Macdonald, visited the southern shores of Teso at the mouth of the Mpologoma River. "Getting a canoe," he wrote, "we pushed out reconnaissance as far as the open water of Lake Kyoga and found that not only did this lake extend a long way to the north-east, but also that this canoe passage through the papyrus and sudd which fringed the bank of the lake was so difficult as to be impassable in the face of a few determined men armed with breechloaders."[35] Macdonald directed that all canoe crossings should be blocked, leaving their defense to the Waganda. Accordingly, Kakungulu reconnoitered the area, including the island where the defeated portion of the rebel army under Rehan Tobi had sought refuge, only to discover that they, like their comrades earlier, had fled to "Wakeddi land." Their cattle were "recovered" by Kakungulu.

A few months later, in June 1898, Kakungulu set out on a punitive expedition against Gabula. But, since his enthusiasm for pillage led him to direct his efforts against other Basoga communities as well, including some who had helped the British against the mutineers, he was ordered by the government to withdraw. The following month a communication from Grant notified the Foreign Office that Kakungulu wanted to settle in Busoga. Permission was apparently denied.[36]

Eastern Equatoria?

The War of 1897–99 aborted Macdonald's military expedition charged with exploring "certain territories within the British sphere of influence, but lying outside the actual limits of the East African and Uganda Protectorates."[37] The intention of the British government, as the Uganda Protectorate became more clearly defined, was to extend effective control eastward "so as to comprise Lake Rudolf

35. Major Macdonald to Marquis of Salisbury, Feb. 15, 1898 (PRO FO/403/261.90).

36. Gray, "Report," Appendix A. In Gray's miscellaneous notes relating to Kakungulu, he cites a communication from Grant to Cromer, July 1, 1898, as his authority.

37. Major Ternan, Aug. 25, 1897; arrangements have been made for troops for Major Macdonald's expedition, etc. (PRO FO/403/243.90).

within its administrative sphere"[38]—a notion of eastward expansion, ultimately to the borders of Ethiopia, that appears several times in the colonial record and was echoed by Protestant missionaries.

When the expedition finally set out in August 1898, its task, ostensibly, was to secure by treaty a continuous block of territory up to five degrees north. The route that was followed ringed Teso, and repercussions were inevitably felt. Their objective successfully carried out, the caravan returned to Save, north of Mount Masaba, at the end of November. For reasons that are not clear, Macdonald ordered Captain Kirkpatrick, the young officer who had accompanied McLoughlin and Kakungulu on their survey of Lake Kyoga less than six months earlier, to detour from the main body of the expedition in order to map the boundary of Karamoja, which was said to lie along the Nakodokododoi River at the foot of the Rift Valley escarpment.[39] Kirkpatrick found the river on August 25, but before marching back to join Macdonald he went with a guide, an interpreter, and seven armed men to a hill some five miles further west. The natives they met offered them food; then, when the officer was separated from his men, they speared and killed him.

A local informant, Aleper, son of the chief whom Kirkpatrick had met in November 1898, provided an explanation of the incident:

> On November 26th Kirkpatrick met the chief of the Nyakwai, Ngoreale . . . The meeting between Kirkpatrick and Ngoreale went well but, unknown to the two leaders, there was a much less successful meeting between a group of Nyakwai women and some of Kirkpatrick's troops. The soldiers flirted so outrageously that the women fled in terror to their "manyattas" [grass huts], perched high among the hills, raised the alarm, and demanded that the strangers be killed. Although Ngoreale on his return advised against violence he was overruled."[40]

Ngoreale's failure had severe consequences for the inhabitants of

---

38. Marquis of Salisbury to Sir A. Hardinge, May 31, 1898 (PRO FO/403/261.128).

39. This account of the Nyakwai incident is taken directly from Macdonald's field report (PRO FO/403/280.154–155). There is no discussion of the incident in Austin (1903).

40. Barber (1964), pp. 7–8.

the Nyakwai hills. Macdonald despatched McLoughlin, Lieutenant Pereira, thirteen Sikhs, ninety-five Nubian and Swahili troops, and one Maxim gun to the scene of the encounter. The villagers lay in ambush among the rocks of the Nyakwai hills but were savagely attacked and defeated. Their chief (named in Macdonald's report as Tomatum) was killed, and five homesteads with their stores of grain were burned to the ground. The next day, November 30, thirteen more homesteads on the northern side of the valley—where the slopes were more easily accessible—were razed. With complacency Macdonald remarked that the Nyakwai would suffer severely from famine, as fresh crops could not be reaped for eight months.[41]

Macdonald attributed the "treacherous" murders of Kirkpatrick and his men by previously friendly Nyakwai to the influence among them of Kabalega's followers, along with, possibly, some mutineers who had been driven eastward the previous August. These, Macdonald knew, would "doubtless have given false ideas of European intentions and warn the tribes to keep Europeans out of their country at all hazards."[42] The map accompanying Macdonald's field report indicated "hostile tracts" bordering the country through which he marched. Northeast of "Lake Choga," these consisted of "Umiro" (Wakeddi), Labwor (with its outlying district, Nyakwai), and "Kimama." All were described as hostile to Europeans and under the influence of Kabalega and the mutineers.[43] Here, then, a rationale for the incorporation of Teso within the Uganda Protectorate was clearly set out for the first time. Indeed, Macdonald anticipated its conquest and drew up a blueprint for the administration of the region. Through a series of levy posts under local chiefs, he proposed the incorporation of an area extending from a patrol post at Save through the fertile districts west of Mount Elgon to Usoga. Annual patrols would be sent out to traverse Karamoja and to pay and examine the levy posts garrisoned with locally enlisted *askaris* (soldiers). The regions north of Lake Rudolf, he suggested, could be visited periodically and a transport service established to keep lines of communication open. Although the new

41. Major Macdonald to Marquis of Salisbury, Dec. 3, 1898 (PRO FO/403/280.155).
42. Ibid., Nov. 26, 1898 (PRO FO/403/280.154).
43. Ibid., Dec. 9, 1898 (PRO FO/403/280.156).

command would be under the commissioner of the Uganda Protec-
torate, it would be premature to introduce civil administration,
Macdonald thought. Instead, Lieutenant Pereira of the Coldstream
Guards might be given command, supported by three lieutenants
and a doctor. An itemized budget put the total cost of £18,000. Not
averse to comparison with the expansive territory northwest of the
Nile, Macdonald proposed that the new command be named East
Equatoria.[44]

The Prospects of the Uganda Protectorate

In July 1899 a special commissioner, Sir Harry Johnston, was
appointed by the British government to inquire into and report on
the condition and prospects of the Uganda Protectorate. Three
matters were of vital concern: the expenses incurred in the War of
1897–99; the relation of Uganda to the neighboring East Africa
Protectorate, where by now railway development was well under
way; and, finally, the future of the territory that lay between the
Protectorate and the administered regions of the Sudan. Although a
northern delimitation of Johnston's responsibilities was deliberately
omitted, within six weeks of his arrival he had set out clear limits
to the Uganda Protectorate: the German and Congo borders in the
south and west; in the east the Rift Valley; and, enclosing the
territories ringed by Macdonald's line of march, the fifth parallel
north. This represented the expansion of the Protectorate far beyond the bounds of effective administration.[45] The pacification and
colonization of the Teso region could not be long postponed.

Between April 1899, when Kabalega and Mwanga were captured, and December 1899, when the special commissioner arrived
in Uganda, there had been several minor encounters with the remnants of the rebel forces in Bunyoro and Lango. Between July and
September, Kakungulu had been engaged in military action in
eastern Bukeddi. The Protectorate government was concerned with
Nubian mutineers, Baganda rebels, and Arab arms-runners and
slave traders harassing the country east of Lake Kyoga. Initially,

44. Ibid.
45. A. D. Roberts, "The Evolution of the Uganda Protectorate" (1963),
p. 102.

Kakungulu reported success in bringing in mutineers; but this was quickly followed by intelligence that the Wakeddi were divided, some behaving well, others joining the mutineers. On a safari north, Kakungulu found Kawere to be safe but was obliged to beat off attacks, which he suggested were of Wakeddi and mutineers combined. He asked for more arms, which were reluctantly sent. The commissioner commented: "I believe, if he stayed quiet, the Wakeddi would also do so, but I am afraid he will raid and I do not wish to encourage him in doing so, which can only bring on attacks from the Wakeddi, and is also quite indefensible on other grounds." If it were really necessary, the commissioner suggested, Kakungulu should be sent one box of ammunition to maintain him, "but he should be informed that no more will be forthcoming and, if necessary, his advanced post will have to be withdrawn."[46]

On October 6, 1899, an attack was launched on the southern shores of the Serere peninsula, the soft underbelly of the Teso region. At Pingire, Kakungulu and his men set out to establish headquarters but were met with strong opposition. Some local forces fought, others joined them. Eventually a fort was established and the surrounding area declared an administrative county. Maraki Magongo was appointed county chief and ninety armed men were garrisoned there.[47]

Johnston's commission in Uganda culminated in 1900 with the Uganda Agreement, which resolved Britain's relations with the kingdoms and the conquered territory of Bunyoro. Johnston, noting that Uganda was by far the more valuable of the two possessions, envisaged a united protectorate of Uganda and East Africa and proposed the location of its future capital on the Mau plateau midway between Entebbe and its outlet port at Mombasa.[48] Two months later almost to the day (in a singularly speedy return communication), the Foreign Office cautioned that he was, perhaps, being premature: no decision had yet been made on fusion of the

46. Sir John M. Gray, (file, n.d.), citing Commissioner to Grant, Sept. 26, 1899.

47. Waswa (MS., n.d.), par. 27.

48. Sir Harry Johnston to Marquis of Salisbury, Feb. 18, 1900 (PRO FO/403/294.25). The Special Commissioner's preliminary report was presented to both houses of Parliament in July and November 1900.

two territories.[49] Only in Busoga and Bukeddi were loose ends to be tied up.

In the event, four months after the Uganda railway reached Kisumu on the eastern shores of Lake Victoria in December 1901, the entire Eastern Province of Uganda (Mau, Baringo, Nandi, Kavirondo) was detached from the Uganda Protectorate and incorporated within the bounds of what was subsequently to become Kenya.

On the eve of his departure from the Protectorate in April 1901, Johnston summoned Kakungulu to Masaba. He could not but be impressed by Kakungulu's achievements and reputation. The entire Protectorate had been built upon force of arms; Kakungulu had established himself as the greatest of the collaborating generals— even if his predilection for unprovoked raiding was to be deplored. Further, the commissioner may well have perceived that a man of Kakungulu's temperament and ability would not always be satisfied with so little.[50] Within the terms of the Uganda Agreement, Bugerere, along with other territories in fealty to Bunyoro before the defeat of Kabalega, had been absorbed into Buganda. Since Kakungulu could not be expected to accept a post as mere county chief within a Mengo hierarchy, the commissioner suggested that he be graded a third-class assistant (equivalent to an assistant district commissioner) with a salary of £200 per annum. Kakungulu's task was twofold: first, to reduce the Langi territory into some kind of order, working outward from his base on the Kyoga peninsula; second, to act as a collector imposing a hut and gun tax upon "his people."

In later years, considerable confusion developed over Kakungulu's precise rank and status in the hierarchy of colonial officialdom. From the very beginning there had been confusion over the nature of his command in Bukeddi. On the identity of "the Wakeddi" and what was meant by "Bukeddi," the views of Kakungulu and various British officers were at odds most of the time; each attempted a definition of the situation according to his own

49. Foreign Office to Sir Harry Johnston, Apr. 25, 1900 (PRO FO/403/294.44).
50. For Kakungulu's understanding of the situation, see Gray (1963), pp. 45–46.

interests. Kakungulu's salary, but not his rank, was evidently approved by the Foreign Office.[51] There is nothing to indicate that it was ever paid.

By 1898 Kakungulu was being treated as a local district officer within the colonial administration and, as such, was seen to represent British power in the Bukeddi region. His career pattern was no longer that of a Muganda general owing allegiance and tribute to the kabaka at Mengo but was, rather, similar to that of empire builders with whom he had shared military action: Williams, Sitwell, Kirkpatrick, Grant, Colville and Macdonald himself. That Kakungulu was an African and they European was an accident of birth to be exploited in campaigns of expansion and abused when those campaigns were over. Father L. J. Van Den Bergh, a Dutch missionary of the Mill Hill Mission, at this time described Kakungulu as "a very useful pioneer and imperialist—notwithstanding his black face."[52]

Jackson, as governor, informed the Foreign Office that Kakungulu had originally been placed

> in charge of that part of the Bukeddi country, in the immediate vicinity of Lake Kyoga in order to check the constant raids into Uganda by the Bakeddi. These raids he effectively stopped, and reduced the Bakeddi to submission. At that time he was not subsidised and paid himself and his followers handsomely in cattle [word illegible] which he took from the natives in his various conflicts with them.[53]

At a certain level—that of imperial relations—anomalies and contradictions were essential if anything at all was to be achieved within the protectorate. Indisputable clarity over matters of territory, jurisdiction, and incumbency came only after the region east of the Nile had been subjected to an extended period of conquest and settlement.

Kakungulu's influence and authority north and east of Lake Kyoga was greatly overestimated. Following on the occupation of Kawere five years earlier, his forces had penetrated no further inland

51. Thomas (1939), p. 132.
52. J. van den Bergh, "Correspondence" (1901), p. 53.
53. Quoted in Gray (file, n.d.), with the citation Jackson to Lansdowne, Jan. 24, 1902.

than a distance of twenty-five miles: a day's march.[54] Indeed, the very area he "conquered," that bordering Lake Kojweri, had been well established by the Banyoro in previous decades as a sphere of trading influence. At the time of Kakungulu's intervention in northern Bugerere, the whole region knew Bunyoro hegemony. Kakungulu's mercenaries advanced within a vacuum created by the collapse of Kabalega. Even more significant, perhaps, than the limited spatial extent of Kakungulu's influence was its frontier heterogeneity. In this island and peninsula region of trading bases and hinterlands, a cosmopolitan population—Bachopi, Banyala, Basoga, Bakenyi, Banyoro, Kumam, Iteso, and many others—had come into being throughout the centuries. Not until 1900, with the backing of the Protectorate government, did Kakungulu move beyond this trading frontier into the unknown territory beyond.

The government's knowledge of Bukeddi at this time came from only two sources: the missionaries and Kakungulu. Of the two choices, Johnston placed his faith in Kakungulu. Of missionary activities, the commissioner reported only failure: "Amongst the naked Nilotic negroes of the eastern half of the Protectorate, missionary propaganda seems at present time absolutely impossible. These people take absolutely no interest in religion or in any subject which is not of a purely material nature," he noted.[55] Here a stereotype of the Iteso is first encountered that will appear many more times in their colonial record. In 1901, materialism is seen to be a barrier to penetration; within a few years it will be viewed as the very key required to unlock the door of capitalist development in the newly created Teso district.

54. Gray confines Kakungulu's sphere of influence to Kelle in the west to the Teso boundary, as well as to an area adjoining Bugondo in Serere (i.e., Ogera), a locality that appears in the missionary record as Lumogera. See Gray (1963), pp. 35–36, and "Report," p. 19; and William Crabtree, "Openings Beyond Uganda: An Appeal for Bukeddi" (1901).

55. Sir Harry Johnston to Marquis of Salisbury, Apr. 27, 1900 (PRO FO/403/294.121).

3. Teso Economy and Society on the Eve of Conquest

> The problem . . . is to move from the circuits of capital to
> capitalism; from a highly-conceptualised and abstracted mode
> of production, within which determinism appears as
> absolute, to historical determinations as the exerting of
> pressures, as a logic of process within a larger (and sometimes
> countervailing) process.
>
> Thompson 1978:355

By the end of the nineteenth century, the vast, unknown expanse of
empty terrain east of the Nile across which Speke had written the
one word "Kidi" had begun to acquire character. As different peoples
were encountered on the hostile shores of Lake Kyoga, more
specific identities developed: the Gang of Acholi were distinguished
from the Kimama of the east, the Ikokolemu or Langi from the
Bakeddi of the Teso region. As the peoples became known, so,
partially, did their territories, although at this time there was no
concerted movement from the center even into the marches of the
newly established Protectorate.

The historiography of the region east of the Nile lies within a
tradition that focuses upon exchange and trade as the fulcrum of
political economy,[1] and it is to the environmental, social, and cultural
conditions of the Teso region that we look first.

Between 1°10' and 2°26' north and 32°57' and 34°16' east lie
open savanna plains that extend as far as the eye can see, from the
scrub and semidesert north of Masaba to Kaberamaido in the west
and further, across Africa, to form the great savanna belt of the

---

1. See, e.g., Richard Gray and David Birmingham (eds.), *Pre-Colonial
Trade in Africa* (1970); John Tosh, "The Northern Interlacustine Region"
(1970); Uzoigwe, "Pre-Colonial Markets in Bunyoro-Kitara" (1972). We
therefore know little about pre-capitalist production in Teso.

sub-Saharan steppe.[2] The short-grass savanna landscape is eaten into by the wide, swampy waterways of the complex drainage system of Lake Kyoga, Lake Bisina, and the Mpologoma River. The average rainfall is slightly over forty inches a year. Temperatures average 85°F. The soil of the region consists of fertile clay and loams in the south and sandy soil in the north. Swamp soils are alluvial clays with sand and silt. Moving from southwest to northeast, following the passage of the rainbelt across the landscape, three ecological patterns merge imperceptibly into one another as rainfall, elevation, and soil type bring about small changes in surface features. Since the vegetation of the Teso region had a marked bearing on land use, which, in turn, affected both precapitalist and colonial political development, and lake fringe swamps affected the distribution and movement of peoples, these three ecological divisions received geopolitical expression. They can be characterized briefly:

1. *The North:* Usuku bordering upon Karamoja, its marches extending to the Labwor hills in the north; Amuria and the northern half of Soroti; generally, the area to the north of the Agu swamp. This was a region of orchard scrub and semidesert. Population density varied between 80 per square mile in the west to under 56 per square mile in the east. Communications became increasingly bad as one traveled north and east; the availability of water limited both pastoral movements and settlement. The wildlife of the region at the end of the nineteenth century included herds of elephant and buck; ostrich were also plentiful. There would always appear to have been more cattle per head of population than elsewhere in the district, in spite of raiding by the Karamojong. This was the southwestern aspect of that terrain stretching to the north of Elgon, between Lake Rudolf and the Nile, ravaged by Ethiopian ivory and slave raiders.

2. Fuller accounts of the Teso environment may be found in L. C. Beadle and E. M. Lind, "Research on the Swamps of Uganda" (1960); J. D. Jameson (ed.), *Agriculture in Uganda* (1970); E. Jones, *Agriculture in Eastern Province, Uganda* (1960); I. Langdale-Brown, H. A. Osmaston, and J. G. Wilson, *The Vegetation of Eastern Province, Uganda* (1962); David N. McMaster, *A Subsistence Crop Geography of Uganda* (1962), pp. 5–32; D. J. Parsons, *The Systems of Agriculture Practised in Uganda: The Teso System* (1960); Harold B. Thomas and A. E. Spencer, *A History of Uganda Land and Surveys* (1938); John D. Tothill (ed.), *Agriculture in Uganda* (1940).

2. *The Southwest:* Serere and southern Soroti. The Serere peninsula formed a shatter zone between the Nilotes of northern Uganda and the Bantu-speaking peoples to the south, the line between them lying along the diagonal of the Somerset Nile, which divides Uganda from northwest to southeast. This zone was characterized by a distinctive rainfall belt, short-grass vegetation, and fertile soil. Population density was around 127 per square mile. At the end of the nineteenth century, the moving frontier of Iteso movement had barely reached western Serere. Game was still plentiful and the peninsula heavily wooded.

3. *The South:* Kumi, Ngora, and Bukedea, lying south of Lake Bisina. By the end of the nineteenth century little indigenous vegetation remained in this area, which was overpopulated, overstocked, and overcultivated. Raiding north of Mount Masaba by Arabs, Swahilis, and Europeans, and the waves of devastation emanating from the southern Busoga trade routes, brought about a pileup of population in the country between Lake Bisina and the Mpologoma Lakes region. Population density in Bukedea was around 166 per square mile; in Kumi around 177; in Ngora around 242.[3]

The populations of the three divisions are known respectively as Iteso, Iseera, and Ngoratok, and though clearly named after the localities they occupy, each also represents a dialect group within what is generally called the Ateso-speaking peoples. Formerly categorized as Central Nilo-Hamites, they are now often termed Central Paranilotes and belong to a subgroup of that family which Lamphear labels Agricultural Paranilotes.[4] From a possible primordial

3. Population density figures take on meaning only in relation to technology. D. Grove estimates that for hand farmers, two acres per head is "rather a large acreage . . . to cultivate" (D. Grove, "Population Densities and Agriculture in Northern Nigeria," 1961, p. 123). See also William Allen, *The African Husbandman* (1965), pp. 185–191. The introduction of the plow was, as we shall see, critical in altering the favorable or "balanced" state of affairs that prevailed in Teso prior to conquest.

4. John Lamphear, *The Traditional History of the Jie of Uganda* (1976), p. 84. For earlier categorizations and discussions of relations between them, see Philip H. and Pamela Gulliver, *The Central Nilo-Hamites* (1953), pp. 9–13; N. Nagashima, "Historical Relations among the Central Nilo-Hamites" (Social Science Conference paper, 1968); Archibald N. Tucker, *The Non-Bantu Languages of North Eastern Africa* (1956). The

point of dispersal in the Didinga hills, bodies of Agricultural Paranilotes moved westward and southward into Karamoja. Some settled around the Labwor and Nyakwai hills, whence further migrations carried the people into Miro (Langi), Kaberamaido (Kumam),
Ngariama, and Teso sometime before 1720.[5] Their economy was
initially based on hunting and gathering, and they became increasingly more agricultural. Iteso traditions indicate that they were
agriculturalists before acquiring cattle.[6] Indeed, it is possible that
Iteso migration from Karamoja was due to the need for both new
hunting grounds and better agricultural lands.[7]

The material culture of precolonial Teso reflects its richly
diversified economy.[8] At least three different types of spears, made
of iron and wood, as well as bows and arrows, were used in hunting
and raiding; a rounded rectangular shield of buffalo hide was carried for defense. Bird and fish traps were made of woven basketry.

---

earlier historiography of the Central Nilotes is confusing and contradictory.
See, e.g., Philip H. Gulliver, "The Karamojong Cluster"(1952) and "The
Teso and the Karamojong Cluster" (1955a); Gulliver and Gulliver (1953);
B. M. Kagola, "Tribal Names and Customs in Teso District" (1955), pp.
41–43; J. C. D. Lawrance, "Rock Paintings in Teso" (1953) and *The Iteso*
(1957), pp. 3–16; John B. Webster (ed.), *The Iteso during the Asonya*
(1973), pp. xxi–19; F. L. Williams, "Teso Clans" (1937); A. C. A. Wright,
Wright, "Notes on the Iteso Social Organization" (1942). The revisionist
assessment by Lamphear (1976), pp. 79–105, is used in the account that
follows.

5. Lamphear, p. 101.

6. This statement is based partly on the evidence of traditional songs
collected in Serere and partly on Webster's statement to this effect: "But the
Iteso are absolutely unanimous that they were farmers before they acquired
cattle" (Webster, 1973, p. 20). Although agriculture is slighted in accounts
of the pre-colonial Iteso economy (partly, it might be suggested, because of
the cattle ethos of their administrator/historians), it would appear always
to have been practiced alongside herding. See, e.g., Lawrance (1957), pp.
11, 135–142. It may be added that most of the songs were about hunger
and food.

7. Kagola (1955), p. 43; Webster (1973), esp. pp. 12–14.

8. See Kathleen M. Trowell and K. P. Wachsmann, *Tribal Crafts of
Uganda* (1953), pp. 35–36, 38, 49–54. Provenance is not given accurately
enough to know whether the types of artifacts in this well-illustrated vol-
ume represent regional specializations.

Wicker work and coiled basketry were also made. Among the agricultural implements, hay forks and small weeding hoes were made of wood. Shell weeding tools were also used. Hoes, finger-knives and hooks, digging spears, and slaughtering knives were of iron. Beaded and thonged calabashes, square winnowing trays of wrapped-twine weave, wooden oblong and round food bowls; flat wooden food trays; wooden ladles and spikes; spoons of horn; and churns, milk-pots, funnels, and platters of gourds were in common use. Three different kinds of stools existed, among them the characteristic Teso three-legged wooden stool. Both a fine black pottery and a common red earthenware were widespread.

Costume, too, attested to the richness of the natural environment. Men wore a single skin hung from the shoulders and large plumed or cowrie-covered headdresses. A rare headdress was fashioned of large iron "horns." Decorations included labrets and noserings; iron beads and cylinders; iron neckrings; heavy coiled metal, ivory, and animal tail bracelets; large iron and pellet ball anklets and tortoiseshell and strung seed rattles on the legs. Women were unadorned, apart from aprons and "tails" made of skin. Babies were carried in saddles made of basketry or hide.

There was no iron in the Teso region: the nearest sources, apparently, were to the west in Bunyoro and to the east in the Labwor hills and at Mount Toror.[9] Its use for agricultural implements and weapons, and even more as ornamentation, indicates extensive trade.

Patterns of Local Production and Trade in Teso

The considerable microecological variations within Teso and the prevalence of famine during the nineteenth century engendered the production of an agricultural surplus, both for exchange and as a hedge against bad seasons.[10] Claude Meillassoux's model of a sub-

9. Lamphear, p. 166.

10. For recent studies of pre-colonial agricultural systems, see Robin Palmer and Neil Parsons (eds.), *The Roots of Rural Poverty in Central and Southern Africa* (1977), and a review of this book by Terence O. Ranger, "Growing from the Roots: Reflections on Peasant Research in Central and Southern Africa" (1978). For the required emphasis on land and labor, see John Tosh, "Lango Agriculture during the Early Colonial Period: Land and Labour in a Cash-Crop Economy" (1978b).

sistence economy seems inapt for the Teso region, not simply for its unquestioning primacy attached to kinship, but for its under-estimation of the role played by commodities in exchange between localities.[11]

Trade was closely associated with a system of agricultural production that coexisted with a local cattle-based kin-and-client system by which the social organization was sustained. Land was held by women. Plots were allocated to a woman on marriage, and she may even have carved them out for herself; these remained in her possession until death, when they were inherited by her cowives or her sons' wives. Each wife had her own granary.[12] In an environment of periodic famine and intermittent food shortages, however, defer-

---

11. Claude Meillassoux, "Essai d'interpretation du phenomène economique dans les societés traditionelles d'auto-subsistance" (1960) and "From Reproduction to Production" (1972). Indeed, it is today generally agreed that "True subsistence economies would appear to occur only in conditions of severe land shortage, or of extreme isolation. (In time of difficulty or disaster, an economy may be driven back, temporarily or permanently, into something approaching a subsistence condition; devastating wars, outbreaks of rinderpest, or a severe depression robbing cash-crop farmers of their markets; many of the economies which look most like subsistence economies prove, on closer examination, to be disaster economies, or to have had their extra-subsistence capacity raided or mulcted by stronger neighbours)" (Marion Johnson, "Cotton Imperialism in West Africa" 1974).

Meillassoux, a structural Marxist, develops a model of the "lineage mode of production." A similar model has been delineated by Catherine Coquery-Vidrovitch, "Research on an African Model of Production" (1977). A more useful model, at least for our present purposes, is Michael Merrill's "household mode of production" discussed in "Cash Is Good to Eat: Self-Sufficiency and Exchange in the Rural Economy of the United States" (1977). For an in-house critique of structural Marxism, see Anthony Cutler, Barry Hindness, Paul Hurst, and Athar Hussain, *Marx's "Capital" and Capitalism Today* (1977). For a critique of Althusserian Marxism in general, see Edward P. Thompson, *The Poverty of Theory and Other Essays* (1978b). The most useful discussions of pre-capitalist formations would appear to remain those of Samir Amin (1976); Eric J. Hobsbawm, "Introduction" to *Pre-Capitalist Economic Formations* (1964b), and the work therein of Marx himself; and Karl Marx, *Grundrisse: Introduction to the Critique of Political Economy* (1973).

12. Gulliver and Gulliver (1953), p. 20.

ence and dependency relations between males, resting on age, gender, kin, and affinal ties, along with neighborly indebtedness, provided the bedrock of the domestic economy and the mechanism for its social reproduction.

There were, most certainly, variations between the domestic economies of the three zones; but, given the homogenization that colonial administration fostered, it is no longer possible to relate these to differences in, for example, inheritance patterns, kinship idioms, or residence patterns. Everywhere certain categories of persons lacked economic power and wealth and thus held low social positions: women, children, and, to a lesser extent, clients and slaves. In the north, where cattle were more numerous, lineages would appear to have been stronger and generation-set organization more developed. Agriculture was limited by the arid terrain and the dislocation of trade in iron hoes at the end of the nineteenth century. As the Iteso moved from the northeast into Soroti and across Lake Bisina, and as fewer men were able to acquire cattle, the property-inculcated lineage system gave way to what is best described as a system of interlocking groups cemented by ties through women rather than by an ideology of patrilineal descent or corporately held property. In the south and west the Iteso at the end of the nineteenth century were almost wholly sedentary agriculturalists residing in large joint-family homesteads for security; in the west, if not in the south, land was plentiful. Throughout the region, nevertheless, ownership of cattle and the labor of women and children provided the principal forms of wealth.[13] Reciprocal exchange and commensality (the sustenance of a wider community than that of the homestead was necessary to spread risk) acted as leveling mechanisms within the agrarian society.

Access, tenuous as it was, to the commodities of long-distance trade introduced Teso to a world mercantilist economy. Those localities where a comparatively rich, sudd-nurtured food-crop economy could be articulated with long-distance trade were those in which expansive political development occurred in the mid-

13. Teso cattle were of three breeds, further attesting to the trizonal ecology of the region. Small Zebu cattle were to be found in the south and throughout; Boran or Karamoja Zebu in the north; and a larger type with an admixture of Hima (Bunyoro and Ankole) in Serere.

nineteenth century: Serere, western Soroti, Toroma, and Agu-Ngora. For much of the region, however, access to trade goods simply reinforced local patriarchs in their control of the domestic economy. Wealth produced by trade was diffused through the kinship system. The ephemeral nature of the *mwami*, or rich man, in Plateau Tonga society has been described by Elizabeth Colson;[14] under similar conditions the Iteso patriarch could have been little more powerful. The most important economic function of trading was insurance against times of scarcity, and it was on achievements in this sphere that the successful leadership of a patriarch was based. But trade in Teso, like that among the Plateau Tonga, mostly remained seasonal and involved no elaborate specialist organization.

Barriers to the expansion of such a precapitalist economy have been clearly set out by Meillassoux. Most important, participation in trade does not lead to a new and different division of labor. Though domestic organization can be adopted to suit trade and though political advantages are gained from it, lineal inheritance patterns, ceremonialism and gift exchange remain the vehicles for the distribution of property. The "traditional modes of production, involving subsistence, and not trade goods, remain the same."[15]

It is generally recognized that simple agricultural productive systems are transcended when cultivators are "persuaded or compelled to wring from the soil a surplus above their own domestic requirements." This has been true especially "when this surplus was made available to support new economic classes not directly engaged in producing their own food."[16] Although some specialization in production existed in Teso in the nineteenth century, this was not divorced from subsistence cultivation; the division of labor found the men engaged in hunting, fishing, and herding, while the women and children bore the brunt of cultivation. Specialists in pottery and basketry were non-Iteso. Ipagero in Serere specialized in pottery,

14. Elizabeth Colson, "African Society at the Time of the Scramble" (1970), p. 52.

15. Claude Meillassoux, *The Development of Indigenous Trade and Markets in West Africa* (1971), p. 61.

16. Quotations from, respectively, Vere G. Childe, *What Happened in History* (1952), p. 73; Jack R. Goody, *Production and Reproduction* (1976), p. 23.

basketry, the making of fish traps, and cattle export. Most traced their ancestry back to the days of Namionjo of Bunyala (that is, about 1880) and ultimately to Buchopi. Ties of marriage cross-cut with those of Iteso clans in Kaberamaido and Kawere. These were the same Bachopi (Jopalwo) who initiated trade with the Langi. For goats, cattle, butter, and later ivory, they traded metal hoes needed by the Langi for both agricultural use and for turning into spearheads. Since neither Langi, Kumam, nor Iteso knew the art of smelting, the Bachopi established commercial links with all.[17]

The open waters of Lake Kyoga clearly provided exceptional conditions for the development of long-distance trading, and the watery inlets and papyrus swamps of Agu and the Mpologoma Lakes region served as arteries along which trade goods were pumped into the interior of Teso. Quite substantial loads were carried by water, for large dugout canoes held as many as thirty men.[18] Specializing within this ecological niche, the Bakenyi emerged as an ethnic group both in service as ferrymen and through the manufacture of salt from papyrus fiber.[19] Through the exchange of salt they obtained rights to bury their dead on Teso soil, for they lived on small islands in the lake.

There were probably, in the mid-nineteenth century, many such groups emerging in response to the possibilities of exploiting new niches and, once established, engaging in trade. A diaspora of movement in the lakeshore region created a crescent of ethnic refinements. The nature of ethnic groups and boundaries being what it is, with minimal distinctive specialization their members served to distribute commodities in a manner adaptive to fluctuations not simply seasonal, but virtually continuous. Variations in crop yield between localities quite close to each other were surprisingly great because of the idiosyncratic rainfall pattern of the Lake Kyoga basin.[20] Social institutions characterized a people both close to subsistence level and, seemingly, ever at risk: rainmaking; pawnship;

17. Tosh (1970), pp. 106–108.

18. R. H. Johnstone, "Past Times in Uganda" (Ms., 1921), p. 8.

19. See David Cohen (1972), pp. 128–133, 137–140, on the Bakenhe fishing people; John Roscoe, *The Northern Bantu* (1915), pp. 145–160. Field research in Serere, 1966–67.

20. Parsons (1960), pp. 15–16.

the loaning and borrowing of cattle and children; and the planting of several varieties of seeds regardless of relative yield. The incremental value of trading contacts resulted in an interlocking of local systems that itself enhanced survival in all but extraordinary times. At times of sustained crisis, coexistence and cooperation gave way to conflict.

Although exchange and barter were most common, the use of currency had localized distribution in the Teso region. A cowrie currency entered the area from Busoga through the Mpologoma Lakes network, as well as perhaps from Mumia's in the southeast. This was preceded by the use of ivory discs and beads in the north and west. Throughout the region, chickens, goats, and iron hoes served as units of account. The indigenous economy, in which labor power was supplied and recruited within a kin-client network, was not disrupted by these currencies, since discrete zones of utilization were recognized. As in certain bridewealth payments in contemporary Teso, specific currencies and commodities in the transaction represented specific understandings; material goods symbolized nonmaterial relations, and commodities exchanged were not thereby interchangeable.[21] Labor power was not purchased; it was rewarded.

Long-Distance Trade and Its Diversion

Those who live in potential famine areas develop widespread relations with surrounding peoples. Prior to the advent of capitalism, three major trade routes crossed Teso.[22] The first, and probably the earliest, followed the waterways of Lake Kyoga, transferring goods to and from west and east. The second was a well-traveled caravan route from Karamoja to Mbale, part of that farreaching commerce by which Swahili, Arab, and Indian merchants transported ivory to the coast for transhipment to Zanzibar, Oman, India, and points east. If the first trade network affected mostly the

21. See, e.g., Vincent (1971), pp. 119–125.

22. According to A. C. A. Wright, "Review of the Iteso" (1958), p. 89, the extent of pre-colonial trade in Teso has been considerably underestimated. Little of the evidence he referred to could be found in the Teso archives in 1967.

peoples of the Serere peninsula and the area west of Soroti, the second route, which passed through the southeast of the region, impinged upon the peoples of Usuku, Kumi, and Bukedea. Finally, a third route (of which little is known) passed through the southern portion of the region from east to west—from Mbale through Serere and Bululu toward the Nile Province. Commerce along these major routes was not divorced from the localized trade of the neighborhoods through which they passed, for the resting places of the long-distance traders, Banyoro, Swahili, Arab, and Greek—whether they were peacefully exchanging hoes for cattle or violently negotiating for ivory and slaves—articulated with local trade and, in some cases, stimulated local production, especially of food crops.

Three categories of goods were traded through western Serere to Bunyoro and the southern littoral of Lake Kyoga in the nineteenth century. The oldest trade was in salt and iron; later, trade in mercantile (largely mobile) commodities such as cattle, ivory, slaves, and guns developed; finally, commodities produced for export, such as food crops (bananas, millet, sweet potatoes, peanuts, coffee) and tobacco moved between the fertile crescent of the south and the less advantaged north.[23] Although barkcloth and hides were traded, the people of Teso mostly wore beads, iron bracelets, and iron anklets (all imported items), along with indigenous ostrich feather headdresses and wooden noseplugs, until well into the first decade of the twentieth century—hence the Luganda gloss on Kidi (the east) as Bakeddi, "the naked ones." At the turn of the century, the "naked savagery" of the Bakeddi was contrasted with the wearing of barkcloth and calico by "civilized" Bantu-speakers.

The magnitude of this western trade drew Kakungulu's attention to Bukeddi. Engaged in his youth in trading arms for ivory, Kakungulu began to infiltrate the Lake Kyoga trading network as the century drew to a close. Early aware of the long-established trade between Bunyoro and the Bachopi middlemen on Kawere, he extended his interests from the northwestern end of the lake to the east. From Bugerere, he obtained from across the lake tribute in the form of grain.[24] After 1896 he sent his own traders north of the lake.

23. Uzoigwe (1972). This flow was later reversed as Busoga became depleted and famine-stricken.

24. Commissioner Sadler to Marquis of Lansdowne, Feb. 27, 1904 (PRO FO/403/341.84). See also Gray, "Report," Appendix A.

Breaking into the east-west flow of goods to siphon profits from the small intermediary trading groups, Kakungulu first diverted the traffic of the Lake Kyoga region and, by the turn of the century, had laid the foundations of an independent power base.

The long-distance trading that brought the Kyoga system into the world economy (via Zanzibar, Buganda, and Bunyoro) had very different effects upon the nomadic pastoralists of Teso's northeast. In the Kyoga system, indigenous peoples were able to exploit the opportunities created by long-distance trade. Africans "dominated every stage of the commercial process save the actual transport of goods to and from the coast."[25] In the northeast, on the other hand, the traders were Europeans, Ethiopians, Indians, Arabs, Swahilis, and Goans, as well as local Africans—many of them agents of merchants in Mumia's, Mbale, or Maji. Where their caravans came into closest contact, in Usuku, Karamoja, and Sebei, indigenous trade was least developed.

In both west and east, the main objective of the long-distance caravans was to acquire ivory. Those trading with Bunyoro and Buganda usually left with ivory worth five times the value of the goods they had brought. Grant, for example, recorded in 1862 an exchange of clothing, brass wire, beads, and two flintlocks for 700 pounds of ivory, 7 women, and 50 cows. Contact with the East African coast served to invigorate indigenous trade so that long-distance trade goods could be acquired. The most important changes involved the introduction of firearms, the use of brass and copper ornaments, and, elsewhere than in Teso, the introduction of new food crops such as maize (in Buganda by 1862), cassava (1875), and rice (1878). With Buganda's increasing monopoly over the western trade routes, both Bunyoro and the coastal traders began to look for ways to circumvent the kabaka's control. Bunyoro caravans bartered for ivory among the Acholi, Langi, and Iteso, exchanging ironware; and it was probably at this time that northern Teso trade with Labwor declined. Existing trade routes served to further the flow of new commodities; where cattle had passed before, ivory now moved.

The exploitative nature of foreign hunting safaris among pas-

25. Tosh (1970), pp. 110–111. An attempt by a group of Baganda merchant venturers to enter the coastal caravan trade in 1899 failed (A. T. Matson, "Baganda Merchant Venturers," 1968b).

toralists, on the other hand, rendered their impact quite different. Among settled agriculturalists, goods were being exchanged and, in places, being produced for exchange. Those received from the traders by the Iteso of Usuku and Amuria, however, comprised "presentation and luxury" goods only: beads, ornaments, dancing bells. The commodities taken by the caravans—ivory, slaves, ostrich feathers—were, for the most part, not an integral part of the indigenous barter economy. This changed as international interest heightened.

James Barber describes the area in the late 1890s as subject to the competition of traders from first Mumia's, then Mbale in the south, and ultimately from Maji, the entrepôt for Ethiopian traders. By 1900 the local people no longer accepted beads for ivory, demanding livestock instead; whereupon the traders began to engage in cattle raiding and in hunting elephant themselves. This introduced guns to those who had previously used traps and spears, and so "what for the tribesmen originally had been a trade to sell useless ivory, had become a trade to acquire cattle, and finally a trade to arm themselves with a revolutionary new weapon."[26] British army officers who embarked on the pacification of northern Uganda were to complain that their troops sometimes faced tribesmen armed with superior weapons.[27] By the end of the nineteenth century, Maji, backed by Ethiopian officialdom, had become the main source for arms in Uganda. With Buganda in the throes of civil war and the IBEA Co. struggling to keep its head above turbulent waters, the northern route became the chief source of arms for the rebels in the War of 1897–99.[28]

26. Barber (1968), p. 93.

27. Ibid., p. 99. Flinthooks and percussion weapons had begun to enter Uganda after the Crimean War, breachloaders and needle-guns after 1866. Obsolete European weaponry, consisting largely of Sniders and Marini-Stenny breachloaders, had reached the market in quantity in 1866 (Beachey, 1962).

28. The position was reported to have changed by 1903, when most of the arms were said to have been brought in "from the Unyoro direction by the Wanyoro, many of whom have settled in the Bukeddi country, and have been there for years past" (Commissioner Sadler to Marquis of Salisbury, Dec. 2, 1903, PRO FO/403/340.4).

Conclusion

The international economic system that preceded colonial rule in Uganda thus, during the nineteenth century, underwent two changes. First, the direction of flow of commodities changed from west to east, away from the peripheral kingdoms of the Indian Ocean mercantile system toward the coastal outlets of European and American capitalist systems. The waterways of the Nile were replaced by the caravans (and later the railway) to the East African coast. Second, the commodities themselves changed, as ivory replaced cattle and guns superseded hoes.

With the provisional establishment of the Protectorate in 1894, this shift of indigenous trade across Teso was well under way. All that remained was the economic aggrandizement of the southern districts (and, especially, Buganda) and the underdevelopment of the north. The IBEA Co. and the Uganda Administration that followed it had by 1899 successfully consolidated a power base in Buganda (three civil wars and an army mutiny notwithstanding) and begun to fashion its periphery. A series of "sporting wars" ensued, and not the least of their consequences was the inclusion of the Teso region as a whole within the imperial orbit.

4. Political Organization and Reaction to Conquest

> . . . the anthropologist who optimistically sets out to recover a
> picture of the pre-European political organization from the
> reminiscences of old men, or the declarations of political
> personalities, soon becomes inextricably entangled in the mesh
> of their mutually denigrating lies.
>
> Fortes 1936:46

At the turn of the nineteenth century the population of the Teso
region must have been about 300,000.[1] There are no sources extant
from which one can learn of the political structuring of Iteso society
prior to Baganda conquest; and the structural reconstruction that
follows can be described at best as *archéologie sociale*, at worst as
conjectural history or logical speculation. It is based upon oral
histories collected among the Iteso[2] and upon manuscripts relating
to "the past" in the Teso District Archives.[3] Informed by the known
history of the Karamojong and Jie peoples, and by the superb eth-
nographies of these pastoral peoples by contemporary anthro-

1. Gulliver and Gulliver (1953), p. 9.
2. These include some of the Teso Historical Texts (hereafter THT)
collected by John Webster. (See John B. Webster, "Research Methods in
Teso" (1970), as the basis for his book, *The Iteso during the Asonya*
(1973), as well as my own research, particularly in Serere County in
1966–67).
3. These, by missionaries (e.g., Father Kuyer) and administrators (e.g.,
W. G. Adams) are to be found in the Teso District Archives (hereafter
TDA), miscellaneous file (TDA XMIS/6).

pologists,[4] the reconstruction that follows goes far beyond what any ethnographer would be prepared to do with his painstakingly created data. A knowledge of the region's terrain (since political organization is responsive to environment) and, most important, a comparative persuasion that structural similarities are to be found between specific types of political organization regardless of cultural differences completes an inventory of the resources utilized. In all, there is a built-in assumption that, without evidence to the contrary, continuity in form rather than discontinuity characterized the Teso local scene prior to Kakungulu's conquest.

To span that amorphous political phase between autonomy and hegemony that characterized the end of the precapitalist and the beginning of the colonial era, the reader is introduced to many Iteso whose political careers carry them from one to the other, and to the localities that provided them with sustenance and support.

For those who wish to trace the development of Teso as it moved into the twentieth century, an account of its precolonial organization may prove a somewhat tedious affair: so many of its leaders whose names will be introduced in this chapter "fell by the wayside," defeated in battle or lost in the obscurity of failure. Yet for the people of Teso, these heroes are part of an oral tradition that helps explain why first the Baganda and then the British came to rule over them.

For the purposes of this general account, the names of many persons and places appearing in Teso local traditions have had to be omitted. Here the main concern must be to trace continuities and discontinuities in political leadership and to account for them in terms of structural regularities, especially those of form (that is, modes of political organization), time, and space.

Teso Historiography

For three centuries at least the landscape of the Teso region has seen the movements of countless peoples across its surface. Indeed,

4. For example, Neville Dyson-Hudson, "Factors Inhibiting Change in an African Pastoral Society" (1962) and *Karimojong Politics* (1966); Philip H. Gulliver, *A Preliminary Survey of the Turkana* (1951) and *The Family Herds* (1955b).

contemporary historians of Teso seem unwittingly to reproduce the mythic charter common to so many African societies in their attempts to come to terms with it[5] (see Figure 3). Thus, three eras are delineated: 1) the *Arionga*, a phase of not very detailed, stylized origins and journeys; 2) the *Asonya*, a phase of clan differentiation, characterized by the telescoping of genealogies; and 3) the *Colonial Period*, a phase of remembered genealogical history which, in Teso, can be deemed to have begun with Kakungulu's authorization to collect taxes on the Serere peninsula in 1899.

THE MYTHICAL PAST OF ORAL TRADITION

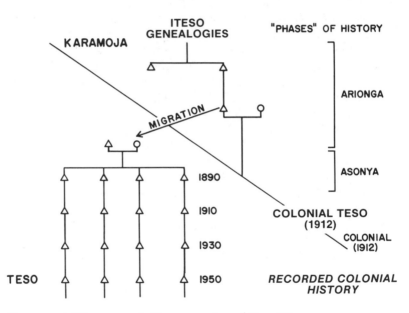

Figure 3. A Diagrammatic Representation of Teso History.

5. For the framework of this charter, see Audrey I. Richards, *Economic Development and Tribal Change* (1960), p. 178, and Peter Rigby, *Cattle and Kinship among the Gogo* (1969), p. 73.

The Arionga is the mythic past of the peoples, "the age of migrations," during which ancestors traversed the lands between Karamoja and Lake Kyoga, then sparsely occupied by Luo settlers. It ended as early as 1600 for the Magoro region and as late as 1800 for the settlers of Amuria and Serere in the far west.[6] The period between these migrations and the coming of the Baganda is known as the Asonya. This, like the Arionga, is of short duration in Amuria, long in Usuku, and intermediate in Kumi, Ngora, and Bukedea. As a concept marking a historical phase in Teso history, the Asonya is not very useful in Serere and western Soroti, where much immigration was from the west (of Banyoro, Bachopi, Bakenyi, and Kumam), and the descendants of "the old men left behind" (the Karamojong) were fewer. The very name Serere (from *iseera*, pioneers) reflects the near convergence of Iteso and Baganda on the peninsula.[7] These "eras," valid reflections of Iteso ethnohistory, are less valuable for the periodization of Teso history.

By the end of the nineteenth century, Teso was inhabited by a largely agricultural people whose histories were not of settlement but of movement. Some of this can be attributed to modes of shifting cultivation, to population pressure on marginal land, and to social pressures, especially generational ones, resulting from natural increase. Movements of greater intensity were probably generated by the spate of diseases—anything but "natural"—that beset the region after the introduction of rinderpest and jigger fleas to tropical Africa.

The ease with which colonial rule was imposed in many parts of the world has been the subject of much debate. In the early days of the IBEA Co. and the Protectorate, Britain was dependent upon a sector of the ruling class of Buganda for the establishment and continuance of its colonial presence. Subsequently, in the Teso region, allies from Buganda were essential for the penetration and consolidation of alien rule. In answer to the question "How could such a tiny handful prevail?" we might well consider (as William H. McNeill did with the Spanish conquest of Mexico in mind) the

6. Webster (1973), pp. 1–7.

7. Ibid., p. xxii; but compare p. 163. Note, however, that "Sera," or "Ngiseera," is a clan name found among various agricultural Paranilotic groups (Lamphear, 1976, p. 84)—as, indeed, is "Iteso."

possibility that occurred to him: the paralyzing effect of lethal epidemics on populations not previously exposed to certain diseases.[8]

Epidemics preceded Baganda and British alike in the Teso region,
and, as among the Aztec and Inca, young adults in the prime of life,
young warriors, were most vulnerable. The relationship between
rinderpest and the sleeping sickness epidemic that extended northward from the shores of Lake Victoria at the end of the nineteenth
century has been explored elsewhere.[9] The earliest phases were
accompanied by specific societal transformations. In 1890, Teso
society was in flux; the movement of peoples and herds destroyed
the immunities offered by *Grenzwildnisse* (no-man's-lands) between one community and another. To the north, east, and south
the integrity of boundary wildernesses had become vulnerable, subject to incursions of increasing frequency and regularity. Even land
that was inherently poor and difficult to work had been put under
the hoe; communities, harassed by those whose cattle stocks had
been depleted by rinderpest, turned to raiding or fell back upon the
shrinking *Grenzwildnisse*. Closer to each other moved old enemies;
raids and local wars succeeded the cattle plague and the famine that
accompanied it.

The same microecological features that caused epidemics and
famines to have varying impacts upon different localities also affected modes of political organization and conflict in the three divisions
of the Teso environment outlined earlier.

1. The north: the modern counties of Usuku, Amuria, and northern Soroti
2. The southwest: Serere and southern Soroti
3. The south: Kumi, Ngora, and Bukedea[10]

8. William H. McNeill, *Plagues and People* (1976).

9. Ford (1971), pp. 480–487; Charles M. Good, "Salt, Trade, and
Disease: Aspects of Development in Africa's Northern Great Lakes
Region" (1972).

10. Data from the three regions is uneven. Extensive use was made by
Webster and his colleagues of oral evidence, specifically for Usuku, Amuria,
and Kumi. This can be supplemented in the south by written Luganda
sources. The inadequate account of the Serere peninsula that follows is
based upon oral testimonies that were incidental to other inquiries (Vincent, 1971).

The North

The predominant characteristic of the north was its sparseness of occupation in the nineteenth century. Its most northerly sections, Obalanga, Acwa, and Kapelebyong, were not settled until well into the colonial era. Elsewhere, politics involved expansive hunting and settlement where the terrain permitted it and conflict where it did not.

As frontier regions, Amuria and northern Soroti—unlike Usuku —evinced a degree of ethnic heterogeneity that became problematic as the colonial grid clamped down upon the movements of its people at the turn of the century. Four ethnic groups came to be recognized: Imiro, Iteso, Iseera, and Kumam. The Imiro (Langi) were viewed by colonial administrators as the natives—the hostile natives—of this region at the end of the nineteenth century, but in fact they were at all times fairly thin upon the ground. The extensive "umiro" zone that appears on Johnston's map glossed a multitude of groups, giving to all the name of those whom the Europeans first encountered. The Imiro entered the northern region from the Labwor hills some time around 1800, retaining ties with kinsmen and affines there for several generations. Macdonald may not have been far wrong in suggesting that the Nyakwai hillsmen who killed Kirkpatrick and his patrol in 1898 were encouraged to do so by Imiro accounts of Nubian resistance to British rule. Reasons for Imiro migration from Labwor are obscure, but their paths carried them both west toward Lango and south into Amuria.[11] According to oral tradition, a group led by Omodoi, from Onyakoi in Labwor, comprised the earliest settlers of Amuria.

Iteso entered the northern frontier regions from the south some seventy or eighty years later. Research into their migrations has been hampered, as N. Egimu-Okuda observes, by the fact that no one on the Makerere research team collected traditions in Soroti county.[12] His own material on this region, for him a peripheral one, raises as many questions as it answers. Another group of immigrants, Iseera, entered Amuria from the Toroma-Kapujan area of

11. N. Egimu-Okuda, "The Occupation of Amuria and the Rise of Omiat" (1973), p. 160; Webster (1973), pp. 9–10. Nagashima calls them legendary (paper, 1968, p. 20).

12. Egimu-Okuda, p. 162.

Usuku, moving westward en masse. By the end of the 1870s they had settled in western Soroti among the Kumam inhabitants of that locality, joining with them to "push back the Langi."[13] It does not seem unreasonable to suppose that this movement northward and westward was part of an effort to enter new hunting grounds in order to meet the demands of foreign caravans for ivory, and it was this that brought about conflict between populations destined to enter colonial historiography as Iteso and Langi.

Very flexible forms of political organization pioneered movement into the stretches of *Grenzwildnisse* between southern Amuria and the Labwor hills, their only "natural" boundaries the swamps they encountered (see Figure 4). "The pattern of settlement . . . was determined by the abundance of wild game. People moved following the retreating animals," and the "people who hunted together in the same hunting sphere settled in this sphere after the animals had been reduced or retreated."[14] Their territories were in a state of comparative flux. Egimu-Okuda writes of "pioneering leaders" who led movements across their northern marches, laying claims to virgin territory for hunting grounds and future occupation.[15] Yet doubtless these leaders were attracted by the caravans purchasing hides and tusks for export to the coast.

By 1897 four leaders had claimed extensive hunting spheres in northern Amuria. Opuna of Atirir in Katine claimed territory as far as the Ootike swamps in Lango. The sphere of Ecungo of Abeko in Orungo extended to the Amare swamp in Obalanga. Egasu of Abya claimed a sphere reaching the Agonga swamp in Obalanga. Most important, however, for recorded history—both of the Asonya and the colonial period—was Omiat of Komolo, whose influence extended throughout most of Asamuk and Acwa, on the western edge of the swampy Akokoroi River.[16] Interethnic hostilities developed, as competition for caravan patronage increased and no-man's-lands diminished. In the following decade, such belts of discord were used to delineate the "natural" bounds of Teso district.

13. Ibid. See also THT no. 88: Group Interview, Orungo, Amuria, conducted by N. Egimu-Okuda, Apr. 25, 1968.
14. Egimu-Okuda (1973), p. 166.
15. Ibid., p. 173.
16. Ibid., p. 166.

Figure 4. Political Fields in Northern Teso on the Eve of Conquest.

Political organization to the east of the Akokoroi River in Usuku appears to have been much more firmly consolidated. John Webster, the historian of this locality, records extensive fighting between what he describes as two large military confederacies. A northern military confederacy was led first by Ocilaje and then by Ocapo, both of Abela in what is today Usuku County.[17] Opposed in civil war was the Itoroma military confederacy, led by Abonya of Angodingodi in Toroma. Omiat of Amuria, who had previously migrated from Abela to Komolo in Wera, chose to ally himself with Abonya in spite of (or perhaps because of) his kinship with Ocilaje. Egimu-Okuda suggests that Omiat's political influence was built upon trade with Banyoro (ostrich feathers and ivory for iron hoes),[18] and that his widening networks reached toward Amuria, Soroti, and Lake Kyoga. The outbreak of the Usuku civil war apparently made him draw back to defend his flank.

According to Webster, after the Great Famine or *ebeli* of 1894–1896, all Usuku was involved in the civil war except the Magoro confederacy (which, as the gateway to Teso through which all had passed, contained kinsmen obligated to both sides) and the *eitela* (parish) of Amusia in Toroma (for reasons that are obscure but may be related to the fact that Okolimong was born there).

At this point, a word of caution is necessary concerning the contingent nature of Iteso military leadership throughout the region. When oral traditions are solicited for information about political structure, it is likely that those who were leading resistance at moments of crisis—whether successful or not—will become imbued with an authority and legitimacy that owes more to the political philosophy of a European educational system than to genuine recollected experience of a Teso past. However, given the segmented nature of Iteso political organization, it seems likely that those military leaders of itela who faced one another in any given confrontation became the leaders of the larger political units amassed behind them for the purposes of that particular affray. Leaders of other itela accepted their command in battle because they were nearest the enemy, knew the terrain best, and could best plan strategy.[19] Later this becomes a critical element of continuity or discontinuity in the early colonial period, since, at the moment of contact, it may simply be the man of that moment who is invested

17. John B. Webster, "The Civil War in Usuku" (1972), pp. 45–52, and *The Iteso* (1973), esp. pp. 47–51.

18. Egimu-Okuda (1973), p. 177.

19. Compare C. P. Emudong, "The Settlement and Organisation of Kumi during the Asonya" (1973), p. 106.

with office, armed, and given an authority backed by force—authority and power such as he would never have known in the indigenous system.

The leaders of the two warring parties in Usuku were Ocapo of Abela and Abonya of Angodingodi. What one has here, it may be suggested, is a zone of intermittent fighting around the higher fertile land bordering the Akokoroi River as it approaches Lake Bisina.[20] On both sides of the river—Komolo on the west, Abela and Angodingodi on the east—pressures on land were considerable. Local informants trace the origins of the civil war to cattle stealing; Webster traces its genesis to the Great Famine. Given the increased caravan activity in this area at the time, and the traders' new practice of raiding for cattle as well as hunting for elephant, both explanations probably contain an element of truth. What began originally as a fight over water holes in swamps developed, apparently, into a full-scale war.

To what extent, then, did concentrated and prolonged warfare serve to institutionalize military command in the Akokoroi Valley? In actual encounters, it would appear that only those itela surrounding battle sites were actually engaged. It seems preferable, then, at least until further evidence is forthcoming, to consider that the military confederacies of northern Usuku were not as tightly consolidated fighting units as were those to the south. From the very nature of the northern terrain, one would expect diffuse political ties rather than centralization. Whereas agriculture and trade provided the economic substrata of the lakeshore confederacies (all of which were densely populated and closely knit), minimal settlement, pastoralism, and raiding in response to caravan demands characterized the north. Northern forces, although they acknowledged ritual leadership over a wide area, were held together less by military leaders than by the cohesive force of raids and feuds.[21]

A second field of activity also engaged, for most of the late nineteenth century, military formations in Ngariam and Magoro. These involved confrontations with Karamojong, as Angissa, the no-man's-land between Usuku and Karamoja, became subject to in-

20. Webster (1973), p. 53.
21. For further examples of such organization, see Jacob Black-Michaud, *Cohesive Force* (1975), esp. pp. 23–32.

creased pressure after the famine. Finally, the region furthest north, lying in Usuku and extending to the foothills of Labwor, was, like the area adjacent to it in northern Amuria, a field of rapid expansion. From this marginal country came a line of prominent leaders, most notably Okadaro, Olokutum, Orwatum, and—on the eve of Baganda entry into the political arena—Okolimong. In 1897, Okolimong was recognized as *emuron* (a seer or prophet) by many in both north and south Usuku.

The Southwest

Problems of reconstruction in the southwest are compounded by the fact that Iseera organization was probably affected a generation earlier than most of Teso, by first Banyoro and then Baganda hegemony. The Serere peninsula was settled in the mid-nineteenth century by small "Iteso" populations moving in from the Asuret region of Soroti. The previous generation was said to have come from Usuku. Clan names reflected the location of settlements in Soroti; thus it was said, for example, that those of the Isureta clan from Usuku took on the clan name Ariekot from a small locality near Asuret. The largest clans in the area appear to be Irarak, Ikarebwok, Icaak, Ilale (from Lale), Igoria, Iguratok, and Imodoi. Oral histories recounted that the land was first cleared by the grandfather generation.[22]

No account was given of military organization. Settlers lived in large homesteads at a distance from one another, and each homestead was fenced with thorn and contained some thirty to forty people.[23] Again, the impression was given that there was intermittent fighting. Deaths were recompensed by payment of cattle or women. Fighting was with spears and clubs.

Several individuals were named as prominent in their localities: Anyamu, son of Omaswa of Arapoo, who "let the Baganda in" from that direction; Amolo of Ongoto; Apuri of Abulayi; Onengyi of Kamod; Omukule of Aojabule; Oluga, "whom the Baganda called Mulangira," of Bugondo; Opoloke of Madoch; and Ocheppa of Atira. (See Figure 5 for these and other localities in the south of Teso on the eve of conquest.) All lived in northern Serere. That

22. Inquiries were conducted largely in the northern and western subcounties, apart from work at Pingire.

23. Field notes, Serere, 1966. Early travelers and administrators often considered these homestead clusters to be villages.

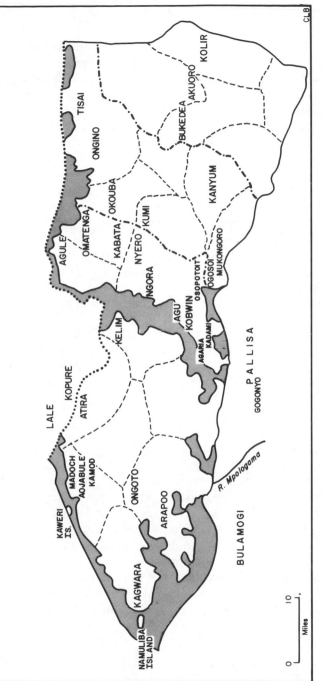

Figure 5. Political Fields in Southern Teso on the Eve of Conquest.

informants did not refer to the men of the south may indicate either that political reputations were, indeed, highly localized and they did not know the leaders; or that Iteso settlement had not extended to the southern shores at that time. The south was inhabited by Bakenyi, but no Iteso respondent could name a Mukenyi leader prior to the appointment of Ali Mwambazi by the Baganda. They did know, however, of Mukankada of Kaweri island ("from whom all the Ipagero of this area come") and Namionjo, the Munyoro chief of the Kagwara peninsula. The northern and western coasts of Serere are as full of Lunyoro-derived place names as those of the south are of Lukenyi-Lusoga ones. Not a single account was given of fighting between these three groups, Iteso, Banyoro, and Bakenyi. On the contrary, the symbiosis of their contact was continually stressed.

Although there is no evidence of political alignments among the Iteso population of Serere, their common social field extended to western Soroti and southern Kaberamaido. Leaders in Obirai, Kamuda, Lale, and Kopure were as well known as those of Serere. Of Obirai, one informant commented: "We heard that Mwanga and Kabalega were caught in that direction."[24] A Musoga who, as a youth, was a gun-bearer for Kakungulu's men, noted that his party (which in the next chapter I call the Northern Expedition) passed from Bululu along the northern side of the lake because of resistance from Serere inhabitants. Fighting occurred, he reported, "if the people carrying guns were delayed. The Iteso feared guns but if they saw that the front column of Baganda had no guns, they would charge to spear them. If they saw guns they ran away."[25] An Ipagero informant supports the testimony that northern Iseera fought the Baganda; after their defeat, his kinsmen moved from Kaweri Island to occupy the empty shoreline. The Ipagero clans involved were Yachwa, Yamia, and Yaiyeru. The Yachwa apparently traded from Kaweri and Namuliba islands until they were "defeated" and "driven out" by the Yamia. Certain Ipagero leaders, such as Kijanjaro and Mukankada, were known to local Iteso, but administrators in Teso failed to recognize the distinctiveness of their ethnic group, viewing them as Banyoro followers of Namionjo of Bugerere.[26]

24. Field notes, Serere, 1966.
25. Ibid.
26. Ibid. See also "Removal of Banyoro" (TDA XNAF/3.135/13) and "Chief Njala" (TDA XNAF/4.331/10).

Clearly, the political organization of the Serere peninsula reflected on the eve of conquest a complexity not found in the rest of the Teso region. This was due to its long association with Buchopi, Bunyoro, and northern Bugerere. Bakenyi movement into the southern part of the peninsula predated that of the Iteso, who indeed appear, on the eve of the conquest, to have been still migrating into the region. Political organization in Serere in the mid-nineteenth century reflected these uncertain conditions.

The South

Kumi appears to have first been settled by Ikumetok some time between 1652 and 1733; the first migrants entered the country from the northern shores of lake Bisina.[27] Responsive to a new terrain, nucleated settlement developed around the homesteads of Big Men, among them Amodan in Nyero, Oitatmun and Imooko in Okouba, Oloit in Kabata, Omasuga in Ngora, and Omuitia in Omatenga. Their homesteads were large and ringed with palisades of thorn-bush. Over time dispersion occurred, and then movement was usually only a short distance away. New clan names were adopted to mark the separation. Localities thus began to take on the coloring of clan, since residential groups were made up largely of kinsmen and their affines. Members of such homesteads were linked within ritual groups. Since these were formed after boys reached marrying age, they are sometimes called age-sets or generation-sets. In Kumi, generation-sets were not contingent military organizations, as they were elsewhere.[28] Nor was the *etem* (administrative sub-county) either a territorial group (as it may have been in Amuria) or a political unit, although it has sometimes been considered such throughout Teso generally.

In Kumi, political organization beyond the domain of the homestead economy was amorphous.[29] An overall military leader united

27. Emudong (1973), p. 87; Gideon S. Were, *A History of the Abaluyia of Western Kenya,* 1500–1930 (1967), p. 52.

28. Emudong, p. 68.

29. This categorical term is adopted from Colson (1970), p. 48. Compare Tosh (1978a), pp. 35–37. Among noncentralized political systems, amorphous polities are usefully distinguished from associational and lineage-based organizations—a point that Claude Meillassoux, for example, does not sufficiently appreciate. Large areas of Africa depended upon "an amorphous network of personal relationships for the ordering of public

each locality or cluster of homesteads, his leadership emergent at times of crisis. Military leadership became increasingly institutionalized (at the expense of clan elders) in the south of Teso toward the mid-nineteenth century. Because such institutionalization occurs with frequency of demand, it may well have developed in response to the new opportunities offered, for it would appear that greater military consolidation occurred parallel to the caravan route that passed from Mumia's through Wakoli's to Lubwa's in Busoga.

By the end of the nineteenth century, the vast expanse of flat, swampy, monotonous terrain that Frederick Jackson viewed from the top of Mount Masaba, stretching westward to Lake Kyoga and the mouth of the Mpologoma, was ringed by military unrest. Between Lake Rudolf and the Nyakwai hills, hunters and traders maintained open season north of Save. South, from Mumia's to Luba's, the country reeled under the repercussions of the caravan trade and the encroachments of Buganda upon her eastern neighbors.

Kumi lay between the two. A civil war raged to the north of Lake Bisina between the peoples of Toroma and those of Komolo-Abela, as we have seen; and, to the south, the inhabitants of Bukedea were waging almost constant military campaigns against those from farther south who attacked them. Closer to home, Karamojong raids against Tisai Island and the Ongino countryside, although thus far repulsed by Okore, the Ongino war leader, were a perpetual threat to a peaceful existence.

Though the waters of Lake Bisina isolated the northern Ikumetok from conflict, settlers in southern Kumi sometimes found it to their advantage to ally themselves with Bukedea and Pallisa to raid southward for cattle, children, and women. Much of the fighting in the southern region occurred within the no-man's-lands around Kolir and Akuoro—"the end of the world"—especially as Bagisu and Ikumetok alike were obliged to exploit the hunting territory more

---

life. These communities had in common their refusal to concentrate authority in the hands of individuals holding political office; to this extent they may be said to have lacked governments though they possessed political structure." Administrators and missionaries, familiar with feudal political structures and patriarchal clan structures (Willis (1925)) failed to recognize that political individuation was inherent in Iteso political structures.

extensively when periods of prolonged drought and famine struck at their communities, destroying the ecological balance maintained during better years.

According to C. P. Emudong, all Bukedea fought under Okoche, and southern Kumi and Ngora joined him on larger raiding expeditions.[30] Affines around Omatenga, which lay between Okouba and Lake Bisina, often supported Okoche's warriors in their campaigns; but those in the far north of Kumi, in Okuba and Agule, chose not to do so. War leaders from the various localities led their men individually to Tamula, where they met with those from other areas of south Teso commanded by their own war leaders. From Tamula, Malinga of Pallisa and Okoche coordinated attacks on the Bagisu and Iyalei. Yet "neither Okoche nor Malinga appears to have really gained command of all the units as one combined force. The other leaders accepted the guidance of Okoche because Okoche was nearest the enemy; he knew the place where they were going to fight and knew much about strategy."[31] Alliances and oppositions were thus contingent in nature and, since they were of short duration, leaders might return from successful adventures with heightened reputations as commanders and strategists but with no extension or consolidation of authority or power.

This cellular structure of military organization, with its individualistic and contingent leadership, required a social cement for concerted efforts to be mounted. This bonding was provided by a ritual leader, an *amuron*. Although local elders held certain ritual powers, and some were specialists in foretelling the outcome of battles and encounters, each military leader (although he might have followed the advice of such seers in deciding whether to lead his followers into raids or battle), once an alliance was joined, subordinated his own *amuron* and accepted a ritual leader recognized by all. Certain war rituals would still be performed locally (rites of separation and reincorporation, presumably), but the important transitional rites

30. Emudong, p. 106. Within political ethnography it has, perhaps, not been sufficiently appreciated that, in spite of the constant conflict between Nuer and Dinka, military leadership never became institutionalized. Should the Teso mode of war organization be characteristic of amorphous polities in situations of expansion, its features go some way towards explaining why.

31. Emudong, p. 106.

were practiced exclusively by the supreme amuron at the site and on the eve of battle. Such extensive and exclusive authority to carry out vital ritual could not easily be separated from political power; and, later, an *amuron* was almost as likely to be made a client chief as was a local military leader or big man. In Teso, Okolimong of Us-uku provides a striking example. In Bukedea toward the end of the nineteenth century, the *amuron* was a woman, Amongin. Whether this was usual is not known; if it was rare, there is no explana-tion.[32]

There is little possibility of the conversion of ritual to political authority within the indigenous system. In other societies, such ritual experts are often individuals who do not belong to dominant kin groups or prominent localities, who operate, as it were, in the interstices of social structure. By virtue of their positions they are seen to be not part of, but above or outside of, sectional interests and divisions and so are able to unite members of diverse groups that, in other situations, may conflict with one another.

Though this cellular structure permitted the greatest possible mo-bilization, lesser occasions brought forth smaller cooperative enter-prises. On one notable raid, for example, warriors from Olupe, Okouba, Kumi, Kelim, and Olungia joined against Oloit of Kabata. Given the nature of political entrepreneurship in Ikumetok society and the opportunities offered by the insecurity of the times, an ambitious notable might attempt to bring together under his hege-mony several itela. He might use force, as did Oloit of Kabata, and so bring forth united resistance; or he might use diplomacy, as did Amodan of Nyero, who successfully united and led Ogooma, Mor-uita, and Amenya at the end of the nineteenth century. Amodan, it was said, attracted followers by his wealth, judicial impartiality and military skill, not by coercion.[33]

The political authority of the indigenous elder rested, largely, on his wealth and the use he made of it. Wealth was acquired both through longevity and through deliberate effort; and its distribu-

---

32. D. H. Okalany, "Mukongoro during the Asonya" (1973), p. 127. One cannot but remark, however, that unlike elsewhere in Teso, extensive territorial ritual relations were founded on the acknowledgment of Amongin's powers. Perhaps, because she *was* a woman, these were not seen to "spill over" into other domains.

33. Webster has an extended note on Amondan in THT no. 18.7.

tion, whether that be of female offspring acquired through marriage or cattle acquired through successful husbandry and raiding, won followers. Where the exchange of commodities took place between different ecological zones, the big men often controlled both access to traders and the disbursement of their goods. The most hierarchical or developed form of political organization in precolonial Teso emerged in the Mukongoro-Pallisa region, where the savanna gave way to the woodlands of Busoga.

The military hierarchy in Mukongoro-Pallisa, in its most developed form, probably in response to Kakungulu's attacks, has been reconstructed by D. H. Okalany as follows:[34]

Under the supreme command of Okoche of Bukedea

Confederacy	Itela	Itela or Battalion Leader	Confederacy or Regimental Leader
East Mukongoro	Mukongoro	Akuku	
	Oladot	Okoboi	
	Onyakelo	Ecapi and Agi	Akuku
	Kodokoto	Mukula	
	Kanyum	Tukei	

Under the Supreme command of Muloki of Bulamogi

Confederacy	Itela	Itela or Battalion Leader	Confederacy or Regimental Leader	
West Mukongoro	Osopotoit	Auk		
	Ogosoi	Doelei		
	Agaria	Otingiro	Auk	
	Kadami	Tukei		
	Kobwin-Agu	Omadi		Osako-Oloit
North Pallisa	Kameke	Osako-Oloit		
	Kisirana	Malinga	Osako-Oloit	
	Kibale	Arikodi		
	Agule	Olinga		
Bulamogi Kingdom	Military structure unknown			

34. Okalany, p. 144.

Several of the leaders had kinship ties with coevals in northern Pallisa. Omadi of Kobwin, for example, was a kinsman of Osako-Oloit of Kameke, who, in turn, was related through marriage to Okoboi of Oladot.[35] Even more important, however, was the fact that military confederacies such as this underwrote trading systems. Muloki in Bulamogi sent bundles of hoes and *matoke* (sweet bananas) to Osako-Oloit in Kameke across the Mpologoma River and to Auk, leader of the Mukongoro confederacy. They sent back cattle, goats, and chickens.[36] Extending across ecological zones, this imbrication of social and economic fields promised to generate less amorphous political forms; but the advent of the Imperial British East Africa Company to the south, and Kakungulu's establishment of his headquarters first in Bugerere and then in Pallisa, aborted such developments.

To what extent conflict rather than cooperation was characteristic of the region in the nineteenth century remains open to question; it has been suggested that "the impression given by much of the colonial literature that whole populations or tribes were constantly fighting each other was a gross exaggeration."[37] Teso informants spoke often of clan fights and mortalities in the precolonial era, but rarely of extended conflict.

Toward the close of the nineteenth century, four political fields coexisted in the southern savanna. In the west, a still expanding field was dominated by Amodan of Nyero; in the center another was precariously dominated by Oloit of Kabata; in the northeast, Okore was war leader of Ongino; and in the south lay the Mukongoro-Pallisa confederacy. To the southwest lay the *eitela* of Omasuge of Ngora. A succession dispute between Omasuge and his son Ijala led the latter to invite Kakungulu's intervention—a course of action that resulted in the conquest of southern Teso—but nothing more is known of political organization in that locality.

Not until after the conquest of the Teso region did any one political authority extend over an area of more than a few square

---

35. Ibid., p. 149.
36. Ibid., p. 148.
37. Helge Kjekshus, *Ecology Control and Economic Development in East African History: The Case of Tanganyika, 1850–1950* (1977), p. 12.

miles. No point within such a domain was more than a day's march away, and only geographical features, especially rivers and swamps, divided one from another. At moments of diastolic expansion such "natural" boundaries were crossed as neighboring big men formed alliances; at times of contraction, *itemwan* became isolable territorial units linked only by trade controlled in the interests of the leaders.

Social and religious interests in a wider community of intermarriage and trade had their ritual manifestation in generation-sets and *supra-itemwan* rainmakers and seers who fostered the well-being of localities in peace and war. For production, exchange, and reproduction, the society required a wider community than the territory dominated by any one big man. Thus were the centripetal forces of big-manship countered in the ritual sphere, as individuals weak in coercion and the mobilization of force arose with spiritual powers to articulate petty political domains within larger, if intermittent, political frameworks.

Conquest and Reaction to Conquest

In 1899, it will be remembered, Kakungulu had been authorized by the special commissioner to extend his activities east of Lake Kyoga. Since 1896 he had been embroiled in two political arenas north and east of the lake. Around Bululu and along the shores of Lake Kojweri he had followed in the footsteps of Namionjo, taking over the mantle of the collapsing Bunyoro dynasty. This region, valued for its entrepôt facilities between east and west, was fringed by hostile Langi, Kumam, and Iteso, who prevented penetration more than a day's march inland. Stationed at forts in Kawere, Sambwe, Bululu, and Lale, as well as in the neighborhood of Serere, Baganda influence spread along preexisting networks. Catechists, mostly young Baganda and Basoga, taught in the garrisons, and prominent men of the area—such as Oluga (Mulangira)—sought to ally themselves with the newcomers and have their sons brought up as Christians. For the most part, however, it was among fellow Bantu-speaking residents of the Serere peninsula (Basoga, Banyala, Bakenyi, Banyoro) that Kakungulu's influence spread.

A second political arena in which Kakungulu's men had been active was the complex lake region that straddled the Mpologoma

River. Like Serere, this, too, formed an eastern aspect of the Lake Kyoga system in which Bantu and Nilotic populations confronted one another. Iteso occupied the brackish plains of Pallisa as early as 1810; and by the end of the nineteenth century Pallisa settlers had engaged Okoche of Bukedea in both trade and war. From market centers in Bulamogi, the Iteso of Mukongoro obtained Banyoro-type iron hoes. Matoke, cattle, goats, and chicken were traded in peace, cattle, children, and women acquired in war. From Bugerere and Bulamogi, Kakungulu and other Baganda raided across the Mpologoma River and were raided in turn. By 1900 Kakungulu's force was an established presence in the Pallisa region.[38]

When Kakungulu received his brief from the commissioner to consolidate and extend his activities in Bukeddi, he despatched two expeditions from Bululu. The first was sent to secure his influence along the eastern shores of Lake Kyoga from Bululu to Bugerere; the goal of the second was to penetrate Teso to the northeast (see Figure 6).

The Southern Expedition

For Isaka Nzige and the three hundred mercenaries under his command, the route lay southward through settled Serere and Kateta toward Gogonyo in Pallisa, making for a locality in which working relations, uneasy as they were, had nevertheless been established. The Baganda force met with little resistance en route, since they were a known quantity in the political equation. What was required of them was a show of force and, more significantly, perhaps, display of the government flag that, under the instructions of the commissioner, Grant had presented to Kakungulu.

The march south from Bululu to Gogonyo was uneventful, probably because it was almost entirely through territory where Bakenyi, Banyala, and Basoga were almost as numerous as Iteso. Yet, if Nzige's march to the south was not distinguished by military action it was, nevertheless, not without incident. En route to Pallisa, he and his men were confronted by John Gemmill, a British adven-

---

38. Gray, "Report."

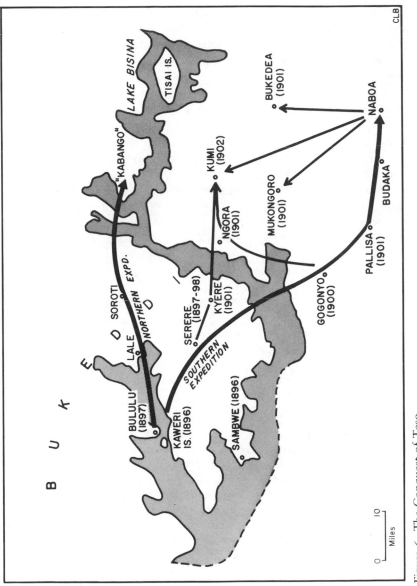

Figure 6. The Conquest of Teso.

turer trading in those parts.[39] Gemmill took it upon himself to disarm the Baganda. In a sense this was a timely blow to Kakungulu's aggrandizement because it obliged the Protectorate government to step in—which it did in the person of C. D. Fowler. Fowler had been sent to Bukeddi to report on the navigability of Lake Kyoga and the Victoria Nile, with a view to asking Kakungulu to send supplies of food to famine-stricken Busoga.[40] Nothing came of this plan, largely because Kakungulu lacked the power to organize such a levy; he had, as seen earlier, given the Protectorate government a somewhat exaggerated impression of his authority. Turning aside from his surveying duties, Fowler set about returning to the natives of Bukeddi the tusks of ivory and cattle that Gemmill had taken from them. Doing so, he made a point of impressing upon the local populations that Kakungulu, not Gemmill, was the true government representative in the area. An influential (but unnamed) chief who protested at this was "summarily dismissed with a caution as to future behaviour."[41]

Here, in the south, Kakungulu received full backing from the British authorities. Not only was an inquiry held into Gemmill's dismantling of Kakungulu's force (he was subsequently imprisoned and deported), but instructions were issued that "no armed parties are for the future to cross over into Bukeddi, and any unarmed food purchasing parties are to report themselves to the Kakungulu." In the indictment against Gemmill, Kakungulu was referred to as "His

39. Gray (file, n.d.). These notes provide a richer account than that in Gray. He cites C. D. Fowler to Nagueries, Bukeddi, June 25, 1900, as his source. Gemmill had earlier been a caravan leader for the IBEA Co. and then for the Uganda Administration, but "his handling and treatment of porters had left much to be desired" (Gray, 1963, p. 39). He had made certain claims against the Administration for losses suffered during the "Nubian Mutiny" and was given 1,000 acres in Busoga in satisfaction of these claims. It is not clear why he crossed to the east of the Mpologoma.

40. Gray (file, n.d.). He cites Johnston to Tucker, Apr. 19, 1900, after he had called Kakungulu's bluff. "He boasted of the peace which now reigns in his province and the abundant supplies of food which could be obtained there. I at once invited him to send the overplus of his produce to Busoga."

41. Gray (file, n.d.). He again cites C. D. Fowler to Nagueries, Bukeddi, June 25, 1900.

Majesty's Special Commissioner's representative in the Bukeddi District."[42]

With some difficulty, for he was confronted in northern Pallisa by the military confederacy commanded by Osako-Oloit, Kakungulu established bases at Gogonyo, Pallisa, and Naboa. His military actions were savage, permanently disfiguring the landscape as villages and crops were destroyed. Both the actions of those to the north (the Iteso of west Mukongoro, who learned from this dreadful example that resistance would be futile) and the reports of European missionaries who passed through the scarred terrain testify to Kakungulu's efficiency.

The Northern Expedition

The second expedition despatched from Bululu set out in the direction of Soroti,[43] perhaps hoping to follow Banyoro trade routes into the interior toward "Teso" north of Lake Bisina, toward Save, or even toward the Ethiopian route. They may well have expected to be passed from hand to hand, as were the Banyoro, or (given their large numbers) welcomed as possible allies in local confrontations. But their passage was charted under very different circumstances. The Great Famine of 1894 and the rinderpest that followed had hit severely in the north; an expedition of 150 men living off the countryside must have appeared to the inhabitants as yet another in the series of disasters that beset them. As the Baganda force moved eastward from the shores of Lake Kojweri, it encountered fierce opposition in the Ajama hills from Kwelo, Kamoda, and their allies. Although they defeated the local population, the Baganda made no attempt to build a fort in this area, pushing on eastward until, finally, stranded in hostile "Teso," the remains of the expedition settled at Kapujan, on the northern shores of Lake Bisina.[44] Here, se-

42. Ibid. He cites the draft of the indictment against Gemmill, July 8, 1900. After his arrest, trial, and imprisonment for the illegal possession of arms, Gemmill was deported. In response to an inquiry of Apr. 9, 1902, from Miss Bella Gemmill, Johnston informed her that her brother had last been heard of in Bombay.

43. Waswa (MS., n.d.), par. 40.

44. The place name "Kabanya" appears in Waswa's manuscript. I take this to lie within South Kapujan, possibly in the neighborhood of Okokorio.

cure among Bakenyi fishermen and ferrymen, Semu Kagwa and his men established a temporary garrison.

As important as the presence of the Bakenyi in Kapujan was the water lily. As in the south the Mpologoma network of lakes and swamps provided a famine granary at the hub of a trading network, so, too, Kapujan was the focal point of an exchange system that in times of famine was crucial to the populations of southern Amuria and Usuku. Water lilies were exchanged for goats in Toroma and Kapujan and also across the lake in Agule and Omatenga.[45]

By 1900, then, Kakungulu's forces had established two beachheads where the local population could support the presence of his garrisons. Between them lay several hundred square miles of untraversed country, a terrain held by innumerable small bodies of fighting men whose pacification would call for both diplomacy and force of arms. Although alien hegemony had been experienced in Serere long before 1900, and administration north of Lake Bisina occurred only after Kakungulu's fall from grace in 1902, Teso's political history, in its official version, lies in the conquest of these three southern counties: Ngora, Kumi, and Bukedea.

The thrust began late in 1901. Assaults had been carried out on Mukongoro, Ngora, and Bukedea under the command of Kakungulu's younger brother, Sedulaka Kyesrikidde. "Few serious attempts were made even to find pretexts for these raids: local Iteso notables were simply summoned to appear before Kakungulu 'to make peace' and then punished if they did not appear promptly enough."[46] Raiding alone, however, became insufficient to achieve Kakungulu's new objectives.

Famine and plague were sweeping through Busoga, and the problem of feeding the country (once the breadbasket of the caravan trade) had become critical. To the east of Kumi, north of Bukedea, lay the most fertile grain district in the region. Known to Iteso as "the thigh of a cow," *akures*, or *amuro itarasit*, this was a center of food production and trade for as far afield as Magoro, Agule, Ongino, and Omatenga to the north and Busoga and Bugwere to the

---

45. Webster (1973), p. 52, and (1972), p. 48.

46. Daudi Musoke, "Ebyafaya bya Bigisu" (n.d.), quoted by Twaddle (Ph.D., 1967), p. 101. This early collection of travel articles, written in Luganda, is described in Twaddle (1969), pp. 193–195.

south. Produce was exchanged at the rate of "one boy for one bull plus some millet or one girl for one cow plus some millet."[47] A coordinated assault was necessary to reach the grain region because the military confederacies of Bukedea and Mukongoro dominated its trade routes.

An alternative approach from the west was made possible through Ijala's cooperation. Seizing upon the succession dispute between Ijala and his father, Kakungulu's troops marched into Agu and thence toward Ngora. Defeating Omasuge with the help of Baganda arms, Ijala set himself up as chief. With Omasuge defeated and Ijala established in his place, the Baganda troops began to make systematic forays into Kumi and Bukedea. The unit in Kapujan was brought south of the lake to Pege Dwarate (near Ngora), which then became Kakungulu's northernmost garrison. Another 250 men, under Sedulaka Lubabule, were transferred from Gogonyo. The local population harassed them so successfully that, although the Iteso were defeated in most skirmishes, it was decided nevertheless to withdraw even further south to Ngora, where they would be under Ijala's protection. Among the members of the Ngora garrison were several men who later became agents for the Protectorate government in Teso.[48] The manner in which their debt to Ijala was repaid will become clear in the following chapters.

With a northern frontier secure—even though it was not as far north as originally planned—other forts were subsequently established on the central plains, especially at troublesome Mukongoro, where Saulo Buzo was left with fifty men.[49] The following year, troops from Serere and Ngora were sent to Kumi, which was fast becoming the center of operations. In spite of strong resistance, the southern Iteso were finally defeated at the battle of Kumi Terai. Following Outa's execution at Kumi and the defeat of Okoche in Bukedea, local resistance collapsed.

Continuities and Discontinuities

The political organization of precolonial Teso carried over into the twentieth century in two forms. First, certain leaders who hap-

47. Emudong, p. 99. He is quoting the elders of Agule in Kumi county.
48. Waswa, pars. 60 and 76.
49. Ibid., par. 61.

pened to be at, or were brought to, the peak of their powers during the years of the Baganda wars were given administrative office under Baganda county chiefs. Second, and more important, the most inclusive unit of the indigenous political system—the etem—became, virtually unchanged, the crucial tier of a newly imposed British four-tier structure of executive chiefs. Above the *itemwan* (subcounties), counties were created; and it later proved politically significant that these counties variously cut across or conformed to earlier cooperative ritual groupings. Usuku County brought together north and south, but in uneasy harness. The etem of Acwa became a subcounty in Amuria, although its cultural ties were with Usuku. The southwest became Soroti and Serere counties, although an early administrator noted that the natural divide between them differed from the administrative boundary. Most important, however, was the division of what had formerly been one ritual sphere of influence in the south with the creation of the three small counties of Ngora, Kumi, and Bukedea. The history of the twentieth century witnesses the interests of a reunited southern bloc reemergent.

As alien creations, the counties were headed by Baganda County, or *saza*, chiefs. Below them, parish, or *miruka*, chiefs and their unpaid subordinates, *elodak* or *erony* chiefs, were responsible for little more than the mobilization and control of labor for public services.

The itemwan received, for the first time, precise territorial definition; indeed, they proved to be the only administrative units whose boundaries remained unchanged in the years that followed. The subcounty chieftainship became the fulcrum of local politics in Teso. Important for their judicial and fiduciary functions, the subcounty chiefs were the first to be given arms. The power of patronage inherent in their office made it the locus of faction struggles, many of them carried over from the precolonial era though not surfacing until several years later.

On the eve of conquest, five diastolic political fields existed in the south. Amodan's influence was expanding even as the Baganda forces were establishing themselves at Ijala's village, little more than five miles away. Ijala called Amodan to Ngora and introduced him to the Baganda as a man willing to collaborate with them. Amodan then "advised his friends in Kumi to accept the new regime."[50] To

50. Emudong, p. 111.

the southeast of Amodan's domain, a plateau had been reached in local feuding. The aggrandizement of Oloit of Kabata had been successfully halted by a coalition of forces from neighboring itelas that supported his rival half-brother, Oluka. Unlike Amodan, who had successfully consolidated power in the west, Oloit's bid had been frustrated. Perhaps with the Baganda presence looming ominously in neighboring areas, there was too much at stake. Any jockeying for position was an all-or-nothing venture, since any position gained or lost was likely to be perpetuated by Baganda force of arms for some time.

We know of twenty-four other Iteso leaders in the southern savanna. (Here something of a caveat must be entered, for in reconstructing the political organization in Teso at the turn of the century, we are solely dependent on secondary sources of varying reliability. Moreover, identifications of big men, by the very character of the role, tend to be somewhat parochial in character.) Two of the greatest military leaders, Oloit and Okoche, were defeated in battle by the invading troops. Oloit was replaced by Oumo, a former client, who was made a subcounty chief by Kakungulu. Okoboi of Oladot was also defeated. Agi was subsequently killed for refusing to recruit labor at Mukongoro.

Many of those who collaborated, among them Ijala and Amodan, were made subcounty chiefs. The value placed on their assistance can be inferred from the gun licenses issued to them when British administrators later took over from Kakungulu. Nine individuals from the pre-Baganda political era were lethally privileged: Ijala (eight guns); Amodan (three guns); Ocheppa of Mukura (two guns); Okore of Bukedea (two guns); Okoboi of Mukongoro (two guns); and Tuke of Mukongoro, Oumo of Kumi, Agi of Kapiri, and Okoche of Bukedea (one gun each).[51]

The differences between this old guard and the men of the next generation is critical to an understanding of the political events of the next thirty years. Emudong writes in general terms of a "division between the youth and the aged. . . . While established military leaders saw much to be gained by collaboration, youth was pre-

51. Information here and in later chapters on chiefs' guns is collated from listings of arms registered in Bukeddi District. These appeared at intervals in the *Uganda Protectorate Gazette* between March 31, 1908, and and Jan. 15, 1911.

pared to test itself against Baganda guns." It was this generation of youths, he suggests, who as they grew to maturity "applied steady pressure on the British to replace the Baganda chiefs with Iteso personnel."[52]

The history of the southern counties was generally characterized by considerable continuity from precolonial times; this was not the case in the north. Possibly only those leaders with the largest herds had survived the rinderpest epidemic as local patriarchs; but whatever the reason, the careers of few of them can be traced into the colonial era. Apart from Abyong of Dakabela, Olume-Ajama of Orungo, and Omiat of Komolo, only the northern frontiersmen— Opuna of Atirir, Ecungo of Abeko, and Egasu of Abya—entered the record, and we shall not renew our acquaintance with any of them until a young administrative officer, J. M. Coote, undertakes a safari in the Soroti region in 1909.

As for the arid northeast, not until after the establishment of British administration at Kumi do the careers of several political leaders begin to bridge the precolonial and colonial divide. The heroes of Usuku's resistance to the Baganda become its recalcitrant chiefs under the British; its collaborators advance apace.

In the Serere peninsula, the matter is more complex due to the earlier incursions of aliens and the polyethnic nature of settlement. Of the prominent preconquest Iseera leaders, only six were recognized as subcounty chiefs: Oluga of Bugondo, Ocheppa of Atira, Olago of Kadungulu, and Okurut, Osamma, and Oiba of Osuguru (Serere). Namionjo was acknowledged chief of the Banyoro, most of whom were settled on the Kagwara penisula and the offshore islands in the north. Ali Mwambazi was brought across from Bugerere to collect tax from Bakenyi kinsmen. Ekora, a client of Olango, perhaps, was made responsible for Basoga residents. Possibly because the Baganda themselves settled in Serere, few chiefs were given arms by the pioneer colonial administration. Of those who were, Oluga received six and Okurut three; "Charo of Serere" (sic) received two and Sedulaka of Kelim one.

Accounts of the conquest dwell upon atrocities. At Mukongoro, for example, cattle and captives alike, it is said, were herded into huts that were then set afire. A Muganda chronicler comments:

52. Emudong, p. 114.

"This was an act of excessive cruelty. But it served its purpose in dealing with such a primitive area."[53] Where no prominent leaders appeared to represent their people, where no villages were to be found, but only fenced homesteads, the Baganda, accustomed as they were to ostentatious deference and acknowledged responsibility, were at a loss to deal even with passive resistance in any other way. The amorphous nature of the polity in Teso served, as does the incohesiveness of people everywhere faced with superior force of arms, to enhance sullen resistance and the reactive adoption of guerilla tactics of savanna and swamp.

53. Daudi Musoke.

5. Hegemony and Pacification: Primary and Secondary Modes

> Let it be admitted at the outset that European brains, capital and energy have not been, and never will be, expanded in developing the resources of Africa from pure philanthropy; that Europe is in Africa for the mutual benefit of her own industrial classes, and of the native races in their progress to a higher plane.
>
> Lugard 1922:617

> The majority of the soldiers and men of action who in Africa have actually been the agents of the acquisitive policy of economic imperialism have been genuinely moved by what to them have seemed the most noble and disinterested of ideals.
>
> Woolf n.d.:290

Teso was no dormant region awaiting its "discovery" by sub-imperialists and the soldiers of Christ. As one might expect of a people engaged in trading and raiding, Iteso themselves reached out for contact with outsiders. So-called Bakeddi chiefs called at the mission stations and *bomas* (administrative headquarters) in Busoga and Budaka several years before the first European missionaries and administrators had established themselves in Teso. The years following the conquest of Teso in 1902 were distinguished largely by the comings and goings of its people, as soldiers, missionaries, and administrators established themselves on its southern borders. Lacking military strength to do more, British hegemony in Teso grew under the mantle of Baganda conquest and, largely, in the guise of missionary endeavor.

The Anglican Church Missionary Society had long anticipated the opening of Bukeddi. Crossing the Mpologoma in 1899, on itineration from Iganga in Busoga, the Reverend G. R. Blackledge first "met the Bakeddi, a wild naked people inhabiting the Nile Valley. They welcomed him, and some five hundred assembled and discussed the subject of a white teacher, and came to the conclusion that as the Gospel had been such a blessing to the Waganda, and had so changed their lives, they themselves were willing to be taught, and would welcome a white teacher."[1] In January 1900 the Reverend T. R. Buckley spent three weeks in Bukeddi visiting Kakungulu, "the chief in command of the whole country." He reported that catechists were preaching the gospel in two locations, at Bululu and Sambwe. There were, he said, about sixty people under instruction, but trained teachers were badly needed.[2]

The first missionaries settled in Bukeddi by chance. Having gone there on safari during a vacation from duties at Iganga, William Crabtree, enthused with a perception of opportunities, wrote to Kampala asking permission to stay in Bukeddi. Regardless of—or perhaps because of—his day-by-day contact with Baganda administration, Crabtree attempted to draw attention to what, in an article written for the *Church Missionary Intelligencer*, he called "openings beyond Uganda: an appeal for Bukeddi." He appears to have set aside his qualms about Kakungulu's administration, setting out instead an argument that Baganda activities in Teso could be made to serve missionary interests. After visiting Bululu and Serere in 1901, Crabtree called for an expansion of missionary effort—not in the east, where Kakungulu was established, but in the region he called "Teso," to the north. Although he was essentially an outsider holding partisan views of the Eastern Province that were at odds with the Gandacentric interests of his superiors, he couched his appeal as counter-Unyoro propaganda, referring to "the notorious slave-raiding king of Unyoro" and "one of the best of the Buganda chiefs, Semei Kakungulu, a sincere Christian." He described "districts which are just now unknown to any white man, but undoubtedly belong to Teso," where the people spoke what he called "the sambwe-language." He further warned that there was no time to lose: here Catholicism, not Islam, became the enemy. "We are getting behind," he urged, "and neglecting first rate opportunities; the Roman Catholics will outpace us and work up to Saveh and Lake Rudolf." Sensitive to the advantages Roman Catholic

1. G. R. Blackledge, "Correspondence" (1900). See also Alfred R. Tucker (1908), p. 294.

2. Roscoe to Baylis, Mar. 31, 1900 (CMS Archives). Compare John Roscoe, "Among the Wild Bakeddi" (1901).

missionaries would enjoy in Teso, he pointed out that several had come to Uganda from Algeria and already knew some Arabic, which "would give them an immense pull over our men if they determined to work up the Nile."[3] He was not wrong.

For the Mill Hill fathers, 1901 was "the year of Busoga," whence the first step was made into Pallisa and, thereafter, the Teso region.[4] In December 1900, Bishop Henry Hanlon and Father Gregorius Kestens set out from Iganga to visit Kakungulu at Masawa. The bishop (like Fowler in Pallisa) was influential in persuading local chiefs that Kakungulu was not an adventurer, helping them to comprehend his "real position" and the futility of continued opposition to his rule. Perhaps in appreciation of this support, Kakungulu gave the Irish and Dutch missionaries a site for a mission station at Budaka close to his own settlement. Once established, however, he was able to control their access to labor, and apparently he did much to make life difficult for them.[5]

Kakungulu was ambivalent in his attitude toward the Roman Catholic mission. Certainly he had, instilled from his earlier days in Buganda, a deep sensitivity to the politics of sectarianism, and he shared Crabtree's Anglican sense of competition with the Catholic fathers. The Mill Hill mission had been introduced into Uganda specifically to counter the nationalistic hostilities of Wa-Fransa and Wa-Ingleza converts in the Baganda coups and countercoups. Cardinal Vaughan of St. Joseph's Foreign Missionary Society of Mill Hill, London (after consultation with Bishop Livinhac of the White Fathers), had submitted to the Foreign Office a plan that missionaries who were both Roman Catholic and English should be sent to Uganda. The existing Nyanza Vicariate was then divided into three sections, and the northeastern part was given to the Mill Hill mission. This became the Vicariate of the Upper Nile by a papal decree of July 6, 1894.[6] Described as "a keen Christian" by the

3. Crabtree (1901), pp. 369–370. The Ateso language, variously referred to now as Lumogera or Lusambwe, was clearly recognized as non-Bantu. Crabtree thought it akin to Arabic.

4. Gale (1959), p. 216.

5. See, e.g., the entry in the diary of Budaka mission (hereafter DBM) of the Mill Hill fathers' Upper Nile Vicariate for Nov. 30, 1903. See also Gale, pp. 217, 226–229.

6. Gale, p. 316, argues that "The English and Dutch personnel of the Mission, and its close cordial relations with the Administration and local

CMS, Kakungulu ws viewed as "a CMS man and a rather fervent one" by the Mill Hill mission.[7] In November 1901 W. R. Walker, on a visit to inspect Kakungulu, was obliged to counter an impression Kakungulu had given the chiefs that only Protestants would gain advancement within the bureaucracy.[8] Nevertheless, as Iteso became chiefs after 1902 they found themselves pawns between Catholic and Protestant missionaries, between the administration, and those who sought to challenge it.

As early as August 1903, "Bukeddi" and "Teso" chiefs began to visit the Budaka mission of the Mill Hill fathers, much as they had earlier approached Mengo through Kakungulu's garrisons in Serere. The names of the first mission visitors were recorded as Muroni, Kanya, Lukojja, and Wafeti; presents were given the visitors, including food.[9] Thereafter, chiefs traveling from Bululu or Serere to the government headquarters at Jinja made the rounds of both mission stations at Budaka, and at both they were welcomed. Whereas the Anglicans at this time placed emphasis on the teaching of reading and arithmetic, Father Kestens, in the tradition of his order, established "an industrial institution" where brickmaking, bricklaying, carpentry, working in iron, roadmaking, and tailoring were taught.[10] Instruction was also given in agriculture and, in deference to the ensuing competition with the "people of the book," some reading and writing. The term "readers" was taken over from the Protestants, since it soon became apparent that it was this aspect

---

'collectors,' cannot but have assisted in breaking down the old party spirit," but this was not universally true. E.g., Father Kestens, who sheltered rebels at the Catholic mission at Luba's, was certainly not in the government's good books. However, Father Christopher J. Kirk, an Irishman, made himself indispensable when he persuaded Kakungulu to leave his Budaka headquarters peacefully (see Gale, p. 228). The greatest successes of the Mill Hill mission in Bukeddi overlapped with Kirk's endeavors there. Father Kirk's career was rewarded with the Order of the British Empire. (See also McGough, 1956.)

7. Gale, p. 221.

8. Ibid.

9. Entries for Aug. 13 and 16, 1903 (DBM). The diary begins with an entry by Father Gregorius Kestens on Sept. 10, 1901.

10. The division of labor between the missions thus began to furnish the nascent capitalist system with both its artisans and its ruling class.

of Christianity that chiefs valued and sought for their sons. At the CMS station, Mrs. Crabtree taught Iteso patients at the dispensary to read.[11]

A breakthrough came in October 1903, when Ijala (who by this time had established himself as Teso's leading collaborator) visited both missions. He was followed four weeks later by "many Bakeddi chiefs."[12] On December 26, visitors are named: Ijala, Mukura (Mukula of Kodokoto), Pakalwana, Tumi, Omadi (of Kobwin), Sawi (a subchief of Ijala), and Nalikodjio (Lukojo of Ngora). Ijala and Mukula returned on the following day as well. As far as one can tell, these are all chiefs from the Ngora region. In April 1903 the visit of two Teso chiefs, Munira and Aurnmo (Aronyo) is noted. (Hitherto, Iteso had appeared in the diary as Bakeddi.) In the following days, groups came from Okaboi in northern Serere, including Teso Chief Kapunta (Oput), with his people.[13] All received small presents.

These must have been rather barren years for the missionaries, with the expectations raised by the conquest of Bukeddi largely dashed by closer contact with Kakungulu and the realization that the Protectorate government was not yet in a position to consolidate its hegemony. North of Busoga, the commissioner reported in March 1903, "the country is inhabited by wild, and in some cases not over friendly, tribes, who have never been brought under our subjection . . . but I am in no hurry to do so, preferring to let them learn through the intervening tribes that they will gain and not lose by voluntarily submitting themselves to our authority."[14]

Although the administration may have been in no hurry to expand its frontier northward, the missionaries were restless. In 1903, both Father Christopher Kirk of the Mill Hill mission and Bishop Alfred R. Tucker of the CMS made safaris into Teso. Kirk's was limited to an area around Ijala's homestead at Ngora, which he made "the starting point of daily visits out to the surrounding chiefs, scattered far and near within a proscribed limit, outside of

11. William Crabtree, "Correspondence" (1902).

12. Entry for Oct. 9, 1903 (DBM).

13. Entries for Apr. 9, 20, and 24, and Dec. 26 and 27, 1903 (DBM).

14. General Report of the Uganda Protectorate for the year ending March 31, 1903 (PRO FO/645).

which it was considered unsafe by chiefs friendly to me to penetrate alone."[15] He used as his interpreter a Musoga youth who had been sold into captivity in Bukeddi. In July 1903 Sambwe's Muganda chief was baptized by Bishop Tucker,[16] but thereafter the activities of the CMS revolved around the Reverend Andereya Butalabudde, a catechist who had accompanied Kakungulu's army on the Southern Expedition and had since resided in the garrison at Kumi.[17]

Kakungulu's Paper Administration

Between 1900 and 1902 Kakungulu nominally administered Teso. Any Baganda conquest of Teso was, in fact, neither deep nor extensive. A line of forts was built Bunyoro-fashion across the south of the region from Bululu in the west to Mukongoro in the east. Its function was as likely to have been to keep out the "barbarians"— naked, warlike northerners—as to establish a line of command across an administered territory. The garrisons were established near the homesteads of prominent Iteso, and the chain of command reached from Kakungulu at the center (variously, in these years, at Budaka, Masaba, and Mpumudde) to each commander, stationed in relative isolation in the Teso countryside.

From their archaeological remains it is apparent that the Baganda forts were slight and could not have housed very large garrisons.[18] Troops were sent out to pillage for food in the surrounding countryside, perhaps an indication that past trading patterns had been punctured. Nor was there any growth of market places, either within the protection of the forts or around their walls. Some local populations were rounded up and sent to work at Kakungulu's Mpumudde headquarters, a measure that smacks of tribute, in-

15. Rev. C. J. Kirk, "Correspondence" (1903).

16. Alfred R. Tucker, "A Journey to Mt. Elgon and the Bukeddi Country" (1904), p. 261. See also Pirouet (Ph.D., 1968), p. 330.

17. References to the work of Butalabudde may be found in Bishop and Ruffell, p. 21; T. R. Buckley, "Correspondence" (1902); Pirouet, pp. 331, 334; Arthur L. Kitching, "Correspondence" (1913).

18. See I. Blackhurst, "The Forts of Kakungulu," final report on the Imperial College Uganda Expedition (typescript, 1965).

spired by the needs of pacification as much as mobilization.[19] A
Muganda chronicler of these times recollects how "the Baganda
used to stay in their forts, from which they would go to their various
duties in the villages under their control," suggesting neither extensive nor unmolested intercourse with the local people.[20] Essentially,
the diffused nature of Iteso social organization made for uneasy
articulation with the tributary administration Kakungulu's commanders aspired to set up.

Set out on paper, the specifics of control in Kakungulu's administration were bureaucratically ordered and unambiguous.[21] To what
extent the men on the spot were able to operate any kind of administration, not to mention a smooth one, remains questionable.
Much of the south and west had been seriously disturbed by fleeing
Nubian soldiers, as well as by the remnants of Kabalega's armies.
Many areas had been pillaged by both sides in the campaigns of
1898. Reliable witnesses wrote of Kakungulu's "scorched earth"
policy; Iteso elders spoke of the conquest in terms of pillage and
rape. The troops, they said, would enter a village, round up old
people and womenfolk, and hold them hostage for the surrender of
fighting men. Cattle would then be seized and food crops plundered.
In localities where the Iteso offered no resistance, homesteads remained unmolested; but the troops lived off the countryside, leav-

19. Twaddle (Ph.D., 1967), p. 146. There is visible in Teso at this period
an emergent form of what Amin would call a "'tribute-paying' mode [of
production] which adds to a still-existing village community a social and
political apparatus for the exploitation of this community through the
extraction of tribute" (Amin, 1976, p. 13). The *"poor* tribute-paying
formation" (ibid., p. 30) created by Baganda conquest was of very short
duration, but its brief existence misled some early missionaries and administrators to speak of pre-colonial feudalism in Teso.

20. Temeo Kagwa, "The History of Bukeddi" (MS., n.d.), quoted in
Twaddle (Ph.D., 1967), p. 136. One indication of consolidation would
have been the establishment of banana groves. Yet, apart from the Serere
garrisons, and a 1901 report that Eriya of Labori was proud of his banana
plantation (*Mengo Notes* 1(2), June 1901, p. 60; cited by Brian W. Langlands, "The Banana in Uganda, 1860–1920" (1966, p. 56), the amount of
banana cultivation remained small.

21. Subjugated Teso was in 1902 divided into two counties, Serere and
Ngora. An account of their administrative infrastructure is to be found in
Twaddle (Ph.D., 1967), pp. 136–143.

ing, in these postfamine years, little behind. Whether there was open resistance or not, covert resentment against the Baganda expressed itself in numerous ways. Late in 1901, when the British began to take over Kakungulu's operation, little had been consolidated but the Bantu fringe of a demesne and a patchwork of Iteso localities in its immediate hinterland; the savanna plains had yet to be crossed. Bakenyi-mastered waterways provided arteries for administration and intercourse in the southwest; the north was a different matter. There the population remained unpacified, since the logistics of troop movements so far from Mpumudde (dependent as they were upon Baganda garrisons in far from secure country) were very different from the south. Pallisa, Bugwere, Bunyole, and Budama—the southern parts of Kakungulu's fiefdom—far surpassed in economic value and resources the two counties carved out in Teso. Both Baganda and British missionaries were active there; corvée labor built roads; Baganda followers carved out estates; and Kakungulu believed himself there to stay.

When the Protectorate government took over the administrative machinery created by Kakungulu, they set about using it to consolidate and develop the Teso region. Whereas Baganda interests had usually been in plunder and the acquisition of estates, those of the British were more managerial. To adopt an analogy of the times, Teso was seen as yet another corner in the colonial estates of the British Crown; the task of administration was to see that the estate was well managed and profitable. The administration moved, first, to put Kakungulu's house in order. The names of all the county chiefs were submitted for approval to A. H. Watson, newly appointed collector at Mbale, in December 1901, and the chiefs were called in for inspection.[22] That the British administration had different expectations of the role of county chief from those of Kakungulu is suggested by the fact that Watson, before sending them back to their garrisons, arranged to have their garden plots in Mbale maintained to await their return. They were now expected to remain for longer periods at their upcountry stations, away from the politicking of Kakungulu's capital. Not only were their appointments at the discretion of the Protectorate government; they had become civil servants subject to transfer from one station to another.

There was, indeed, every indication that Kakungulu's career was

22. There is a full account of this incident in ibid., pp. 188–227.

coming to an end. Sometime earlier the Mengo court had complained of the propensity of Kakungulu and his followers to evade
taxes; but even more disturbing was the fact that so many young
Baganda had been attracted "over the east bank of the Nile" by the
prospects of obtaining estates. "For some time past," Jackson observed, "Kakungulu has been a constant source of worry and trouble, a thorn in the side of Mr. Grant and the Regents."[23] Jackson,
acting as commissioner for the Protectorate, took this occasion to
present to the Foreign Office his version of Kakungulu's career.
Based on a knowlege of the man and his activities that spanned the
years since the arrival of the first IBEA Co. caravan in Uganda,
Jackson's assessment was less flattering than that of Harry Johnston. Kakungulu had, Jackson said, originally been placed in charge
of Bukeddi in the vicinity of Lake Kyoga simply so that he might
prevent raids into Buganda. He had stopped them. He had reduced
the Bakeddi to submission, and although he had not received a
salary, he had paid himself and his followers handsomely in cattle
seized in his numerous encounters.[24] His fighting men, abakungulu,
had certainly been of considerable use to the Protectorate government in its early days. But Jackson appears to be contesting a sense
of obligation that had grown in the consciences of some British
administrators. The Reverend Mr. Crabtree (a perceptive observer
of the Bukeddi scene) was painstakingly guarded in his assessment
of Kakungulu's achievements in June 1901.

> Much might be written about the occupation of the country by the
> Baganda, however, I hardly like to go into many details on a subject
> about which there might be a good deal of diverse opinion. They are
> certainly encouraging people to wear clothes, but they do not seem to
> understand how to encourage trade, by which alone the people can
> become able to buy for themselves. I am not aware of any market in the
> whole of Kakungulu's district. The system of administration is the feudal
> system so familiar to us in Uganda . . . it is too soon to say what
> influence the Baganda will have on the direct evangelisation of the coun-
> try. At first I was disappointed, but perhaps unjustly. The Baganda
> throughout the district are somewhat estranged by their position as
> rulers, and what one might term Protectorate Police.[25]

23. Ag. Comm. Jackson to Marquis of Lansdowne, Jan. 24, 1902 (PRO
FO/403/318.144).
24. Ibid.
25. Crabtree (1901), p. 58. Another missionary, John B. Purvis, who was

Crabtree's comment on the lack of trade is significant: that colonization—even in the form of subimperialism—destroys indigenous forms of commerce and handicraft has nowhere been more apparent than in Teso.

As Kakungulu's sphere of interest had shifted from Bugerere to Pallisa and thence to Budaka, complaints began to reach Entebbe.[26] It was said that the people were "practically destitute, practically no cattle left for people to pay tax in"; moreover, Kakungulu had

---

posted to Masaba, was less restrained. A sensitive reporter of this phase in the history of the province, he wrote in his autobiography, *Through Uganda to Mount Elgon* (1909), pp. 359–360:

> One of the greatest difficulties that we have had to contend with in the work at Masaba is the unsettling of native mind and mode of life by the incoming Government administration.
>
> In 1903 the actual work of dealing with the natives was done by the Muganda chief, Semei Kakungulu. . . . He had placed his agents in various parts of the country to rule it on lines similar to the feudal system of Uganda, and he was answerable for the general condition of the district to the British official at Budaka, situated some twenty miles from Masaba. . . . New assistant collectors were appointed from time to time, and gradually a new order of things was evolved. . . .
>
> I am convinced that this step was taken for the good of the Bagishu; but after some four years' residence in the district I am bound to say, having earnestly and carefully weighed the seriousness of the statement, that during the years of my residence which mark the introduction of law into Masaba there seems to me to have been much less peace, less security of property, and more, very much more, bloodshed than during the period I lived there without direct British administration. . . .
>
> My memories of the troubles between the Administration and the people of Masaba are altogether painful, for in almost every instance my sympathies are with the native , as I am sure would be those of any man who had been asked by the men of a clan to beg back the women who had been taken prisoners; to console the relatives and friends of a dead woman whom they deposited at my door, and said to have been one of four, besides men, shot that day by the native police; and obliged to turn the vestry into a hospital for the wounded shot by native hut-tax collectors and their men without any provocation whatever.

26. Ag. Comm. Jackson to Marquis of Lansdowne, Jan. 24, 1902 (PRO FO/403/318.144). See also Gray (1963), p. 44; Twaddle (1966), esp. pp. 26–28.

actually extended his district to the western slopes of Mount Masaba, where he had proclaimed himself kabaka.[27] Walker, a junior
administrative officer, was sent to reside temporarily at Kakungulu's headquarters. For three weeks it looked as if Kakungulu
would resist this usurpation of his powers. Then, in February 1902
(chiefly, it would appear, through the persuasion of Father Kirk),
Kakungulu lowered his Union Jack and evacuated the boma without incident. As he put it: "At the end of 1902 I was driven out of
Bukeddi."[28] Walker, with twenty police askaris, was ordered to
open an adminstrative station at Budaka, and the British government took direct responsibility for the administration. The government acceded to Kakungulu's demands for a twenty-square-mile
estate at Masawa, north of Mbale, for fear of open rebellion—a
danger at this time that should not be underestimated. "Rebellion
was something Protectorate officials had to live with in the early
1900's and the thought of it was constantly in their minds; rebellion
rebellion was also publicly discussed by Kakungulu and his followers."[29]

In 1904 a further crisis occurred within the administration. It
took the form of a request from five of Kakungulu's county chiefs
(three of them from Teso) that they should receive their orders not
from Kakungulu but directly from British officers. They were immediately reprimanded and charged with disloyalty, and Kakungulu
was authorized to punish them.[30] Hindsight suggests that the objective reality of the situation was better appreciated by the county
chiefs than by the British. Their change in status since the freebooting days when they had first led Kakungulu's forces into Teso
was not lost upon them. Not only could they not protect their
interests at Mbale, but they could not be certain of acquiring land,
establishing estates, or exploiting labor in the manner to which
comparisons with Buganda had accustomed them. They were at a
point at which their advancement might be seen to depend as much
on loyalty to the colonial administration as to Kakungulu. The
validity of their perception depended upon their understanding of

27. Ag. Comm. Jackson to Marquis of Lansdowne, Jan. 24, 1902 (PRO
FO/403/318.144).
28. Gray, "Report."
29. Twaddle (1966), p. 27.
30. Twaddle (Ph.D., 1967), p. 198.

the relationship between Kakungulu and the British—not at all simple to determine. There were to be considered, on the one hand, the conflicting views of various distinguished British officials about Kakungulu's status, not to mention those of the missionaries, as well as the projection of it that Kakungulu himself engendered. On the other hand, the chiefs could base their assessment upon the events they had either witnessed or heard about and upon the day-by-day behavior of the individuals involved: Jackson, Grant, Watson, the Crabtrees, J. B. Purvis, Kestens, and Kirk, as well as Kakungulu.

The impact of their recall on Iteso living in the vicinity of the Baganda forts can only be conjectured. To most, a change of personnel might mean little; but to those who had come to operate in intermediary positions between county chiefs and people, the appointment of new men must have been critical. Some had become clients in the Baganda regime, a personalized pursuit, and a succession crisis such as this would have entailed at grassroots level the opening of opportunities to their rivals. For many, the actions of the government must have seemed extraordinary; for to seek the patronage and protection of the strongest, as the Baganda civil service chiefs had done, was intimately a part of Iteso political culture, extended to Teso's occupiers.

Local reaction was soon manifested in outbreaks of disorder and violence. The legitimacy of the Baganda presence was called into question and this, not insignificantly, where the Baganda had been first and most firmly established: in Serere. At the beginning of the year the Mill Hill fathers at Budaka had been gratified by the visit of a catechist from Kaboi (located between Bugondo and Serere). He had brought them news of the building of a neighborhood church; in July they were stunned by a rumor (which turned out to be false) of Mulangira's assassination.[31] Visiting Ngora in June, the collector was unable to travel beyond the borders of Kumi County because of the fighting that had broken out in the southwest.

Watson reported the unsettled condition of the region to the provincial commissioner, who suggested that Kakungulu be sent on a tour of northern Teso to reestablish Protectorate authority.[32] Not

31. Entry for July 18, 1904 (DBM).
32. Twaddle (Ph.D., 1967), p. 201. He cites Boyes to Hayes Sadler, Aug. 13, 1904 Entebbe Secretariat Archives (ESA A/27/6).

only was it clear that the colonial government wished to employ
Baganda chiefs only through Kakungulu, but it was also apparent
that his forceful presence was needed among the Teso natives if law
and order were to be maintained. Until the government was able to
operate from a position of strength in the eastern province, continuity was the order of the day.

Kakungulu was despatched on safari in August 1904. He began
at Kyere and from there went on to Tira, Soroti, Gweri, Kapiri,
Mukula, Kumi, Tulituli, and Bukedea. Of his reception by the people and his impact on conditions prevailing in these areas, there is
no account. His addresses in *baraza* (assembly) were, essentially,
preparing the way for the newly appointed county chiefs, commu-
nicating their legitimacy. His presence must have smacked of real-
politik to those who had been clients of the deposed men and those
who had seized upon the interregnum to challenge the government's
authority. But Kakungulu was also preparing the way for an increase in active participation by British officers in the area—perhaps
to an extent that he himself did not fully realize. From the speech he
gave at each stopping place, echoes are gleaned of his pride in past
military glories. Significant, too, in retrospect, are his remarks on
race and dominance. Above all, however, the tone is that of a
colonial officer on tour; its emphasis is on pax, tax, and the work
ethos.[33]

Kakungulu's pacificatory visit was clearly sufficient, and it was

---

33. A summary of Kakungulu's speech is reproduced in Twaddle (Ph.D.,
1967), pp. 202-203. Kakungulu greets those gathered at each baraza:

First of all, I am delighted to see you Bakedi. . . . I have been sent to
you, not to stir up trouble or fight, but to visit all of you, my friends,
who live in the places I have already visited and those to which I am
going.

You know that when I first came here, I came as a child. All the
Bakedi, everyone who was a fighting man from Bululu to Masaba, came
and fought against me. Where now are the people who defeated me?
Nevertheless, you must understand that both I and the Europeans want
peace, not warfare.

. . . You should also realise that the Europeans have learnt to be
reasonable. Therefore if you have any matter you want to raise, or if
some Muganda has harmed one of you, do not say, "As they are all
Baganda, how can they judge the Mukedi's case fairly?" Rather bring

followed by a new spate of missionary itinerations. Not surprisingly, Kirk, in April 1905, found that conditions had deteriorated since his earlier visit.[34] At Ngora the catechumenate was "in bad state," in spite of its thirty-one readers and its Asian trading store.[35] Ijala, along with Mulangira of Serere, one of the earliest chiefs to encourage catechists to work from his homestead, reported some of the conflicting pressures that chiefs were under. Thus, when Kakungulu had visited Ngora on his safari, he had told Ijala to give up his son to him "to read." Thinking he could not refuse Kakungulu, the chief had obeyed, although both he and the child's mother, had wanted him to be schooled with his brother at the Mill Hill mission. To what extent this was true, or to what extent Ijala used

---

your case before the chief appointed for your area. Should that chief fail to deal with the case to your satisfaction, he will bring it to me—I, Kakungulu. If I fail to solve it, I will take it to the European who rules this area. If the European fails to resolve the matter, he will take it to the one at Jinja, the one at Jinja to the Commissioner, and so on until the case is decided, and we know who is actually in the wrong.

The Government wants you to work and pay taxes. That is what we Baganda do at home. . . . Remember how in the past I told you to cultivate chillies, groundnuts, simsim, and to prepare sisal fibre. When these come to maturity, they will help your payment of taxes considerably. For how long can you pay your taxes by cows?

So we should all be friends. We are all the same flesh, though we ourselves usually tend to think otherwise. There is no distinction between Muganda and Mukedi. The European has suggested that if a chief gives a cow for tax, he should take goats from his men, since tax is for huts in general, not only those of certain individuals. If there is anyone present who has been wronged by a Muganda or a Mukedi, let him stand and say so. Indeed, anyone who has anything to say, let him speak. That is all I have to say now.

34. Entry for Apr. 1, 1905 (DBM).
35. The store belonged to a Alidina Visram, and Kirk purchased Amerikani cloth there. This is the earliest reference I have found to Asian trading stores in Teso. An Intelligence Report of 1905 indicates that there were "Hindi shops at Bululu, Serere, Angorla (Ngora), Kumi, Makurrah (Mukura), Kapiri, and Seroti (Soroti)" (12 KAR Intelligence Report no. 1, July 26, 1905; encl. Uganda Protectorate Intelligence Report no. 25, PRO FN/487/879; CO/879:88).

this incident to have sons brought up in both denominations, is not clear.

From Ngora, Kirk went on to Mukuru, by this time a catechumenate of twelve readers. He found it in excellent condition; the chief had run up a small latrine beside the church and appointed a caretaker. But the catechumenate around the homestead of Omadi of Kobwin was in a bad way, with only ten readers. To Kirk's gratification the young chief, Sawe, came to say that he wished to read. Sawe was presented with a medal and chain in front of Omadi and the assembled people of both chiefs, and he promised to build a catechumenate. The following day Kirk set out with him to see his village. There is no record of his impressions, but their encounter must have been satisfactory; for the next day, when Kirk had arrived back at Ijala's village, Sawe came again, carrying a gift. The Serere chief, Molo, also went to see Kirk at Ijala's place and also promised to build a catechumenate.

On April 10, Kirk set out again from Ijala's to visit Kabaya's catechumenate of twenty readers. A large number of men and women had thatched the roof of the church. He arrived at Mulingira's the following day and met the chief's fourteen readers, before going on to Seko (seventeen readers) and the catechumenate of chief Nalikodi. This was the largest catechumenate visited on the itineration; forty readers worked with the catechist, Patrisi Mukedi. A ceremony was held to baptize the son of the recently deceased chief Nalikodi. The following day Kirk traveled to chief Tukei's homestead in Mukongoro, where he inspected the small church, met thirty readers, and baptized Tukei's small son. In quick succession he then visited Nabunula (23 readers), Dinira (15), Ngola (10), and Kamia (17), then returned on April 19 to Budaka mission. The day after Kirk's return from Teso, Teso (in the person of Molo, the Serere chief who had sought him out at Ijala's) came to him. He stayed overnight at the mission, sealing an agreement to build a catechumenate in his village.

Not long after, Kirk learned of Kakungulu's reaction to his Teso safari. Kakungulu had apparently called a *lukiko* (a council meeting) and ordered the chiefs (Tukei in particular) not to build churches. If they did, he would deprive them of their chieftainships.[36] Ten

---

36. Kakungulu's hostility to the Christian missions at this stage in his career (and later) was possibly grounded in his experience of what, in

days later, Kirk received news from Chief Mulango that Kakungulu's men had seized some of his property because he had built a
church. We can presume that Kirk appealed to the government and
that Kakungulu was warned not to permit sectarianism to intrude
upon his governmental duties. As Kirk's safari makes clear, Roman
Catholic activity at this time was largely confined to Mulangira's Serere and Ijala's sphere of influence around Ngora.

Anglican activity in Teso was even more constrained, still
officially reliant as it was on the Rev. Andereya Batulabudde,
Kakungulu's interest notwithstanding. In 1905 Batulabudde was
sent on an inspection of Teso forts. He visited "the Teso district—or
Terere" (a revealing modification) and Bululu. His report "showed
that very little had been done for the [people of] Bukeddi . . . There
are some places in which a few Baganda Christians are struggling to
teach the Bakeddi, but it is very hard work. The languages of the
Bakeddi are very difficult for the Baganda to learn."[37] Crabtree
asked that six missionaries be sent immediately.

Apart from the fact that Kakungulu's penetration of Teso had not
been as deep or effective as those who believed in his prowess
thought, the very nature of Iteso society operated against evangelization in the manner to which missionaries had become accustomed elsewhere in Africa. The difficulties of language were early
commented upon; a further obstacle lay in the fact that conversion
of the masses could not be achieved through chiefs. In Teso, the
chiefs who asked for teachers were few. Father Kirk, indeed, found
on his first visit to Ngora in 1903 that approaching chiefs was not
at all useful, for all the chiefs would do was consult their womenfolk. Since Kirk was apparently asking whether they would like
their sons to accompany him to Budaka to read with his mission,
such behavior does not seem unaccountable. Kirk, however, mis-

---

Luganda, was called *okusenga:* the apprenticeship of young men at a chief's
headquarters. Services were offered to important men in return for the
opportunity to learn superior knowledge and manners and, perhaps, be
favored with a recommendation for a minor chiefship as the opportunity
arose. Missionaries found themselves accepting applicants who wished to
"senga" them (Rowe 1966), pp. 179–180; see also Ashe (1895), pp.
126–127, a practice Kakungulu would clearly, and rightly, have seen as
undermining his authority and power.

37. Pirouet (Ph.D., 1968), p. 362.

read the situation. "The usual proverb out here," he told his English readers, "is: if you get the chief, you get the tribe; but in this part of His Majesty's dominions that saying must be reversed and run thus: if you get the headwoman to read, you get the chief and his tribe."[38] Apart from the difficulties of language and the lack of chiefs, the very acts of Kakungulu also, surely, alienated as many as they attracted to Christianity.[39] Not until the Protectorate government took over the administration of Teso was conversion to Christianity seen by Iteso as a necessary first step toward control of their own destinies.

The Advent of British Administration

The creation of Teso district was characterized by all the deficiencies of Victorian imperialism: the nature of indigenous political development went unrecognized and was unconsciously downgraded as African political units were labeled "tribes;"[40] colonial

38. Kirk, "Correspondence" (1903), p. 249.

39. Between 1906 and 1908, three Baganda and six Iteso were baptized into the CMS. None played any subsequent part in the history of the Church—an unusual phenonemon (Pirouet, p. 342). Roman Catholic records do not begin until 1912.

40. This in spite of earlier (and concurrent) recognition of kingdoms and feudalities. The notion that tribal organization represents a phase in some colonial administrative history is still strongly contested by some scholars. *"The Notion of the Tribe* assaults the generally held concept of 'tribe' by attacking the notion of highly discrete political units in pre-state society. Although we are accustomed to think about the most ancient forms of human society in terms of tribes, formally defined and bounded units of this sort actually grew out of the manipulation of relatively unstructured populations by more complex organised societies. The invention of the state, a tight, class-structured political and economic organisation, began a process whereby vaguely defined and grossly overlapping populations were provided with the minimal organisation required for their manipulation, even though they had little or no internal organisation of their own other than that based on conceptions of kinship. The resultant form was the tribe" (Morton H. Fried, *The Notion of the Tribe,* 1975, preface).

On the use of the term in Africa, see, e.g., Raymond Apthorpe, "Does Tribalism Really Matter?" (1968); Colson (1970), pp. 30–32; May Edel, "African Tribalism—Some Reflections on Uganda" (1965); Beverley Gar-

officials misinterpreted local institutions and found in them a gener-
alized uniformity; above all, an artificial homogeneity was imposed
upon an area inhabited by peoples as much opposed to one another
as to European rule.

Because of the nature of politics east of Lake Kyoga at the end of
the nineteenth century, the conquest of Teso was not a once-and-
for-all affair. There could be no formal diplomatic treaties between
heads of states as there had been in central and western Uganda,
since there were no states. Just as in Teso indigenous political forms
were fashioned by ecological factors, especially those of location
and continuity, so, equally, were patterns of contact fashioned between administrators and conquered people: existing differences
between north, south, and southwest affected both the timing and
the nature of contact. The immediate and subjective form that the
"problem" or "crisis" of penetration took for British administrators
in Teso in their efforts to establish and maintain relations with
peripheral groups, and the extent to which interaction and conflict
among the leading elements of Teso society conditioned the nature
and success of that process, varied from region to region.

In succeeding Kakungulu, the first task of the British administration was to define the political community.[41] If we choose to see,
in the years that followed, the British administration as holding the
ropes, as it were, around an arena in which local combatants strug-

---

trell, "The Ruling Ideas of a Ruling Elite: British Colonial Officials in
Uganda, 1944–1952" (Ph.D. thesis, 1979), pp. 149–155; Peter C.W. Gutkind and Peter Waterman (eds.), *African Social Studies: A Radical Reader*
(1977), pp. 1–14; Holger B. Hansen, *Ethnicity and Military Rule in Uganda* (1977), pp. 18–32; Nelson Kasfir, *The Shrinking Political Arena*
(1976), pp. 28–46; A. Mafeje, "The Ideology of Tribalism" (1971); Alpheus Manghezi, *Class, Elite and Community in African Development*
(1976), pp. 95–98; Aidan Southall, *"The Illusion of the Tribe"* (1970), and
"From Segmentary Lineage to Ethnic Organization" (1975); Twaddle
(1969). There is a need to explore tribalism "as an ideology, produced
under concrete historical circumstances and articulating the interests of a
particular social group" (Mahmood Mamdani, "Class Struggle in Uganda," 1975, p. 36).

41. The two paragraphs that follow appeared in Joan Vincent,
"Colonial Chiefs and the Making of Class," (1977), pp. 144–145.

gled for local power, we become aware of the topological characteristics of such an arena—pulled as it is first in one direction and
then in another, first including and then excluding different localities, groups, and subgroups from the Teso scene. At moments of
potential interregnum, such as in 1908, when the British took over
from the Baganda (or, for that matter, in 1962, when the independent nation was established), such elasticity became politically
significant.

One of the first tasks of the Mbale Collectorate was to establish
Teso's boundaries. A northern limit to the Protectorate had been
established on paper with the line of treaties obtained by Macdonald in 1898. This delineation of an area of some thirty-five
hundred square miles for possible inclusion in Uganda provided full
scope for a district officer to carve out a colonial estate of some
magnitude. Individual empire building by pioneer administrators,
British and Iteso, occurred; but in the final analysis, the exact location of boundaries was as much a response to the societal forces
that penetration encountered as to an administrative ideal of what
a colonial district should be. For the first twelve years of British
government the boundaries of Teso district ebbed and flowed, as in
one locality those whose communities were raided tried to come
within its orbit (the northwest) and in another rebel leaders tried to
challenge its integrity (the northeast). In the south and west the
problems were of a different nature: there the task was not one of
military penetration and consolidation, but of countering disaffection. In the north the armed patrol engaged the people, in the
south missionary endeavor.

Pacification: Primary Mode

In June 1908 Stanley N. Ormsby was given charge of the newly
created Mbale Collectorate.[42] One of his first tasks was to tour the
country north of Lake Bisina. Although in 1901 and again in 1904
Omiat of Amuria had petitioned the Baganda to intervene in northern affairs, they had not in fact done so until 1907, when, led by
Enosi Kagwa, they established a garrison at Abela. Omiat and Ka-

---

42. The Mbale Collectorate included Bukeddi, Karamoja, Labwor,
Turkwel, Turkana, and Dabossa. The rest of the former Central Province
became the Jinja Collectorate (Busoga).

gwa's forces staged a standing battle with those of the "northern military alliance" at Obore Otelu in 1907 but were defeated. A year later the Baganda established a base at Katakwi and advanced from Abela into Usuku and Ngariam. By this time the various prominent men of the localities were bargaining among themselves, with Omiat, and with the Baganda for positions in the new structure of power that had entered the region. Nevertheless, administration remained weak, the new territory was not consolidated, and few northern leaders were entrusted with arms.

Ormsby confirmed Kagwa's appointment as agent in Usuku; a few months later John Methuen Coote, the assistant collector, reported that he was doing good work, "getting in touch with the natives." He observed that "these Teso people, although similar in custom and language to the Bakeddi are a great deal more independent in manner and bearing and will require careful handling and frequent supervision by the Agent."[43]

By 1910 *bomas* (fortifications) and camps had been erected at Magoro and Usuku (at Okolimong's homestead) and one at Kelim was nearing completion. Most chiefs were reported as genuinely pleased to be brought under British administration and anxious to bring their country into line with the rest of the district. Several of them apparently asked that traders might be sent up into their country "so that their people might obtain iron hoes." The district officer in Kumi, F. H. Newman, was somewhat less sanguine about the "Teso" than Coote. With prescience, he observed the "tractable spirit displayed by the majority of them," leaving unspoken his condemnation of the rest. Indeed, resistance to authority was imprinted on the landscape. In any colonial district, the making of roads is perceived as one of the first tasks of an administration, as well as a measure of its success or failure. In Teso, the intractable minority made no tracts, if the pun may be forgiven. Where the

---

43. This quotation and much of the information in the following four paragraphs is taken from Kumi Station Diary, Apr. 1909–Dec. 1912 (TDA VADM/3/1). Note that, during this time, "Teso" was used to signify the country north of Lake Bisina only. Thus an entry for Aug. 18, 1909, read: "Mr. Jackson went to Teso [from Kumi] to inquire into row there," and again, on Sept. 5, 1909: "News received from Teso that there is the likelihood of a fight," etc.

Ormsby safari had passed six months before, the administrative tract had been cleared that Newman found in fair condition for the most part. In southern Usuku, ominously, five or six miles remained uncleared.

The first approach of the Baganda into northern Usuku had been made through Okolimong, the ritual leader of the northern military alliance. Despite his considerable age, the British administrators had recognized Okolimong as the most powerful of the local chiefs. Perhaps the district officers, young men themselves, were struck by the fact that most Iteso chiefs were comparatively old, but coming as they did from a gerontocratic society, they were prepared to accept this. Nevertheless, they expected of Okolimong a more substantial population base than he, as an emuron, actually controlled; from the start, considerable power was vested with Barimo, a young client of Okolimong's whom the British considered his katikiro. Lacking a deployment of forces on the ground, however, Barimo's authority was under challenge from several neighboring big men in 1909.

A spate of safaris was conducted into the north between June and October 1909. The frequent and unannounced appearances of British officers and troops were considered to have a pacifying effect— whether upon the natives or upon "Greeks and a Somali" said to be raiding their herds is uncertain. On a visit to the Nyakwai hills in August 1909, Newman noticed that the people had returned to hunt together in the uninhabited country lying between them. He took this as an indication that peace had been restored, but it might well have been a concentration of people withdrawing from areas of close administration. The Nyakwai hills were deemed some twenty-five miles north of the district boundary, and this probably marked the first visit of a British officer since Macdonald's expedition eleven years earlier.

Whether in response to the more visible presence of the colonial administration or whether the result of a diminution in fighting among themselves, a series of rebellions occurred in Usuku over the next six years. These first involved refusals to appear before government agents and to provide provisions for garrisons. The specific row that took first Newman and district officer Morris, then Jackson, the provincial commissioner, northward in August 1909, is not known, but their descent upon the local scene appears to have had no effect. The following month, news was received of the likelihood of a fight between one of the subchiefs and the agent. The two Kumi officers again set out rapidly for Usuku, and the provincial commissioner again diverted his safari to cross Lake Bisina. In April 1910 Subchief Lekiteki refused "to see the agent at Usuku when summoned. He, too, wanted to fight." Food had to be brought in from surrounding areas, since the chief refused to support the garrison. Newman again descended on Usuku, where he presumably took disciplinary action, receiving the provincial commissioner's approval.

The effort required to bring the peoples north of Lake Bisina into the Kumi fold had become increasingly apparent. The success of the rebels was acknowledged by an announcement that the government was "disinclined to press these people [since] they are north of the lake, rather wild and require time." When a few months later a deputation of Bokora chiefs arrived at the government boma at Usuku requesting protection from Jie raiding, to be followed three weeks later by two other chiefs from Manimani and Chodomoi, the provincial commissioner lost no time in sending a telegram to Kumi ordering "no further negotiations with Bokora chiefs." The villages of the Bokora chiefs lay in the neighborhood of Anamuget, and the district officers quickly took recourse to Macdonald's map to find the Kakinyi River (Akinyo on the map), on which the Swahili interpreter said Anamuget lay. It was clearly "out of bounds." The provincial commissioner's ruling was wholly in keeping with Protectorate policy at that time (a policy first enunciated by the Foreign Office to Jackson in 1901 and reiterated subsequently), but it also reflected the success of the Usuku rebels.

Although the administration recognized its inability to bring the warring peoples of "Teso" (as the early administrators called Usuku) and Karamoja into the administrative net, their warlike reputation somewhat ironically won them the attention of the central government. Thus, on August 26, 1910 a recruiting safari for the King's African Rifles was conducted in Teso country. But the rebels had generally won their battle to be left alone, and attention was centered not upon the north but upon Serere and Soroti.

Ultimately, however, the time came when an effort had to be made to collect taxes from the villagers of Usuku. For two seasons, the people rested passively under a fairly light yoke; but then intimations of serious disaffection were manifested at a baraza in Kelim.[44] Attendance at the baraza was slight, but that in itself would not have taken on significance in Usuku. It was then learned that several groups of people had taken up arms against their chiefs. Ikabata of Kelim and the agent, Yonosani, confirmed that it was impossible to collect taxes in the area. That same month, subcounty chief Ojenatum reported a village burned at Old Nariam and four head of cattle killed by raiders. Here the Iteso had resisted the Baganda in 1908; and even after the defeat of Ojenatum, at that time their military commander, many remained unconvinced of alien supremacy. Although Ojenatum had been made a chief, his control had lessened considerably in the four years since he had mustered seventy porters for Coote in exchange for hoes, beads, serengini, and clothes.

One subchief in particular, Ojotum, had continued to be resentful and uncooperative. In August 1913, Ojotum's cluster of eight villages near Ngariam decided to move away from the administered area to Karamoja. En route, they attacked a CMS reader and fled when the agent went to inquire into the matter. At this point, Ojotum was outlawed.

Shortly afterward, at Adachal, Chief Amuge of Kelim reported that some of his men, like those of Ojenatum, had fled to Karamoja to avoid the tax. Amuge seems to have been an exceptionally cooperative chief. While others in the area went in fear of their lives, refusing even to obey summons to baraza, he reported on January 4, 1914, that some of his subchiefs were offering armed resistance. Those led by Chief Akordet refused to come in to attend baraza. On January 5, J. G. Rubie, the district officer, called a baraza at Ngariam. Further emigrations were reported, followed by news of the murders of two tax collectors. It became apparent that what had been reported as emigrations were, in fact, the massing of followers around a rebel leader. Whether Akordet was attempting to establish his autonomy at Kaikamussin (a no-man's-land), between Ojotum's rebel bands and the administration's forces, or whether he was a protector or ally of Ojotum is not clear. Whatever the case, his individual stance led to his deposition at the end of 1913 and the

44. The account that follows is taken from "Disturbance in Usuku County" (TDA XNAF/9.252/14).

appointment of Opolot, son of Okwari, in his place. Matters then escalated. The entire population of one Ngariam parish fled to the Mount Kamalinga region, taking their cattle with them, as well as the cattle of a neighboring chief who was well-disposed to the British. The cattle were recovered on the slopes of Mount Kamalinga, but the thieves had fled.

Rubie and his men marched back to Adachal, where Chief Amuge and the agent reported that two more subchiefs, Banyali and Ogwakoli, had offered armed resistance. Banyali (brother of Ochomode) was said to be harboring Ojotum. Both men were arrested. The next day Rubie went to Ojotum's village and found all the men gone. Continuing to Kelim, he there received news that Chief Amuge and all the people of his village had been massacred. The raiders had fled to Karamoja, taking cattle and women with them. Rubie immediately informed Kumi, and a telegram was sent to the provincial commissioner requesting additional police to quell the makings of a major disturbance. Rubie then marched back to Adachal.' On the way he heard that Ojotum had collected an armed force and was now threatening to attack Chief Ojenatum at the Ngariam home in which he had taken refuge. Rubie's men carried spears and shields at the ready, but they were not molested on the march. Detouring to pass again through Ojotum's village, where they seized sixty-two head of cattle in reprisal, they arrived at Ngariam in the evening.

The attack on Chief Amuge's homestead had been made at dusk on the evening of January 10, 1914, and had been quite unexpected. Amuge himself was struck down by Ochomode in a cotton field outside the village. Four men and thirteen women and children were killed, and the village was left burning as raiders retreated into the bush. Rubie's force undertook to bury the dead. The agent at Amuge's village reported that Ochomode's men had also advanced upon his boma but, seeing that he was armed, had not attacked. Scouts were sent out into the countryside to find out more about what was happening. The next day the district commissioner, R. Paske-Smith, arrived. The villages of Subchiefs Ojotum, Banyali, and Ochomode were deserted. Since burning their villages would not have been practicable at that season (cotton was ripe but not food crops), Rubie requested permission to follow the offenders into Karamoja.

The crossing of district boundaries in order to follow up on incidents that occurred in Teso does not seem to have been at all unusual. One exgovernment chief of the Bokora, for example, said that his first sight of government troops occurred when two European officers and about twenty African soldiers entered Bokora to seize cattle in reprisal for a Karamojong raid on Teso. Lopuko, the chief, thought there would be no difficulty in annihilating such a small force, but they nevertheless delayed their attack until the troops had collected the cattle and were hampered by herding the animals. Lopuko demonstrated how the warriors had advanced when the Karamojong attacked and how the troops had knelt down back to back and opened fire at the charging tribesmen. The Karamojong, he said, had fallen in great numbers. After an enthusiastic first charge and later two half-hearted attacks, the tribesmen had had enough. They fled, leaving the field to the troops.[45] No documentary confirmation of the incident was found, but if it is not one of Rubie's exploits in Karamoja, it would certainly have been very like one.

On March 21, 1914, half a company of troops were sent to Usuku along with the district commissioner's patrol from Karamoja.[46] Nine days later, the murderer of the two tax collectors was caught, and an indemnity of five to ten head of cattle, one woman, and goats was claimed by relatives. The government saw to it that forty head of cattle were paid in place of the woman. Claims for damages were assessed. An exagent in Amuge's village, Ibrahim Musole, along with Abdul Aziz, a Baluchi shopkeeper, claimed compensation for nine head of cattle stolen while they were coralled with Amuge's herd. Villagers returned and began planting crops. Amnesty was promised Ojotum's followers if he were "presented for trial." There being no response, the Usuku County Council undertook his capture.

For those who have in mind something like the local government system of England and Wales when they read a typical colonial report describing the organization of Teso district into county councils presided over by chairmen, Paske-Smith's account of the arrest of Ojotum may contain an element of surprise. The Usuku County Council then con-sisted of eleven men: Ngyangata, Angyiro, Abun-

45. Barber (1968), pp. 126–127.
46. TDA XNAF/9.252/14.

ga, Okanya, Alukuri, the aged Ikabata, Okurut (the former military leader), Ojenatum, Ocapo (former northern supreme military commander), Opolot, and Barimo: a mobilization of leading warriors armed with spears, muzzle loaders, and Snider rifles. Of the event Paske-Smith wrote: "The County Council obtained news that Ojotum was living at a certain village. The County Council surrounded the village at daylight and called on Ojotum to surrender. Ojotum refused and attempted to break out of the village with several followers. Ojotum was shot dead by one of the Chiefs and three of Ojotum's followers were shot." The report of the incident concludes: "The Chief Agent in the County, Yonosani, reports that general relief is felt over the county at Ojotum's death and he considers the natives will now settle down quietly."[47]

The period from 1907 to 1915 saw not only the pacification of Usuku but also the penetration and consolidation of the northwestern parts of the district. It was in response to an appeal from a Langi named Oyara, for protection against raiders, that Rubie and John Postlethwaite set out to determine the boundaries of the district. Postlethwaite writes of the "vagueness of the boundary set to active administration . . . in the north, a boundary which was in no sense tribal and a constant source of irritation . . . Accordingly, [they] pushed out further afield, determined to embrace at any rate the whole of the Teso tribe."[48] This was a matter of no consolation for Oyara, and cattle raiding and family feuding continued in the area.

Six months later, the provincial commissioner set out comprehensive guidelines for the newly created Teso district. First, no further agents were to be appointed, and the district officers were to tour the outlying regions as often as possible. Second, no attempts were to be made to collect tax from "these remoter areas." Finally, it was suggested that, "to natives such as Oyara who profess to have grown weary of customs handed down by their forebears, you should say that they are at liberty to move into more closely administered areas."[49] It is perhaps a commentary upon the commis-

47. Ibid.
48. John P. Postlethwaite, *I Look Back* (1947), p. 44.
49. "Correspondence with provincial commissioner," 1912 (TDA XADM/10A).

sioner's lack of sympathy for Oyara's plight that the administration's problem later turned out to be, not one of turning prospective citizens away, but rather of keeping those they had firmly in their place.

When on July 11, 1912, the Kumi Collectorate was formally constituted Teso district (under the Uganda Order in Council of 1902), the era of expansion enjoyed by Kumi's pioneer administrators came to an end. The boundaries of the district were clearly set out as follows.

> Commencing at the junction of the Kiboko River with Lake Gedge the line proceeds in a north-easterly direction to a point on 20 north latitude due south of the highest point on Kamalinga Mount. From thence it runs in a north-westerly direction to the western extremity of Lake Kirkpatrick the shore of which it follows to the outlet of the Asua River which it follows to 33°30′ east longitude. From thence it runs due south till it intersects the swamp east of Lake Kwania; thence through Omunyal Swamp to the north-eastern extremity of Lake Kioga which it follows to the most easterly point of Namlimoka Island. It then follows the eastern area of Lake Kioga to the junction of the Gogonia and Mpologoma Rivers. From thence it follows the boundary of Bukeddi District to its point of commencement west of Lake Gedge.

From the junction of the Kiboko River with Lake Gedge, the Bukeddi boundary ran

> in a southerly direction to the junction of the Sipi River with the Siroko River which river it follows to the point at which it is joined by the Nalukuba River which river it follows to its source. From thence it passes between the hills Omiton and Mpoga thence along a natural depression to the source of the Naminassa River which river it follows to its junction with the Lwere Swamp the southern shore of which it follows to the Mpologoma.[50]

An idea of the Uganda government's view of Teso and the surrounding region may be gleaned from Figure 7. That this is still a somewhat amorphous, although formative, phase in the Protectorate's expansion is suggested by the placing of the name "Teso" north of Lake Salisbury (Bisina) and the now archaic spellings of Siroti (Soroti), Nakwai (Nyakwai), River Mpologama (Mpolo-

---

50. *Uganda Protectorate Gazette,* July 11, 1912.

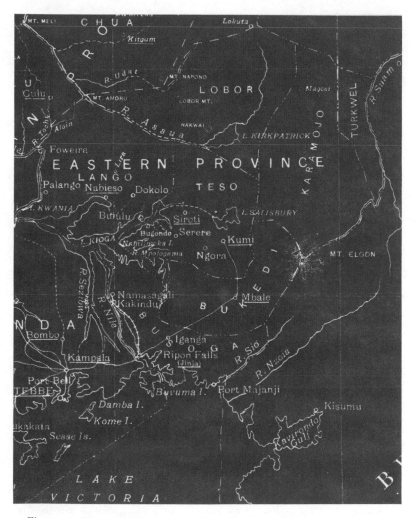

Figure 7. Teso District, 1912. Uganda Annual Report, 1912–1913. FN 645. Group 1, 1900–1932. Govt. Publ.

goma) and Lake Kioga (Kyoga). Yet compared with Speke's early map (Figure 1) and Vandeleur's map of 1898 (Figure 2) the gradual filling in of the empty terrain east of Lake Kyoga and west of Elgon (Mount Masaba) is apparent. The far northwest remains untamed.

Three years later, in 1915, the district commissioner was able to report that "with the exception of certain Miru peoples living near the Lango-Labor border," all the natives of the district were fully administered and the organization of native government complete.[51] Finally, accompanied by a patrol of the King's African Rifles, Paske-Smith set out to pacify this last redoubt. Langi who raided and murdered were punished, and stolen cattle were returned to their owners. Those living within the Teso border, irrespective of tribe, moved their villages closer to the agent's post. Oyara, having found protection, achieved his place in the administrative records, competently making a road and proposing to grow cotton—a tax-paying member of the Teso public at last.[52]

Pacification: Secondary Mode

Six months after the establishment of the Mbale Collectorate in June 1908, Assistant Collector J. M. Coote undertook a tour of what was to become Teso district. His first stop was at Kumi, where the new headquarters was being built, the second at Ngora, where plots had to be allocated to the CMS and Mill Hill missions. Father Kirk had purchased land from an Etosot Omadi, for Rs.75 on July 22, 1908, the CMS from Areko for Rs.70. As far as we know, this is the first occasion on which Teso land is treated as a commodity. A reproduction of the agreement appears in Figure 8. Both deals were negotiated through the collector.[53] Coote's scrupulous attention to detail ensured that the two mission plots were identical in size. On January 14 he had the Roman Catholic mission plot marked out following the marks pointed out by Ormsby and found its area to be 47 acres. The following morning he measured the CMS plot and found it to be 58.76 acres, whereupon he returned that evening to add 300 feet to one side of the Roman Catholic plot. His evenhandedness might have reflected an awareness of tensions between Protestant and Roman Catholic in Uganda, or it might simply have been a result of his upbringing in southern Ireland (Coote was

51. Teso District Annual Report, 1915 (TDA XADM/9).
52. Ibid.
53. The Mill Hill plot at Ngora was purchased from Chief Madi (DBM, July 22, 1908). The CMS land was acquired by Stanley Ormsby, according to John Roscoe, "A Brief Report of a Tour through Busoga and Bukedi," Sept. 29, 1908 (CMS Archives G3.A7/o). J. M. Coote's diary, "A Tour in the Teso Country" (1909), names Areko as the seller.

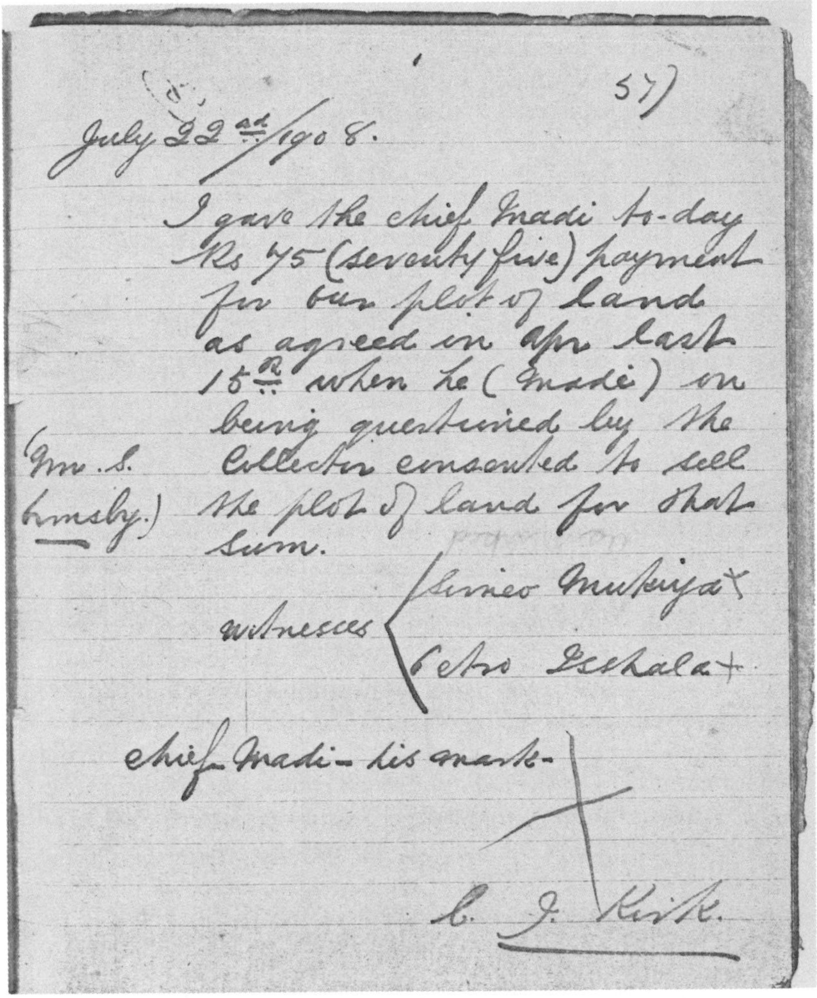
57)

July 22nd/1908.

I gave the chief Imadi to-day Rs 75 (seventy five) payment for our plot of land as agreed on Apr. last 15th when he (Imadi) on being questioned by the Collector consented to sell the plot of land for that sum.

(Wm. S. Grimsby.)

witnesses { Simeo Mukiya + / Petro Isikala +

chief Imadi – his mark – X

C. J. Kirk.

Figure 8. The Omadi-Kirk Land Sale Agreement, 1908. Source: Diary of the Budaka Mission, Book IV. Mill Hill Mission archives, St. Joseph's College, Mill Hill, London.

the second son of the twelfth Baronet). He was certainly aware that the CMS was one of the few pressure groups operating upon the Protectorate government at that time and knew that he would subsequently be held responsible for his actions, should any complaints be made. Whatever the truth of the matter, his journal records the incident in momentous detail.[54]

The efficacy of Christian missions in detaching Africans from their indigenous societies and reorienting them toward the needs of the newly imposed colonial structure is well established. Margery Perham has written of the education offered by missionaries as an acid that eats away at the mortar of ancient structures,[55] but at this point our concern is with the role of the missions in inculcating those values and procedures—the work ethic, the clothed state of grace, monogamy and the Western-styled nuclear family, individualism, time and work discipline, sabbatarianism—that provided an ideology for the capitalist economy.[56] Christianity "provided the framework for the structuring of a new order which, with imperial rule, was . . . overtaking . . . Africa."[57]

The mission schools at Ngora seem to have taken a long time to get off the ground. During their itinerations in the early days, missionaries were obliged to spend considerable time persuading chiefs to send them pupils, since there was far more demand for missionaries to send teachers to chiefs' homes. Not only did a young catechist living in the home, accepting food and shelter, bring prestige to the chief, he also served as a bridge to the European power structure. Fine distinctions between missionary and administrative officer had not yet emerged.

Missionaries recruited aggressively. Innumerable stories are told of Iteso fathers hiding their children from catechists, and the district files contain numerous charges of one mission against the other. The administration remained neutral if not unconcerned. One district commissioner, for example, said after hearing complaints that the

54. Coote diary.

55. Margery Perham, *Colonial Reckoning* (1962), p. 36.

56. Compare Edward P. Thompson, *The Making of the English Working Class* (1963) and, esp., his "Time, Work-Discipline, and Industrial Capitalism" (1967). A useful anthropological study of Christianity and the early days of industrialization in Pennsylvania (partly because it fails to address the politics of control) is Anthony F. C. Wallace, *Rockdale: The Growth of an American Village in the Early Industrial Revolution* (1978), esp. pp. 350-400.

57. Donald A. Low, *Lion Rampant: Essays in the Study of British Imperialism* (1973), p. 139.

CMS was telling people that the Roman Catholics eat children, "Don't think I am partial, being a Protestant. To me it seems to make no difference whether the savages become Protestants or Roman Catholics.[58] To the individual "savage" it was to be a matter of some importance; the overall structuring of change in Teso was such that, with or without good will, with or without impartiality, discrimination evolved. To the Protectorate government, dominated by men to whom economy, parsimony, and efficiency were gospel, this appeared a wasteful reduplication of evangelical effort. It was suggested in Uganda that, as elsewhere in sub-Saharan Africa, there should be discrete spheres of occupation marked out for each Christian mission; the first such proposal was made by the assistant collector at Mbale after a tour of the Eastern Province in 1908. In the long term, Christian sectarianism was to have a markedly divisive effect upon Teso, since, given the close association of the established Anglican church with the colonial government, the Roman Catholics, seeking advancement for their educated converts, were, irrevocably, structurally, in competition with the CMS. The question inevitably arose: to what extent did this remain within the bounds of a loyal opposition, a proposition exacerbated at this time for the government by its tangential "Irish problem"?

The missions differed in their penetration of the district and in the organizational frameworks they established. The Roman Catholic mission aimed at establishing stations at distances of about twenty miles from one another, from which itinerations could be made into the surrounding countryside. Catechumenate organization placed local converts, catechists, at regular points within this large area. These were visited by a priest every six months. Father T. Matthews described how catechumenates were designed.

> Let us suppose a . . . Mission-station area is a piece of ground twenty miles square (i.e. twenty miles each side). Some are more and some are less . . . Now let us build our station in the middle of this piece of land. Let us also suppose that the land is well and evenly populated. We want to get at everybody in the . . . area, in order to keep all up to scratch. To do this, we divide this big square of 400 square miles into decent pieces— say of 3 1/3 miles square . . . Thus we get 36 pieces. Each piece has

58. District Commissioner to Father Hurkmans, Nov. 18, 1914, on education of the natives, missionary work (TDA XEDU/3.109/13).

people enough to keep one man occupied, as we shall see; and that man is the catechist. In order to do his work well, the catechist must know his people: and he knows them well *only* when he visits them. The population is very *shifty*, not to say *nomad*: yet always on the move for one reason or another . . .

. . . If twice a week he visits every house in which there is a Christian or a catechumen, very little happens without his knowing it. If he finds a sick person he reminds those who look after him to keep him au courant concerning his health. When he finds the sick person in danger of death he tells the priest, personally or by letter. If he finds youngsters kicking about a rag or fibre ball instead of being at school or catechism, he boxes his ears, for it is useless reporting such cases where there is *no compulsory education* . . . If he finds some Catholic children attending Protestant schools, (of which there are plenty) he keeps at it till he gets them out . . . If he finds people getting too fond of the bottle, losing their heads, singing, dancing, fighting and causing a nuisance, he warns them that there is a place called *"H. M.'s Guesthouse."*[59]

The Anglican mission in Teso, while similar in its practical implications to that of the Mill Hill fathers, was modeled more closely upon Protectorate administrative structure. The smallest unit of Protestant organization was the village, "a small area, very much smaller than the civil muluka [subdistrict], covering a few square miles, within which little groups of huts cluster around a very primitive little village church." Several churches under one central church formed a muluka. A group of muluka churches formed a pastorate. "Ideally these would correspond to the civil *gombololas* [subcounties], but actually in view of the present shortage of native clergy, they are considerably larger." Pastorates combined into rural deaneries, each extending over some two to six thousand square miles. Teso district formed one such rural deanery, within the archdeaconry east of the Nile.[60]

The techniques of the CMS and the Mill Hill mission differed

59. Father E. Grimshaw, "Some Notes on the Apostolic Vicariate of the Upper Nile, 1895–1945" (MS., n.d., orig.), pp. 17–18.

60. Willis (1925), pp. 28–31. Church councils operated at the muluka, pastorate, and deanery level by 1925. Bishop Willis pointed out with some pride that the diocese with its synod brought together European and African delegates from throughout the Protectorate—a higher stage of development than that reached by the civil administration. As he noted, the first

considerably for winning converts and even the interest of the people. Both missions were hampered by a lack of funds and workers, and efforts to train Iteso youths as catechists were unsuccessful. The Roman Catholics persuaded chiefs to build ecclesia, or chapels, but villages then had to wait until teachers or catechists arrived often several months later. The Iteso youths sent to them were often poorly supervised, sometimes behaving so badly that chiefs turned them out. The replacements they asked for were, not unnaturally, slow in coming. The CMS had a similar problem in training teachers speedily enough. In 1911, the CMS had thirty-five Iteso youths placed as teachers; but after one or two years, just as they were becoming competent, they had to leave the district in order to embark on further training.[61]

A significant difference between the two missions lay in the ability and readiness of the Roman Catholic missionaries to conduct classes with as many as 600 pupils in one class, trained by the European fathers themselves. In the CMS pastorates, on the other hand, some 23,463 readers were taught by 270 native teachers, many of them Baganda and Basoga. No wonder Archdeacon Buckley wrote to his bishop in 1914 asking for reinforcements east of the Nile. "We have formidable competition in the RC missions who bid fair to carry position after position through sheer force of numbers unless we are in a position to extend our work."[62] More and more men were forwarded to the mission field by St. Joseph's Society in the hope of counterbalancing the politically dominant Protestants; the CMS used the numerical preponderance of the Catholic fathers to appeal for more recruits for the Bukeddi mission. Thus, in spite of its divisive social effects, missionary competitiveness served to generate a greater output of schools, dispensaries, and workshops than might otherwise have been the case.

Legislative Council was not established in Uganda until 1925; even then, it had no African members. What the bishop did not observe was that the paradistrict ecclesiastical organization of the CMS also served to generate the organization of sectarian opposition to it in the form of the Malaki Church, as we shall see shortly.

61. H. G. Dillistone, Ngora, annual letter, Dec. 9, 1911 (CMS Archives G3.A7/o).

62. Buckley to CMS, July 22, 1914 (CMS Archives, G3.A7/82).

Finally, the actual sequence of events in missionary pacification differed. The CMS established its first station at Ngora in 1909, but not until the 1920s did it expand further to build stations at Bukedea (1923), Kalaki (1925), and Soroti (1930). The Mill Hill fathers, on the other hand, both because they were less dislocated by the war and by virtue of their international organization, were able to build in Soroti in 1914 and Kaberamaido two years later. Subsequently, stations were established at Toroma, Bukedea, Okidetok (in Serere), and Amuria.[63] Thus, while the Anglican mission maintained its supremacy at Ngora and Kumi, in the south, the Roman Catholics penetrated more successfully into the more heterogeneous, peripheral parts of the district. As might have been expected, not only did it dawn in Teso that administration and Church were both representations of the same dominant authority, but, further, the very essence of the new capitalist economy—uneven development of its regions—received ideological expression in the confrontation of its two European missions.

63. Brian W. Langlands and G. Namirembe, *Studies on the Geography of Religion in Uganda* (1967), pp. 43–49, 55–57.

6. The Colonial Establishment

Afterwards the King held a great council and very deep
speech with his wise men about this land, how it was held, and
with what men. He then sent his men all over England,
into every shire, and caused them to find out how many
hundred hides were within that shire, and what the King had
himself of land and cattle, and what rights he ought to
have yearly from that shire. Also he caused them to write
down . . . what or how much each man that was settled on
the land held in land and cattle, and how much it was worth.
So very narrowly did he cause the survey to be made that
there was not a single hide nor yardland nor—it is shameful
to relate that which he thought no shame to do—was there
an ox, or a cow or a swine left out, that was not set down
in his writing.

Anglo-Saxon Chronicle, 1085

The history of administrators and their client chiefs, missionaries,
and, to a lesser extent, Asian merchants and alien entrepreneurs of
Teso is to be found in archives and history books. Parochial songs
and stories tell of local heroes, big men, and villains. But the lot of
the developing peasantry and emergent rural proletariat (except
where the names of unfortunates enter the criminal records) can
only be excavated in aggregate. Only as statistics—as taxpayers,
converts, laborers, consumers—are the common people of Teso to
be found, and from these is their condition reconstructed.[1]

1. Rich as they are by colonial African standards, the Teso District
Archives do not lend themselves to the detailed historical reconstruction
required to meet today's standards of historical anthropology. See, e.g.,
Alan Macfarlane, *Reconstructing Historical Communities* (1977), esp.
pp. 29–80; Vincent, "Agrarian Society and Organized Flow" (1977b);
Edward A. Wrigley, *Nineteenth-Century Society: Essays in the Use of
Quantitative Methods for the Study of Social Data* (1972), pp. 1–6.

The African Population of Teso District

The first population figures available, those of 1909–1910, reflect the administration's lack of access to the northern part of Kumi district. The people of Serere and the south, designated Bakeddi, were accounted at 85,430 males and 105,955 females. No explanation appears to have been sought for the disproportion between the sexes. The people of the north, designated the Teso, were estimated to number around 30,000—a gross underestimation born of ignorance. The total population of Kumi district was, therefore, thought to have been around 220,000.[2]

Poll tax that year was extracted only from adult males; estimates of age were arrived at by examining teeth. The figures reveal little more than the greater efficiency of tax collection in the south (where 11,006 paid tax) and, to a lesser extent, Serere (3,081) than in the north, where only 6,896 taxpayers were located.[3] From later, more reliable census figures, we know that for much of this period the population of the south was about twice and the population of the north about three times that of Serere. Given that the area of the south was between 565 and 932 square miles (depending upon whether Bukedea was included within Teso district), that of Serere 497 square miles, and that of the north 2,369 square miles, we arrive at population densities of around 114 in the south, 73 in Serere, and 40 in the north (excluding Soroti town).[4]

The 1911 District Census, while representing Serere and the south in their correct proportions, continued to underrepresent the north (see Table 1). What begins to appear in this census, however, are the administration's cultural perceptions of the district in the making. Geographical labels, as well as ethnic identifications, were still disorderly and confused. Nevertheless, the problems that the district administration perceived as lying before it can be seen. Not only "primitive classification"[5] reveals the cultural ethos of

2. Kumi District Census, 1911 (TDA XCST/1).

3. Kumi Station Diary (TDA VADM/3/1).

4. Brian W. Langlands, *The Population Geography of Teso District* (1971), p. 45. Compare estimated population densities after 50 years of colonial administration: north, 56–80; Serere, 127; south, 177–242.

5. Emile Durkheim and Marcel Mauss, *Primitive Classification* (1967).

Table 1. *Census of Kumi District, 1911*

Division	Population	
Central		
Kumi, Ngora, Mukura,		
Kapiri, Mkongoro	78,501	
Bakenyi	1,330	
Total		79,831
Bukedea	19,360	
Bagwere	3,258	
Total		22,618
Soroti	42,526	
Bakenyi	506	
Total		43,032
Northern	48,552	
Bakenyi	460	
Total		49,012
Serere	54,073	
Bakenyi	2,097	
Total		56,170
Total Africans		250,663
Asians		64
Europeans		3
Grand total		250,730

SOURCE: Adapted from Census, 1911. TDA. XCST/1/78A.

classifiers. The 1911 census showed clearly that the district was not one "tribal area," and that if cultural homogeneity within the district were a goal, its boundaries required relocating.

Most of the native population fell into a single category that received no tribal label in the local census but appeared as Bakeddi or Wakeddi in the Kumi District Book. "Teso" was kept for the country and people north of Lake Bisina.[6] Kumi district was clearly perceived as part of northeastern Bukeddi, and Wakeddi were to be found throughout the district in overwhelming majority. Five administrative divisions were recognized: Kumi, Bukedea, Serere, So-

6. See Chapter 5, note 43.

roti, and Usuku. The population of Kumi (which then included Ngora) was 79,831 and that of Bukedea 22,618. Serere had a population of 56,170, Soroti 43,032, and Usuku 49,072. Two minorities were recognized: the Bagwere and the Bakenyi.[7] The Bakenyi were to be found in all but one of the divisions (Bukedea), and in largest number in Serere. The Bagwere, on the other hand, were to be found only in Bukedea, where they formed one-sixth of the population. A racial classification complemented the tribal categorization: 64 Asiatics and 3 Europeans were to be found in the district in 1911, making a total population of 250,730. Racial and ethnic heterogeneity was not uniform throughout the region, as was made clear by census enumerations in 1921.[8] In general, polyethnicity came into being with the moving frontier.

Polyethnicity on the Colonial Frontier

The precolonial frontier in Teso reflected the emergence of ethnicity with the exploitation of economic niches. Thus the Bakenyi were to be found along the shores of the Serere peninsula and the Agu swamp, a distribution that rendered them the largest minority within each of the region's three ecological zones. Similarly, while Banyoro concentration lay in Serere and western Soroti on account of their long-established trade across Lake Kyoga, by 1921 some were also found in small numbers where the capitalist economy was developing most rapidly, in Kumi and Bukedea. Here, earlier than elsewhere in the district, Bahima from Bunyoro were employed as herdsmen by southern cattle owners. Of the remaining precapitalist frontiersmen, Baganda distribution reflects appointments to government positions (evenly throughout the district), acquisition of estates (mainly in Serere but also in the south), and involvement in trade. The success of an administrative move in 1913 to restrict the acquistion by "aliens" of the land in the bush and to foster their settlement in roadside colonies[9] cannot be judged from any remaining population records.

7. Kumi District Census, 1911.
8. *Uganda Protectorate Census of 1921.*
9. "Native Land Settlement" (TDA XNAF/9.44). See also "Reduction of Baganda Agents, 1913" and "Transfer of Baganda Agents to Other Districts, 1913–1923" (TDA XNAF/4.36 and 4.345). It is not clear how the Baganda acquired their estates or the aliens their trading plots, but

An anomalous category of the population remains the Basoga. For one thing, administrative classification grossly oversimplifies the cultural patterning of the Mpologoma region, Bugerere, Bulamogi, and the numerous groups that became incorporated into the tributary state of northern Busoga. The large number of Basoga in southern Serere reflects the distillation of the eastern Kyoga social network described earlier, especially the extensive marriage ties of Bakenyi and Basoga, as well as the entry of further Basoga into Teso as a result of displacement from their home region. With a head start in the acquisition of capital, many Basoga in Teso, having invested their cash earnings in apprenticeships and tools, became, with the opportunities opening around Kumi and Gondo, an early artisanry. Others entered trade, especially in the three southern counties, and thus became elements within the urban-Muslin-commercial complex of Teso's expanding economy.[10]

Increased ethnic heterogeneity between 1911 and 1921 reflected Teso's increased involvement within the new economy. In 1911 the Kumi District Census revealed a population of 4,393 Bakenyi, 3,258 Bagwere, and 243,102 other Africans, most of them Iteso. Unnamed within that census had been two groups of considerable economic and political significance: the Banyoro and the Baganda. Their roles in commerce and government permitted their acquisition of land, and in spite of the discriminatory relocations of elements of their populations, their wealth was greater than that of the local natives. Culturally, they were well placed to act (as were the Bakenyi to a lesser extent) as intermediaries or brokers for the "civilizing mission" of European Christians and administrators.

By 1921 the Protectorate census had revealed a more complex patterning of population in Teso district (see Table 2). Five divisions were still recognized by the administration but under new labels. Bukedea lay within the district in 1921 and, along with Kumi, made up the "south." The vast expanse of the "north" was labeled Omoro (there was no separate recognition of Usuku and Amuria). Over

---

presumably it was by purchase (e.g., Vincent, 1971, p. 238).

10. The career histories of Gondo residents, collected in 1966, showed that most Iteso artisans had worked apprenticeships with Asian (usually Hindu) entrepreneurs, whereas Bakenyi had received their training from Basoga fellow Muslims (Vincent, 1971, p. 164).

Table 2. *The Native Population of Teso District, 1921*

	North		Serere	South		Total
	Omoro	Soroti		Kumi	Bukedea	
Sons of the soil						
Iteso	64,699	44,002	30,811	77,620	32,276	249,408
Bakenyi	0	383	1,380	1,014	0	2,777
Cultural intrusions						
Langi	5,664	7	0	0	0	5,671
Bagweri	0	1	0	21	735	757
Bagisu	0	6	0	16	340	362
Badama	0	0	0	0	18	18
Precapitalist frontiersmen						
Banyoro	0	260	1,516	4	30	1,810
Baganda	32	555	1,215	291	203	2,296
Basoga	22	94	1,524	1,211	291	3,142
Industrial immigrants						
Kavirondo	0	28	0	26	0	54
Acholi	0	19	0	0	0	19
Sebei	0	15	0	0	0	15
Swahili	0	7	8	13	27	55
Others[a]	0	5	0	2	0	7
Total	70,417	45,382	36,454	80,218	33,920	266,391

SOURCE: Adapted from Native Census, 1921. TDA XCST/1.36.
[a]Includes Banyema, Basiba, Basese, Alur, Nubi, Somali.

five thousand Langi were still included within Teso's border.[11] Increased ethnic heterogeneity in Soroti was due to the move of administrative headquarters and the subsequent growth of commerce there. Elsewhere, heterogeneity developed with the expansion of cotton ginning. Although most operatives were Iteso and Bakenyi, ethnic specialization grew up around subsidiary employment, as among Acholi night watchmen (*askaris*), Swahili foremen, and Basoga porters.[12]

11. *Uganda Protectorate Census of 1921.*
12. It is not clear to what extent employers *preferred* nonlocal employ-

If we separate the sons of the Teso soil (Iteso and Bakenyi) from, as it were, the culturally intrusive groups (Langi, Bagweri, Badama, and Bagishu) whose presence later led to the redefinition of the district's boundaries (the Langi of Omoro being included in Lango district and the Bagweri and Bagishu of Bukedea in Bugisu), two patterns of immigration emerge. The first involved Banyoro and Baganda, frontiersmen of the preindustrial mercantile system of the Lake Kyoga region. Coming from the west, pockets of these populations were to be found largely in Serere and western Soroti. With Kakungulu's conquest and the advent of British administration, certain Baganda were then appointed to localities in other regions. The density of their settlement reflected, first, their distribution at the district's successive administrative centers, Kumi and Soroti, and, second, their residence (since at one time they acquired estates) in the most fertile agricultural areas. The banana groves of Serere and Bukedea bore witness to their presence. The second pattern of immigration involved individuals rather than groups and brought from surrounding areas those most responsive to the newly developing capitalist economy in Teso—those who, for the most part, were also the most disadvantaged within neighboring economies, as in Busoga and Acholi. Their settlement patterns reflected the government of African migration by colonial authorities, since most were single men, "wandering men" or "tramping artisans,"[13] the costs of their social reproduction borne, for the most part, in the peripheral regions of their origin.[14]

There was a miniscule amount of labor migration *out* of the

---

ees. In Gondo, most non-Iteso were regular workers dependent on ginnery wages during the cotton season; local Iteso tended to be hired weekly. Skilled and managerial positions were filled by Mbale and Jinja residents who lived locally only during the cotton season (Vincent, 1971, pp. 35–36).

13. For the historical importance of this control, see Eric Hobsbawm, *The Labouring Men* (1964a), pp. 34–63. African dimensions are documented by Helmuth Heisler, *Urbanisation and the Government of Migration: the Interrelation of Urban and Rural Life in Africa* (1974), esp. pp. 89–102, and discussed analytically in Joan Vincent, "The Changing Role of Small Towns in the Agrarian Structure of East Africa" (1974a), pp. 268–272.

14. For a sustained development of this idea, see Michael Burawoy, "The Functions and Reproduction of Migrant Labor" (1977).

district in 1921. In all, 435 Iteso, 76 percent of them male, were to be found in Bulamogi county, Busoga. Given the proximity of this county to Serere (as well as to Pallisa), it lay within the social field, especially the marriage field, of Teso residents. Farther afield than this were only two Iteso, one in Buddu and one in Masaka.[15]

Demographic Changes

Whether the development of Teso's economy was accompanied by an increase in its population is questionable. Changes in boundary delineation make assessment difficult, but it would appear that population rise over the decade, if it occurred, was exceedingly slight—from an (under-) estimated 250,663 in 1911 to 266,396 in 1921. There may even have been a population decrease, if the extent of movement into Kaberamaido, Lango, and Karamoja were known. Where comparable figures are accurate (for Serere, for example), a loss of population occurs that is of devastating proportions: from 56,170 in 1911 to 36,454 in 1921.[16] The reasons for this will become apparent.

Teso's population characteristics have puzzled geographers and demographers. Its low rate of growth in each intercensal period from 1911 to 1969 was much less than the average for Uganda. Its population density increased only from 74 per square mile in 1921 to 132 per square mile in 1969; and "a district which was moderately closely settled in 1921 might have been expected to show a high density by now."[17] Whereas Teso was the fifth most densely populated district in the Protectorate in 1921—and we have seen how missionaries and administrators alike addressed themselves to Teso's "overwhelming" numbers—it was only the tenth most populated district in 1969. The following chapter addresses some of the factors to which this is possibly attributable: epidemics, famines, and widespread gonorrhea and syphilis, among others. Sterility was commonplace and polygyny (among pagan, Muslim, and Christian) a cultural ideal. The interdependence of these and other features has

15. O. Dak, *A Geographical Analysis of the Distribution of Migrants in Uganda* (1968), p. 112.

16. Kumi District Census, 1911; Native Census, 1921–25 (TDA XCST/1.36); *Uganda Protectorate Census of 1921*.

17. Langlands (1971), p. 3.

never been worked out; explanations for Teso's distinctive demography remain elusive.

They do not, however, remain obscure. Recent European studies by historical demographers and social historians have explored similar population responses to nascent capitalism. The Teso case, distinctive as it is, may be seen to lie at the end of a continuum. Unlike Buganda, the first region of Uganda to experience capitalist industrializing agriculture, Teso lacked an indigenous dominant class that was able, to some extent, to control development. Further, the pace of its incorporation into the modern world system had been, unlike that of Buganda, the matter of a moment.

The Tax-Paying Population

The main purpose of district censuses was, of course, to arrive at an estimation of tax potential. The skeletal record of tax collection in Teso is short and unadorned: its chilling aspects become apparent as we begin to flesh out the bare facts. With the signing of the Uganda Agreement in 1900, a hut tax of Rs.3 was introduced throughout the colonial territory. The Poll Tax Ordinances were first applied in Bukeddi from April 1, 1909, and the amount of tax demanded of the natives was steadily increased between 1909 and 1927. Beginning at Rs.3 in 1909, it was raised to Rs.5 in 1914 and to Rs.7.50 in 1920. With conversion of the currency to shillings in that year, a poll tax of s.15 was introduced in 1921 that was maintained until the end of the period with which we are concerned.[18]

18. Thomas and Scott (1935), pp. 223–225. The best account of the Protectorate's fiscal policy remains Roger Van Zwanenberg, with Anne King, *An Economic History of Kenya and Uganda, 1800–1970* (1975), pp. 275–296.

Indian rupee coinage was introduced to the East African Protectorate in 1898, replacing the Maria Theresa dollar. The first branch of the National Bank of India opened in Entebbe in 1906, but the coin was not adopted outside of government circles; the cowry was in general use. The East Africa and Uganda (Currency) Order in Council, 1905, established the Indian rupee; the silver rupee of the IBEA Co. was still recognized. The East African florin was introduced in July 1920, following upon extreme fluctuations in the rupee–sterling exchange rates during the war. Throughout the period, economic crises were aggravated by government action in the area of currency reform.

In Teso, the first installment of tax was received from Chief Oumo of Kumi on October 4, 1909.[19] Tax was doubly welcome, first because it represented "one of the first signs of a native's submission to authority" and, second, because tax collected by the chiefs in that year (Rs.62,949) represented a considerable increase over that obtained in earlier years, when the people had to "draw on their stock."[20] At this time, expenditure in the district amounted to Rs.10,339, of which nearly a third went to government agents and chiefs who received a rebate on all taxes collected. This expenditure, totaling Rs.3,147, was the only "wage" they received.

Exactly how many Teso chiefs had been appointed or recognized in the district at this time is not known; Coote's safari journal suggests that he is still discovering them as he travels from place to place.[21] It is not clear how far down the line, so to speak, the funds from rebates had to be redistributed. Chiefs "employed" their own katikiros and askaris. At this threshold between big man status and contract chief, the exact nature of obligations, reciprocities, and exploitations is uncertain.

Before the imposition of colonial rule, it can be assumed, big men or patrons were accustomed to receiving gifts from clients in the form of food (chickens and goats, especially)—mechanisms of a precapitalist nontributary polity. Bigmanship expanded with and flourished upon the newly imposed statelike conditions of colonial rule. For any chief remaining from the precolonial system, the employed followers would have been kin, affines, and clients. One would expect considerable variation throughout the region according to the extent to which Iteso social structure had been affected by Baganda overrule. Big men in Serere, Kumi, and Bukedea had the most opportunity for aggrandizement. In Soroti and Usuku they were more likely to be constrained by the indigenous redistributive system. The records cannot help us. Although we might tabulate

19. Entry in Kumi Station Diary, Oct. 4, 1909.

20. Kumi District Annual Report, 1909–10 (TDA XADM/9).

21. Coote (diary, 1909). Coote toured Kumi, Serere, southern Soroti, Amuria, and Usuku between Feb. 1 and Mar. 1, 1909. His diary records the sudd-cutting operations of the Agu swamp; the lawlessness of Serere; cattle thefts; the appearance of early cotton plots; a visit to Okolimong; game safaris; and the foundation laying of the administrative headquarters at Kumi.

cases of chiefs brought to justice at Kumi for the misuse of office, such records more likely reflect the closeness of the administration, both literally and metaphorically, than the actual occurrence or frequency of abuse.

A momentous decision, taken at the top level within the Uganda Protectorate, not only widened the gap between chiefs and commoners, but went a fair way to entrench and perpetuate it. Agents were, at that time entitled to 10 percent of the tax they collected, chiefs to 5 percent. Early in 1910, Baganda agents were removed from the sides of the district's most efficient and cooperative chiefs. Four men—Oumo (Kumi), Ijala (Ngora), Kamundani (Nyere), and Pakalwana (Kumia)—thereafter began to accumulate a full 10 percent of the taxes they collected.[22] In March 1911 Ocheppa (Mukuru), and in March 1912 Tuke (Kapiri) and Kariebi (Kachumbala), were granted the same privilege.[23] Thus, by 1912, seven Iteso chiefs, all from the southern counties, had begun to acquire large and official cash incomes that far exceeded anything available to other Iteso at the time. As a symbol of their elevated office, each chief was given a tax collector's box, a practical insignia shared only by the remaining government agents.[24] Though Buganda agents certainly formed a privileged elite in colonial Teso, there was in their economic aggrandizement no basis for the formation of a dominant class. A considerable portion of their wealth was, in all probability, sent out of the district to Mbale rather than invested in local concerns. The southern Iteso chiefs were a different matter.

But what did the poll tax mean to the common people? From the outset, the payment of taxes was deemed an individual matter for each adult male. A chief paying a cow in tax should collect goats from his followers, as Kakungulu put it.[25] One of the rationales underlying the introduction of cotton as a cash crop was that it would permit each adult male to pay tax without parting with

22. Kumi District Annual Report, 1909–10.

23. District Commissioner to Provincial Commissioner, Apr. 17, 1912 (TDA XADM/10.A).

24. Ibid., Feb. 12, 1912. The government agents were Anderea (Malera),Yakobo (Bugondo), Daudi (Wera), Yakobo (Toroma), Yonosani (Serere), Reubani (Kyere), Yailo (Usuku), and Temeteo (Orungo) (TDA XADM/10.A).

25. Twaddle (Ph.D., 1967), p. 203.

cattle. Another was that a modicum of cotton cultivation provided necessary investment. A third was that a grower might, after selling his cotton crop and paying tax, have surplus cash for discretionary (that is, extrasubsistence) purchases. Nevertheless, that a poll tax was introduced in a society made up for the most part of groups with communal, not individual, rights in cattle and land, and that, within the district, not all the African population belonged to that society (that is, Iteso) was to have specific repercussions for agrarian development.

Tax records for 1910–1927 are incomplete (see Table 3),[26] but, for the early part of this period, the correlations between administrative consolidation, increased cotton production, and income from taxation are clear. Most striking is the large rise after the move of the district headquarters to Soroti, accompanied as it was by more efficient administration and marketing in Amuria and southern Usuku.

The European and Asian Populations of Teso District

If the burden of imperialism in Teso was borne by its African population, its profits fell, largely, into non-African hands. Yet, in spite of this, it was not until 1919 that "nonnatives" paid a higher tax (s.30 per annum) than "natives."[27]

Colonial censuses and tax records shroud European and Asian residents in Teso in anonymity, and it is necessary to make a devious approach to them through an analysis of voluntary contributions to war relief funds in 1915–16. In 1915, the sum of Rs.741 was donated (in amounts ranging from Rs.1 to Rs.50) by eighty-eight individuals.[28] Given that the individual contributions were made public, it can be assumed that they partially reflected estimation of self and perception of social position within Teso's colonial hierarchy.

26. Files used for Table 3 were "Teso District Annual Reports, 1912–21, 1922–31" (TDA VADM/4/1–2); "Cash Books" (TDA VFIN/1/1–18); "Native Poll Tax Ticket Registers, 1911–19, 1923–24, 1926–28" (TDA VFIN/2/1–5).

27. Thomas and Scott (1935), p. 225.

28. "Uganda War Relief Fund," *Uganda Protectorate Gazette*, Feb. 15 and 27, Mar. 15, and May 15, 1915.

Table 3. Poll Tax in Teso District by Region (in Rupees
[1910–1920] and in Shillings [1920–1927])

Year ending March 31	1910	1911	1912	1913	1914
South	33,018	68,343	78,849	94,533	95,343
Serere	9,243	27,585	32,700	37,146	41,130
North (Soroti Town)	20,688	42,261	51,537	64,155	79,842
Total	62,949	138,189	163,086	195,834	216,315
	1915	1916	1917	1918	1919
South	158,720	155,885	156,095	156,965	– –
Serere	66,274	61,525	63,700	64,045	– –
North (Soroti Town)	133,570	128,075	130,760	130,190	– –
Total	358,564	345,485	350,555	351,200	344,340
	1920	1921	1922	1923	1924
South	– –	– –	19,701	22,245	23,904
Serere	– –	– –	10,622	11,798	12,560
North (Soroti Town)	– –	– –	88,932	793,567	902,355
Total	502,332	531,715	119,255	827,610	938,819
	1925	1926	1927		
South	23,843	22,788	– –		
Serere	13,161	13,432	– –		
North (Soroti Town)	948,380	954,409	– –		
Total	985,384	990,629	1,267,417		

SOURCE: Annual Reports, TDA. XADM/9 and David J. Vail, A History of Agricultural Innovation and Development in Teso District, Uganda, Syracuse: Syracuse University Press. 1972, p.
146.
NOTE: From 1910–1921 Bukedea county lay within Teso district. From 1910–1921 poll tax
was collected in rupees and thereafter in shillings. Fluctuations in tax revenue are attributable to
changes in currency (see Chapter 6, note 18); increases in poll tax (i.e. from 3s. to 5s. in 1915;
to 7.50s. in 1920 and 15s. in 1922); and by the considerable variation in annual incomes. Tax
defaulters were sent to prison. These figures are not at all reliable; different totals appear in
Provincial annual reports (TDA. XADM/5) and in Native Affairs reports (TDA. XNAF/5).

Eighteen Europeans contributed a total of Rs.380. The district
commissioner, W. G. Adams, headed the list with a contribution of
Rs.50, but pride of place had to be shared with J. Mackertich, a
provisions merchant of Gondo. Three individuals contributed
Rs.30: the district agricultural officer, the local manager of the

British East Africa Company, and the district agricultural officer. Three, including the CMS missionaries, contributed Rs.20. Eight Europeans, all in Soroti, each contributed Rs.15, one at Kyere and one at Ngora each contributed Rs.5. The colonial hierarchy appeared intact, with the district commissioner at the top, down through the Department of Agriculture, lower echelon administrative officers, and missionaries, to members of the Department of Public Works.[29] Twelve of the eighteen Europeans were stationed in Soroti, two in Ngora, two in Gondo, one in Kyere, and one in Kudunguru.

Whereas the distribution of European contributors reflected the spread of cotton production and missionary endeavor in the district, as well as the new establishment of Soroti as district headquarters, the distribution of the Asian population mirrored that other dimension of the expanding economy: the growth of small towns, minor townships, and trading centers throughout the Teso countryside.

The range of Asian contributions was far greater than that of Europeans. Three individuals (or firms) gave Rs.20, six gave Rs.15, and seven gave Rs.10. The contribution of these sixteen Asians totaled Rs.220, nearly one-third of the total for the district. The remaining Rs.156 came from eighteen donations of Rs.5 and thirty-six of smaller sums. The Asian community of Kumi was tapped by F. C. Mehta, and in this township considerable wealth was manifested, as well as marked differentiation within the commercial sector. The largest corporate subscriber was H. M. Jamal, of the General and Trading Company (Rs.30); other businessmen gave Rs.20 or Rs.25; two donated only 50 cents. Although Kumi had by 1916 the smallest Asian community in the district—for most firms had followed the administration to Soroti—it raised the sum of Rs.113. But the heart of the Asian population was by this time firmly beating in Soroti, where Rs.342 was collected. Of this, Rs.255 came from two businessmen, Molvi Abdullah Shah and Lala Thanduram Lakram. Not only had large capital interests entered the district, but there was beginning to be a move toward wholesale monopolies.

In Ngora, two collections were made: one from Muslim Asians

29. For a discussion of Uganda's colonial hierarchical elites, see Gartrell (Ph.D., 1979), pp. 38–88.

and Arabs of the commercial sector and the other from Europeans. In Gondo, A. M. Fernandes (a substantial subscriber to the earlier appeal) was in charge of the collection from Asian traders. His "constituency," while entirely Asian, had a richer complexion than that of Ngora: fewer Muslim Indians and considerably more Hindus appeared in the subscribers' list. The sums collected for each Asian community do not suggest an egalitarian distribution of wealth. Goan Catholics and Hindus made the largest donations and, proportionately, more Hindus gave than Muslims. This religious breakdown reflected a distinction within the Asian community between the public (government service and the cotton industry) and private sector (small businessmen.) This was further reflected in differences with respect to acquisition of land, intermarriage with Africans, residence in rural areas, and, later, manifestations of violence against Asians. Socially, Hindus and Goans on the one hand and Muslims and Sikhs on the other formed inward- and outward-looking sectors within what was perceived by others as a solidary Asian community.[30]

The explanation of this particular structuring of the Asian population within Teso lies in the wider political-economic system of which it was a part. Even a cursory study of the state and caste systems of the Indian subcontinent shrieks of the historical place of the Muslim trader in its cattle and grain economy. With the expansion of empire, and the linkage of India with East Africa (a linkage that took the specific form of the importation of personnel: clerks, soldiers, laborers on the railroad), a further element entered the Ugandan scene: Catholics, Sikhs, and Hindus from Goa, Uttar Pra-

30. See H. Stephen Morris, *The Indians in Uganda* (1968). "It is the Indian under the direction of the Englishman who has been the civiliser of East Africa. It is the coolie who has made the railway; the Indian artisan who fills the railway workshops; the Sikh who forms the backbone of the military forces, . . . the Bangali and the Goanese who staff the railway station offices, the post-offices, and the subordinate posts in the Government departments; the Parsee and the Goanese who conduct the greater part of the retail trade" (Herbert Samuel, *The Uganda of Today*, p. 395, quoted in Gregory, 1971, p. 66). Teso's experience was very different from Samuel's Gandacentric view of economic development, a matter of some significance for the later political condition of Asians in Teso District in the seventies.

desh, and Gujerat. Asian occupational specialization in the Teso economy reflected these historical processes. If the polyethnic structure of Teso's political economy in 1911 was largely a reflection of its precapitalist involvement in a larger Indian Ocean mercantilist economic system, that of 1921 testified to its closer involvement in the capitalist world system that had supplanted it. And, in this, European and Asian joined.

In November 1916, a second fund-raising drive was carried out on behalf of the British Red Cross and the Order of St. John.[31] On this occasion the sum of 3,348 rupees was collected, nearly five times that donated to the Uganda War Relief Fund the previous year. This was due entirely to the fact that this time Africans were required to contribute. For each of the five counties, agents were responsible for collecting donations, but since there is no nominal breakdown of individual Africans as there is of Asians and Europeans, status differentiation cannot be inferred. Kumi County, which had the largest population (93,432) in 1915, forwarded the second largest contribution (Rs.530); pride of place went to Serere (population 49,552) with Rs.673. Soroti County, with approximately the same population as Serere in 1915, contributed Rs.467; and Usuku (population 47,770) and Bukedea (population 35,226) contributed Rs.360 and Rs.191, respectively. In 1916, African contributions amounted to Rs.2,790.05, compared with Rs.470 from the European community and Rs.558 from the Asian sector. Even in charitable support of the European war effort the African population of Teso was heavily milked.

Occupational Structure

The occupational structure of Teso in 1921 (see Table 4) shows how small was the capital-intensive sector of the economy.[32] Unfortunately, the census is of limited value for reconstruction, since its categorization derives from the tribal preconceptions of colonial authority. Although the occupations of Bateso and Bakenyi are

31. "British Red Cross and Order of St. John, Subscription List," *Uganda Protectorate Gazette*, Nov. 15, 1916.
32. *Uganda Protectorate Census of 1921*.

Table 4. Occupations of Male Natives in Teso, 1921

	Iteso	Bakenyi	Total	Percentage of Total
Chiefs	98	4	102	
Subchiefs	267	16	283	
Clerks	56	6	62	
Teachers	260	2	262	
Government employees	116	0	116	
Commercial employees	269	0	269	
	1,066	28	1,094	.97
Agriculturalists	1,616	0	1,616	
Cattle owners	22,312	74	22,386	
Fishermen	135	93	228	
No occupation (includes children)	60,835	848	61,683	
	84,898	1,015	85,913	76.15
Artisans Carpenters	66	4	70	
Blacksmiths	300	0	300	
Bricklayers	180	0	180	
	546	4	550	.49
House servants	780	16	796	
	780	16	796	.71
Other occupations	728	42	770	
	728	42	770	.68
Laborers	23,145	287	23,432	
Cattlemen	258	0	258	
	23,403	287	23,690	21.00
Total	111,421	1,392	112,813	

SOURCE: Adapted from Native Census, 1921. TDA XCST/1. 36.

enumerated, nowhere are there to be found employment statistics relating to any other category. The impact of capitalist penetration on the countryside may be inferred, but not a comprehensive profile of labor.

However, a reclassification of the occupations of the male natives of the district suggests the dynamic process under way in the agrarian society by 1921. An emergent top stratum consisted of those with education, salaries, and opportunities for advancement—chiefs and subchiefs, clerks, teachers, government and business employees. These numbered 994 out of an employed population of 51,130. They formed a privileged category of fewer than 2 percent of Teso's native sons.

The bottom stratum of the agrarian society was made up of a rural proletariat, laborers who numbered some 23,432 in 1921, a figure approaching 45 percent of the total. This large proportion reflected the effort expanded in Teso during the years from 1907 to 1921 on construction works (bridgemaking, roadmaking, factory construction) and, above all, porterage as the cotton industry developed. Between these two strata was the middle sector, made up, first, of those who remained in established rural occupations—agriculture, herding, fishing—and, alongside them, literally and categorically, those who had become the artisans of the industrializing agricultural economy: carpenters, blacksmiths, bricklayers, and others. The middle sector numbered, in 1921, some 550. The mobility (and alienation) of their labor places them along with the rural proletariat; in some instances in a colonial system this would be most apt. In Teso, however, a second consideration, the fact that much advancement in this domain lay in the control of missionaries and Asian businessmen, suggests that artisans belonged in the middle sector. So, too, did the comparatively large number of servants who were almost entirely employed by Asians and Europeans.[33]

The Christian Population

There is no reconciliation possible between government and mission statistics on religious persuasion in Teso district. The Protec-

33. The servants were entirely male, including ayahs (children's nurse-maids). The structural implications of the gender of house servants in East Africa, both during colonial times and more recently, along with the role of European women in the labor market, has yet to be explored.

torate census of 1921 indicates a clear numerical supremacy of Protestant over Roman Catholic by nearly 3:1, as well as the diminutive number of Muslims (594) in the district.[34] Even more apparent, the overwhelming majority of the population (249,871 out of a total of 266,546) belonged to no universal religion and were categorized as pagans (see Table 5).

These figures do not correspond with those of the missions. For example, the CMS in 1921 claimed a following of 23,463 readers and 270 teachers.[35] The government recorded a total of 11,521 Protestants. Similarly, in the same year the government enumerated a Roman Catholic population of 4,410 in Teso district; the *status animarum* (annual accounting of the saving of souls) of the Mill Hill mission indicated a following of 1,650 converts and a school population of 5,215.[36] The Mill Hill statistics (some of which are reproduced in Table 6) provide, nevertheless, valuable information on the process and success of Christian proselytization. The total Catholic population increased from 90 in 1913, when only the Ngora mission station was in existence, to 204 on the opening of the Soroti station the following year. Thereafter the Church population increased continually (apart from a minuscule drop in 1919) until 1924, when it fell by around 13 percent. It then continued to rise annually until it reached 6,162 in 1927—a steady process of conversion from under 100 to over 6,000 in a matter of only fourteen

Table 5. *Religious Affiliations in Teso, 1921*

	Protestant	Roman Catholic	Muslim	Pagan	Total
Bateso	10,704	3,801	109	234,794	249,408
Basoga	150	112	157	2,723	3,142
Bakenyi	18	19	21	2,719	2,777
Baganda	470	377	210	1,239	2,296
Banyoro	146	89	33	1,543	1,811
Total	11,488	4,398	530	243,018	259,434

SOURCE: Adapted from Uganda Protectorate Census, 1921, Table 60.

34. *Uganda Protectorate Census of 1921* .
35. H. G. Dillistone, annual letter, 1912 (CMS Archives G3 A7/o).
36. The status animarum was published annually in St. *Joseph's Advocate.*

Table 6. *Mill Hill Mission Records for Teso, 1913–1927*

	Baptisms				Christian	Children
	Infant	Adult	Marriages	Funerals	Population	in School
1913	9	1	2	5	90	1,521
1914	16	7	2	4	204	2,578
1915	10	20	3	30	278	5,500
1916	11	23	2	–	390	5,355
1917	14	35	3	–	434	3,698
1918	15	41	2	–	540	2,869
1919	13	64	7	–	535	2,866
1920	24	104	6	–	719	4,489
1921	50	45	18	–	1,650	5,215
1922	79	180	36	–	2,064	8,104
1923	105	504	62	–	3,438	7,978
1924	175	780	142	593	3,049	9,590
1925	125	229	36	195	3,500	7,260
1926	165	630	167	637	4,220	12,498
1927	326	1,461	228	699	6,162	12,186

SOURCE: Status Animarum Vicariate—Apostolic of the Upper Nile, *St. Joseph's Advocate,* 1913–1927.

years. The sociologically significant dimensions, in a sense, are those of marriage and burial—public ceremonies of the Church rampant. It is to be remarked how few these were before 1920. Thereafter, the sharp rise in the total population is most apparent, as it doubled between August 1920 and August 1921.

Local field inquiries (working with informants, genealogies, and life histories) might well suggest that some significance be attached to increased prosperity from good cotton harvests and from the administration's policies of promoting educated Teso-born chiefs. That the missions were the vehicles of modern education and that the natives of Teso wanted this education had been apparent from the start. Unfortunately, there are no comparable statistics for the CMS, and the relationship remains a matter of speculation.

7. Development and Underdevelopment

What is wanted for Uganda is what Birmingham has got—an
improvement scheme.

Chamberlain 1897:136

Pauperism, political economy, and the discovery of society were
closely interwoven.

Polanyi 1944:85

Ideologies of development come to the fore when a territory in
relation to the world capitalist system is undergoing an interregnum. This has occurred three times in sub-Saharan Africa—in
the 1960s, after World War II, and in the first decade of the twentieth century.

The Development Decade 1908–1917

The decade from 1908 to 1917 was Teso's first development
decade. Disturbed by the changes in British colonial policy and
practice that had occurred during his career, Sydney Olivier noted:
"That word [development] recurs incessantly in State papers and
governors' speeches as describing the principal aim to which regard
must be had . . . not only in the interests of European adventurers
in these new colonial enterprises, but in framing conceptions of the
interests of natives, which are presumed to be bound up with
'development'." In determining native policy and deciding what
manner of obligations shall be primarily placed on them Olivier

asked "what attitude shall be adopted . . . towards the question of their own indigenous economies?"[1]

It has been suggested that imperial expansion often brings about economic degradation in conquered territories, as natural economies are taken apart so that bits of them can be integrated into the international economic system.[2] This is not simply the development of underdevelopment, but a dimunition of specific measurable economic attributes: local handicrafts, indigenous trade in foodcrops, the distribution of landholdings, and so on. Accompanying these changes, new ideologies and values are inculcated both by colonial officers and by missionaries. The reorientation of the indigenous economy has known effects: inferior nutrition results for some elements of the population, an increase in labor demands for others. Women in agrarian societies fare less well, and for all, increased economic differentiation within the population leads to the betterment of the few at the expense of the many.

In Teso, the process of transition from a largely subsistence economy to one in which a cash crop—cotton—was grown for export took on not only a capitalist but a regional dimension. Thus, while the north was slowly brought into the modern sector of the economy, much of it remained like neighboring Karamoja, a backward region; and while Serere and the Kyoga shores of Soroti had much of their former vitality eroded by the demands of colonial mono-

1. Sir Sydney H. Olivier, *White Capital and Coloured Labour* (1929), pp. 56–57. Olivier views development as the third phase of colonial policy, i.e., exploitation through the development of territories (white commercial capitalism exploiting colored labor in Africa). He notes (p. 10):

Within the lifetime of my own generation, and very impressively within the experience of those who, like myself, have been continuously associated with the affairs of British Crown Colonies and Protectorates, the whole colour of the influentially prevalent and actively effective ideas about Imperial relations with our dependencies of mixed population was changed. The keynote of that change was sounded by Mr. Joseph Chamberlain in the historical phrase that our Imperial possessions must be treated as "Undeveloped Estates." . . . When I joined the Colonial Office in 1882 . . . no one thought of the Colonies as milch-cattle for England, "estates" to be "developed" or exploited for the benefit of the Mother Country.

2. Rosa Luxemburg, *The Accumulation of Capital* (1972), p. 417.

culture with its export requirements, the south bloomed. As a result, it was in the southern counties of Teso district—Ngora, Kumi and Bukedea—that those most able to take advantage of the economic developments emerged and prospered.

The Agu swamp that divided south from north also marked off those who advanced within the new political economy from the underprivileged. Initially, it will be remembered, a marked difference of soil types was to be found within the Teso region. While all topsoils were shallow, those of the north were light with a high sand content; heavier clay loam and alluvial soils were to be found only in the southern counties and in isolated swamp valleys. The best soils in the district were those of the south, in the "cow's thigh" of Bukedea, and in a few parts of eastern Serere. The soils of Kumi, Ngora, and the remainder of Serere ranked next in quality, while the entire area north of the Agu swamp and east of Soroti was very low in fertility. Further to the detriment of the disadvantaged north, Usuku and Amuria counties had only a single, prolonged rainy season, whereas southern Teso was characterized by two distinct rainy seasons with a six- to ten-week dry spell between them. Serere, while it shared the bimodal rainfall pattern of the south, had a total annual rainfall comparable with that of the northern counties (forty inches annually, compared with fifty in the south) and so was intermediate in developmental prospects. We saw earlier how the introduction of iron hoes from Bunyoro and Labwor stimulated trade in the region, especially in cattle, hides, and ivory; but given the natural limitations of soil and climate, only 2.9 million acres of the 4,306 4,306 square miles of Teso district could be considered potentially arable. A cattle economy predominated in the north.

The actual moment of Kakungulu's entry into southern Teso and the gradual consolidation of colonial rule in the decade that followed had found the north severely disadvantaged. Drought and locust attacks of 1894–1896 had engendered famine in much of the region; double indemnity ensued when rinderpest followed the crop failure almost immediately. Vail's "educated guess is that two-thirds of all cattle in Teso died of the plague and drought."[3] In the south, on the other hand, there were peanuts (introduced in the

3. David J. Vail, *A History of Agricultural Innovation and Development In Teso District, Uganda* (1972), p. 15.

1890s) and sweet potatoes to fall back on when the millet crops failed. By the 1890s land in the south rather than cattle was the prime resource.

Chronology of Events, 1908–1917

The events of the development decade in Teso can be narrated in short order; the processes involved require more elaboration.[4] In 1908, the headquarters of the new Collectorate was established at Kumi, and steps were taken to render it, along with the bomas of agents and chiefs, an oasis of civilization in the African bush. In the same year the Anglican mission inaugurated a new Diocese of the Upper Nile, and the Reverend Arthur Kitching was instructed to open a station at Ngora. Kirk, whose mission had been experimenting with various crops at Iganga and Budaka, joined Kitching, W. Holden, and Ormsby there to inspect the sites. In that year trade was depressed in the restricted United States markets in ivory and skins, and the price of cotton was low on the Liverpool market.

The following year the administration initiated regular safaris in the Collectorate. Coote traveled in the west and north; Bishop Tucker accompanied Dr. Albert Cook on a tour of Serere and the south, returning to England to appeal for funds so that the country could be opened to Christian endeavor. Rev. H. G. Dillistone arrived at Ngora and opened a school for the sons of chiefs. The Lake Kyoga Marine Service came into operation. Cotton prices began to rise in Liverpool.

By 1910 the lands on either side of a fifty-mile route through Kumi district from Mbale to Gondo had been opened for cotton cultivation. Although growing seasons were by no means clear, the export crop had begun to come in to the headquarters at Kumi from as far afield as Soroti and monthly records were accumulated with considerable gratification (see Table 7). When, in March, the district commissioner traveled from Gondo to Kumi via Soroti, cycle paths were secure, and a triangle of intensive roadside and estate production had begun to take shape. Canoes provided regular ferry services from Agu to Kyere, even if the traveler had at times to

4. The account that follows is derived from Kumi Station Diary; Teso District Annual Reports; and Department of Agriculture Reports (TDA XAGR/1.47/13/47, 1.19, 1.8, 1.85/13, 1.1, 1.G, and 1.2).

Table 7. *Cotton Sales in Kumi District, by Season*
November 1909 – July 1912 (in pounds)

1909–1910	November	0
	December	0
	January	56,264
	February	257,751
	March	391,301
	April	308,810
	May	84,315
	June	892
	July	32
	Total	1,099,365
1910–1911	November	40,653
	December	560,026
	January	1,038,161
	February	648,155
	March	154,094
	Total	2,441,089
1911–1912	October	69,748
	November	464,770
	December	1,144,357
	January	1,008,861
	February	1,411,927
	March	933,019
	April	774,841
	May	396,903
	June	62,239
	July	6,918
	Total	6,273,583

SOURCE: Kumi Station Diary, Nov. 1909–July 1912. TDA. VADM/3/1.

complain of the independence of Bakenyi ferrymen. The Agu swamp dividing the southern counties from Serere was bridged by a dry season road; but the journey north still entailed a four- to five-mile canoe passage from Esera to Okokorio (Kokolyo), a small settlement of natives and Swahili under a Muganda agent. An alternative route from Kapiri to Kapujan was more frequented after the district headquarters was moved to Soroti in 1914.

As early as 1910, the provincial commissioner, F. C. Spire, was able to send London a favorable report of development in the southern counties of the Collectorate.

> Considerable improvement in the general attitude of the native has taken place during the year. This is evidenced by the large increase in the poll tax collected; payment of this tax being one of the first signs of a native's submission to authority. This improved demeanour is particularly noticeable in the central part of the district, around Kumi, Ngora and Mukura, where the chiefs have now a very good hold over their people; so much so that the experiment is being tried of allowing the chiefs at Kumi and Ngora to rule without the aid of a Govt. agent. Umu and Njala, the two chiefs concerned have each engaged their own clerk and so far the experiment has proved entirely satisfactory. The central baraza, which meets in Kumi every Monday, is always very largely attended and is so successful that an appeal from its decisions is practically unknown. The excellent and law abiding disposition does however not yet extend to the Serere and Soroti districts where the people are still very backward and robbery with violence is not an uncommon occurrence. The great difficulty here is the lack of power and in some instances lax attitude on the part of the chiefs, who are consequently of very little assistance to the Administration and whose duties have in many cases to be performed by the D.O.'s. Unfortunately no better material exists at present.[5]

In 1911, recruiters from the Mabira rubber plantation in Busoga attempted to tap Teso's labor supply, with little success. The first plow—that primordial indicator of agrarian progress—arrived in the district, along with a government plow instructor. At the developing ports of Gondo and Lale, cotton was shipped first to Kakindu and then to Namasagali for conveyance by the Busoga and Uganda railways to Mombasa and thence to England. Cotton production grew from 0.5 to 2.8 thousand tons between 1909 and 1911.[6] When

---

5. Annual Report by Provincial Commissioner, 1910 (TDA XADM/5).

6. "Teso Statistical Time Series: 1909–1939," in Vail (1972), p. 146, Table 10. The statistical sources cited by Vail (p. 147) for this table are Uganda Protectorate: Annual Reports or Blue Books (TDA XCST/1); 1929 Cotton Commission Report; and Tothill (1940), p. 78. The 1911 production figure was not surpassed until 1921, when a new type of seed was introduced.

the Protectorate government requested the withdrawal of Baganda agents, Teso's district officials protested vehemently.

In 1912, Teso district was proclaimed. The development of its infrastructure proceeded apace; the Department of Public Works began systematic road and bridge construction; sudd cutting continued in the Agu swamp. Cotton production expanded, and limitations on marketing alone seemed to hold back an expanding economy.

The year 1913 saw the first gazetting of Iteso county chiefs, an indication of the competence of that small group of men who first received arms and then safes as tokens of trust and delegated authority.[7] For the population of Serere and Ngora, orders to cease work on sudd clearance provided, probably, the most welcome event of the entire period. Everywhere work continued on the roads, however, and cotton production continued to expand. As armed patrols penetrated deeper into Usuku, cotton production reached a record 8.8 thousand tons.[8]

The move of district headquarters to Soroti in 1914 was accompanied by the northern relocation of a large section of the Asian community. On the outbreak of war, administrative and departmental staffs were reduced, and missionaries left to become army chaplains. Rinderpest hit the district, plague broke out again, and the cotton crop was jeopardized by falling prices.

During the war years the district administration shrank in upon itself, conserving its limited energies. Plague lessened briefly, to increase again in 1916. Manpower was drained from the district for the King's African Rifles and for battlefront porterage. The capital of those who remained was tapped by appeals for war charities. Development in the district was at a standstill.

Cotton production in 1917 dropped to 2.9 thousand tons. The development decade was at an end. Food shortages were felt throughout Teso; drought hit even the most fertile zones; rinderpest again decimated herds. Epidemics of influenza, smallpox, and dysentery struck the population. Morale was at a low ebb, culminating in the disquiet that spread throughout the district as Europeans were rumored to be about to take over the land.[9]

7. Teso District Annual Report, 1914–15 (TDA XADM/9).
8. Vail, p. 146.
9. It would appear that the people of Teso clearly recognized (as their

The Introduction of Cotton

Whereas elephant herds and cattle had first attracted alien enterprise to the Teso region in the nineteenth century, it was the potential for cotton growing that spurred British initiative in the area at the beginning of the twentieth. In January 1901 Benjamin Crapper, cotton magnate, had pointed out to the Oldham Chamber of Commerce the declining position of the Lancashire cotton trade in the world market. Barely a year later, Kristen Eskildsen Borup, a Danish-Canadian lay missionary, superintendent of the CMS Industrial Mission in Kampala wrote to his London headquarters appealing for funds. The CMS was unable to raise the sum required, at least £3000, and the treasurer brought Borup's letter to the attention of a "remarkable group of men" who combined "philanthropic interest in what was still the 'Dark Continent' with some experience of business."[10] The group was made up of Thomas Fowell Victor Buxton, president of the Anti-Slavery and Aborigines Protection Society and treasurer of the CMS; Alfred Buxton, his cousin, of Messrs. Prescotts' Bank in London; Henry Carus-Wilson, who had spent some time in Uganda; and Henry Edward Millar, managing director of an import and export commission firm. In July 1903 they launched the Uganda Development Company, with a capital of £15,000, of which 10,000 shares of £1 each were offered for subscription. Its directors were Robert Barbour, Justice of the Peace of Chester; the two Buxtons; Millar; Carus-Wilson; and Samuel Hen-

---

responsiveness to rumors about railway expansion, forced labor, and land alienation demonstrated) that much that happened in the Uganda Protectorate reflected the priorities of neighboring "white" Kenya. Further research in Foreign Office and Colonial Office records, along with analysis of Kenya and Uganda as semi-periphery and periphery, would probably indicate that their judgment was not very wide of the mark.

10. Cyril Ehrlich, *The Uganda Company, Limited* (1953), p. 8. Data on the Uganda Company support the contention of Kuebner, Platt, and others that British capital exports were mobilized by small-scale speculators rather than by large London banking houses. The precariousness of the financial undertaking (see J. O'Connor, "The Meaning of Economic Imperialism," 1970) is suggested by the schedule of dividends earned between 1903 and 1927 on £100 invested (Ehrlich, pp. 54–55).

ry Gladstone of Bovington, Hertfordshire.[11] The CMS was willing to sell the Kampala industrial plant to the company on the understanding that mission work connected with the industrial training and education of natives would continue; the directors of the company were in sympathy with the objectives of the CMS. Borup's services were placed at the disposal of the company until such time as the business became remunerative. "The main object of the Company [was] to provide a business-like solution of the 'labour question' in Uganda, and in so doing to make the business pay."[12]

At this point the interests of the CMS, the Uganda Development Company, and the Oldham Chamber of Commerce converged. Cotton, their prospectus noted,

> is found growing wild in Uganda, and a sample recently submitted to a Manchester expert was pronounced by him to have a distinct commercial value. It is intended to make experimental plantings of several of the best varieties of cotton and should these plantings be successful, steps would be taken to promote the growth of the article on a large scale for export.[13]

The first meeting of the board of directors was held five months later.

> In the minutes of that meeting appears an inconspicuous resolution. "(7) That the thanks of the Directors be conveyed to the British Cotton Growing Association for the free grant of cotton seed recently made for the use of the Company" . . . a modest record of an incident which was to determine the future of a country larger than the British Isles.[14]

Cotton cultivation was adopted in the Protectorate for reasons reflecting the special interests of the British government, the Christian missions (especially the CMS), and the British textile industry, respectively. The government wanted a crop introduced which

---

11. William Ewart Gladstone, his relative, opposed the acquisition of Uganda. Kathleen M. Stahl, *The Metropolitan Organisation of British Colonial Trade* (1951), p. 277, names Sir Robert Williams, chairman of William Deacons Bank, as a prominent director. Alfred Buxton later became chairman of the London County Council.

12. Ehrlich, p. 12; Stahl, p. 279.

13. Ehrlich, p. 9.

14. Ibid., p. 10.

would permit its growers to pay their taxes in cash rather than kind; the missionaries wanted to inculcate the work ethic in order to modernize those whom they considered primitive and to clothe the heathens; and the British textile industry simply wanted the cotton. Within the United Kingdom there was a strong opposition to subsidizing imperial ventures. As late as 1903, 84 percent of the Protectorate government's expenditures were covered by United Kingdom subsidies; not until 1915 did revenue meet expenditure. This was entirely due to the opening up of Teso. Between 1906–07 (when seed was distributed only to chiefs in Buganda) and 1911–12 (when cultivation was widespread in Teso) the Protectorate's export figures more than trebled. Cotton, which comprised 9.84 percent of the Protectorate's exports in 1906–07, made up 90.28 percent of its total exports in 1926–27.

Gresham Jones, bishop of Kampala, described how his missionaries, Borup in the west and Purvis in the east, "began in 1904 to distribute cotton-seed among the chiefs." Subsequently, he noted, the cotton of Teso had become "an asset of imperial importance."[15] As early as 1908, Ormsby reported that cotton planted at Kumi and Serere was doing well,[16] and in April 1909 A. R. Morgan, the Protectorate government's cotton inspector, arrived at Kumi on an inspection tour. During the first two days of his stay he examined bags of cotton sent in by Chief Ijala of Ngora and looked over a cotton plot at Malera. He then set out on tour of the district, traveling to Soroti and Atira, into Serere country, and then across Lake Kyoga before returning to Entebbe.

Cotton cultivation, at this time, was carried out on purely experimental lines; each Muganda agent had established in his village model plots ranging in size from one to eight acres. The agents were under the direct supervision of administrative officers at Kumi. By 1910, it was planned, individual cultivation would replace village cultivation, although it was anticipated that some persuasion might be required for this transition. It was "a most difficult matter to get the people to take up a new crop and more especially cotton, as they

15. Herbert G. Jones, *Uganda in Transformation, 1876–1926* (1926), p. 123.

16. Teso District Annual Report, 1908–09 (TDA XADM/9).

cannot see any object, owing to their entire indifference to money matters, in growing anything but food products."[17]

By the following year, four thousand acres were under cotton cultivation in Kumi district. The largest yield came from fields between Serere and the lake at Bugondo, where cotton appeared to thrive in the particularly fine, free-working black soil. But nine months later a different picture emerged. Various seed types had been under trial at Entebbe. A Ugandan cotton seed was used in 1909, a mixed staple in 1910, and in 1911 Sunflower Allen was introduced. Kumi district was used as the Protectorate's laboratory, and reports were not promising. Plots of an Egyptian strain at Serere had not done well, although at Lale the crop was better. The best region remained that between Serere and Bugondo, extending southward to Sambwe. At Soroti, where a nine-acre variety test had been carried out, the results were poor, and on plots along roads from Soroti to Lale and Gweri results were only moderate. The best reports came from Kamolo and Kyere, where five hundred pounds of cotton per acre was obtained. The Kyere cotton had been sown early; but, although the trial plot was one of the best in the district, the general cultivation around the Kyere village was "only fair."[18] Cultivation on large, carefully supervised acreages was clearly superior to that on individual plots. Here the interests of the administration and the missionaries clearly began to diverge from those of the industry. For poll tax collection to be successful and for heathens to become civilized, the encouragement of individual peasant cultivation was desirable, even necessary. For the maximization of profits from cotton growing, plantations or estates that permitted greater supervision evidently provided a greater return from investment. The two were clearly incompatible.

What actually happened in Teso is not absolutely clear to this day. That close supervision of cotton production, if not actual control, was maintained by the administration as late as 1919 is apparent. The government relied heavily on chiefs. The district agricultural officer for fourteen years in Teso, R. G. Harper, wrote force-

17. A. R. Morgan, cotton inspector, "Tour of Serere County," Apr. 1909 (TDA XAGR/7); see also Kumi Station Diary, Apr. 9–12, 1909.

18. Coote (diary, 1909).

fully of what he expected from the administration in a memorandum to Kampala in August 1919. He had just returned from touring the southern part of the district and was incensed by the hasty and careless preparation and sowing of cotton plots. "At this date, and after ten years of instruction," he wrote, "careless cultivation, whether of cotton or foodcrops, cannot be tolerated and should be a punishable offence. Chiefs and sub-chiefs must learn that they have as much responsibility in regard to the cultivation of their areas as they have in collecting tax and administering justice."[19] To remedy matters, Harper proposed that cotton instructors should travel with the county chiefs throughout the region, assuming equal responsibility for cotton cultivation.

There was a great deal at stake. In the earliest days of cotton in Teso, certain chiefs had refused to plant it, and in several areas cotton plots had been rooted up.[20] Although this was no longer the danger by 1919, the demands of the cotton market were rigorous, and Teso's long-stapled cotton could be grown only under the strictest edicts.[21] Planting had to be at an optimum date, so that the first rains engendered germination and early growth and the following hot, dry season the maturation of the cotton boll. The spacing of seed in rows (all other crops were sown broadcast) was imposed by regulation, as was the burning of old plants.[22] Very little peasant initiative was encouraged, and close administrative control was enforced. Since cotton growing conflicted with food crop cultivation—the planting and weeding of peanuts, "grass rains" millet, and late millet especially—sanctions were required to maintain production. Before considering this in the context of the interdependencies that made up the Teso agricultural system (Chapter Nine), the impact of new technology must be noted.

19. R. G. Harper, "Circular" (TDA XAGR/1/no. 8).

20. See, e.g., entries in Kumi Station Diary for Sept. 27 and Oct. 22, 1909.

21. Gartrell (Ph.D., 1979), pp. 387–389.

22. For an assessment of today's disciplined conditions, see Joan Vincent, "Teso in Transformation: Colonial Penetration in Teso District, Eastern Uganda, and its Contemporary Significance" (1978), p. 9.

The Introduction of the Plow

Limited changes in technology accompanied the fundamental social changes in the conditions of production and exchange from precapitalist to peasant commodity production in Teso. The introduction of iron hoes, facilitating the earlier preparation of sun-baked soils, had occurred prior to colonization. The early administration brought Banyoro hoemakers to look for iron in Teso, and the Anglican mission donated £20 to train local blacksmiths; but neither effort was deemed successful.[23] Iron hoes were then imported from England and America.

More significant was the introduction of the plow—not so much for its improvement of agriculture as for its social consequences. An increase in social differentiation is a recognized concomitant of plow agriculture, and in Teso, as elsewhere, the greater involvement of men in cultivation, the development of private ownership of land, the creation of a landless class, even monogamy and tighter control over women's fertility were allied trends.[24] Plows were first made available to Oumo and Ijala, the prestigious chiefs of Ngora and Kumi. The first school was opened at Kumi in 1910, nearby chiefs sending their oxen to be trained. In 1912 two plowing instructors were appointed, and by 1924 there were five; this dropped to three in 1926–27.[25]

The first instructor was the overseer of a cotton seed farm in

23. John D. Tothill, "Ploughing as a Factor in Native Agriculture in Uganda" (typescript, 1935), p. 1, suggests that the CMS received a grant of £20 for training smiths—but Vail, p. 94, states "the Anglican mission donated £20 to train local blacksmiths."

24. See, e.g., Jack R. Goody, *Technology, Tradition, and the State in Africa* (1971), pp. 25–26; see also Ester Boserup, *Woman's Role in Economic Development* (1970), esp. pp. 53–65. In principle, movement occurs away from shifting hoe cultivation, polygamy, and institutionalized premarital sex to plow cultivation, monogamy, and greater control over women's reproductive powers. A longer-term study is required to document this trend in Teso, although field data collected in 1966–1970 would appear to bear it out.

25. Only one appears in the staff list until 1915, and the post is not filled until 1920 (Vail, pp. 94, 98).

Busoga, who traveled with an Indian wooden plow that had been made at the farm, a team of oxen, and a carpenter with the necessary tools for making another plow on the spot at Kumi. Whereas government policy appeared to favor local initiative and what today would be called intermediate technology, the missions, in conjunction with the Uganda Company, initiated instead the importation of British-made Ransom metal share plows.[26] By 1917, the main suppliers of agricultural implements in the two East African protectorates were England, the United States, Germany, Denmark, Italy, and India.[27]

Local chiefs supplied sixteen oxen, which were worked with the Busoga team. These came from Oumu and Ijala, who, in August 1909, had been instructed to buy "cattle" for training. The plowing instructor also toured the district giving demonstrations, and by March 1910 six chiefs (probably six of the seven given cash boxes—Oumu, Ijala, Kamudani, Ocheppa, Juko, Pakalwana, and Kariebi) had purchased Indian type plows, at a cost of Rs.12 for the plow and Rs.3 for the yokes. In April, twenty acres were plowed for cotton at Ngora. Six more Indian plows were sold. The instructor also received a consignment of iron plows (Howard's Invicta) from England; these cost Rs.60, and a European firm in Soroti began to

26. Tothill (MS., 1935), p. 1. William Smith Syson was the local agent for Ransom. A builder's manager, Syson accepted a special agreement on May 18, 1909, to serve CMS as an industrial agent. He accepted a home connection in 1914 and resigned in November 1931. Compare Vail, p. 94.

27. A report submitted by Henry P. Starrett, American Consul at Mombasa, *East African Markets for Hardware and Agricultural Implements* (1917), indicated that the American share in the importation of hardware and agricultural implements in 1917 ranged somewhere between 5 and 30 percent, dependent upon the commodity. No distinction was made between Uganda and British East Africa (Kenya) in the report, but the importance of fostering agricultural development and vehicular transport was noted. The breakdown was as follows:

Building materials:	less than 5%
Cutlery	20%
Fencing materials	20%
Agricultural implements and machinery	30%

The total value of these imports in 1915 was £121,640; in 1916, £334,186. (Statistics on arms and ammunition imports were affected by the abnormal war conditions and were not included in the report.)

import them. In 1912 a plowing school under a European instructor was established at Kadunguru. By 1915, about 100 plows of various kinds were in use throughout Teso district. By 1920 the number had risen to 210, and several ginneries had begun to market them. By 1924 there were 1,000 plows in Kumi County alone, and cash was flowing freely for their repair as instructors on safari carried spare parts. By 1926, *dukas* (Indian shops) were stocking spares in most of the small trading centers.

Development economists tend to be euphoric about Teso's plow cultivation, although they note that it remained "the only sizable and widespread capital investment in Teso farming." Teso, writes Vail, "was unique in Uganda and extra-ordinary in sub-Saharan Africa for the speed and thoroughness with which ploughing became standard practice." Its success he attributed to (1) its appropriateness to Teso's ecology and cattle resources; (2) its capacity to break a seasonal labor bottleneck that was restricting acreage and output expansion; and (3) the development of an "effective input supply mechanism."[28]

Yet, although the industrial manufacturers of Europe and America benefited from the development of this new market, and although the cash flow increased through the widespread sale of plows, cotton production in Teso did not increase, and there were serious long-term deleterious effects. Among these were: 1) loss of soil fertility; 2) loss of social components in labor relations between *gros paysans* and their clients; 3) increasing expenditure on oxen and machinery by the landholding generation with concomitant intergenerational costs (cows were needed for the marriage payments of the young); 4) the aggrandizement of certain individuals at the expense of others and of 5) certain regions at the expense of others.

First, however, let us establish that the increased use of plows did not lead to an increase in cotton production. An inquiry was not made into this matter until 1935, but a clear trend was discernible

28. Vail, p. 92. See Victor Uchendu, *Field Study of Agricultural Change* (1969), p. 32; Victor Uchendu and K. R. M. Anthony, *Agricultural Change in Teso Distirct, Uganda* (1975), pp. 36–39. Plow sales clearly reflected the consolidation of effective administration. While wooded Serere always had fewer plows, by 1929 the northern counties had outpaced the south.

earlier.[29] Between 1923 and 1927 the average yield per acre was 281 pounds. During the same period, plow use increased from 1,564 to 8,816. The reduction in yield was attributed to declining fertility of the soil due to lack of resting and rotation. On the other hand, food crop production (for which the plow was not used) showed no decline. Food crop yields were, however, never systematically measured or estimated, and given that millet, the main staple, was usually planted after cotton in the rotation, one cannot be sure that judgment was sound on this matter. What was certain, however, was that, for the average cultivator, declining crop yields did not lead to a greater acreage put under the plow.

In most places, throughout the period, peasant cultivation remained the standard mode of operation, with the plow a somewhat expensive implement, leading as it did to erosion and the rapid impoverishment of good land.

The total plantings of cotton in 1923—245,000 acres—were less than one acre per capita, little more than twice that grown *under compulsion* when the crop was first introduced. But what had become apparent was the large acreage of cotton cultivation by the few and, as we shall see, the lack of land use by the many.

The Development of Small Towns

"Like the rabbit produced from a conjurer's hat, the ramparts of the town identify an enterprise not an entity," and the internal class relations of towns mirror the complex processes of political and economic change.[30] Agrarian society is dominated by the relationship,

29. Teso District Book (TDA VADM/5/6). See also C. C. Wrigley, *Crops and Wealth in Uganda* (1959a), pp. 19–22, and Vail, pp. 70–77. For a detailed analysis of the ownership, control, and use of plows in one Serere locality in 1966–67, see Vincent (1971), chap. 9, "The Politics of Agriculture."

30. Philip Abrams, "Towns and Economic Growth" (1978), p. 27. On the historical significance of the development of country towns, see Fernand Braudel, "History and the Social Sciences" (1972), pp. 18–20, 24–25, and *Capitalism and Material Life, 1400–1800* (1973), pp. 373–440. With special reference to African economic development, see George C. Bond, *The Politics of Change in a Zambian Community* (1976), pp. 28–30; Charles Good, *Rural Markets and Trade in East Africa* (1970); Peter C. W. Gutkind, "The Small Town in African Urban Studies" (1969); Anders

the antagonism, between town and country, and in Teso this has its roots in the development of small towns at the sites of agents' bomas and mission stations. Foremost of these towns was Kumi, where an urban history documents living conditions on the frontier of colonial expansion. From its establishment as an administrative station, its tentacles reached out to inculcate "law and order," to participate in the development of agriculture first in its own surround and then further afield, to market cotton, and to create a home market. As a center of urban growth, Kumi (and, even more, Soroti afterward) manifested "the social realization of power created in the countryside" it drained.[31] Kumi, the small town, in microcosm reflected the development of the district.[32]

Cotton experts and stock inspectors arrived; porters from Serere, without permission, left. An Entomological Research Committee stayed over in August 1911; German prospectors, Swahili and Arab traders, ivory merchants, and "an Austrian Expedition" passed through Kumi en route to Karamoja. Chiefs came in to the station to receive their hut and later poll tax percentages; officers went out with plows and a harrow (for Oumu). Agents came in to receive measuring poles for cotton plots. Throughout, officers left on safari. Sudd cutting operations were continued in that abortive attempt to establish a channel from Ngora to Lake Kyoga.

Hjort, *Savanna Town* (1979), pp. 3–12; David Parkin (ed.), "Introduction" to *Town and Country in Central and Eastern Africa* (1975), pp. 3–44; Jaap Van Velsen, "Social Research and Social Relevances: Suggestions for a Research Policy and Some Research Priorities for the Institute of African Studies" (1974); Vincent (1971), pp. 85–103, 257–274. In Vincent (1974a), I argued the importance of anthropologists' studying rural politics and the changes that occur in small towns and their *umlands*; but as Clive S. Kessler has pointed out: "We need not . . . argue apologetically that small townships are simply manageable or convenient to us. Because of their own distinctive features and functions, they are themselves intrinsically important, even crucial. The dynamic forces of the great transformations of modern history have for centuries expressed themselves, in various ways, in the opposition or 'cleavage' between town and country" (Kessler, *Islam and Politics in a Malay State*, 1978, p. 247).

31. Abrams (1978), p. 6.

32. The substantive data in the following four paragraphs are taken from Kumi Station Diary (TDA VADM/3/1).

Officialdom was not yet up to bureaucratic ideals; headmen were punished for selling government property; peculation was rife; Ijala (of all men) earned a rebuke for cutting off the ears of an offender. A chief, a subchief, and two readers in Malera were convicted of murder.

All around Kumi the infrastructure of the district grew. The site of an agricultural school was marked out at Ngora by Dillistone of the CMS; district officer Morris approved it. A plowing school was started in January 1910. Medical stores were received "at last," along with a platform weighing machine, which was to be installed in the marketplace. A football match was arranged between the CMS (Ngora) and Kumi. District headquarters defeated the mission two goals to one.

Barazas were held at the end of each month, and chiefs came in from all sides to attend. Empire Day (May 24) was commemorated with police sports, as in British East Africa, Zanzibar, India, and throughout King Edward's realm. On the sovereign's birthday staff and labor were given a holiday. No holidays were taken on Easter Sunday and Monday in 1910 because too much cotton was pouring in and there was too much work on hand. On Christmas Day 1911, Mr. F. H. Newman "presented to police, Station staff and to Indians three bullocks. Merry Christmas." A marketplace was laid out on June 18 and completed on June 30. In between, work continued on a prison and a store. New roads were aligned and grass planted. At the station, cotton, corn, peanuts, and rubber trees were grown. Manure was delivered from Mbale. Chickens were kept. Kumi was taking on an urban quality: on August 12, 1909, an unknown man was found dead near the station; "no local chief or his people able to identify (the) body"; the kinless "wandering man" of capitalism had arrived.

In all these events, local, territorial, national, and global manifestations interrelate: the local big man, the economic development of the Protectorate, the established Anglican religion, national commemorative events, international interests and participants. The development of capitalism engendered the growth of other small towns throughout the countryside. Bomas and catechumenates began to service cotton production, as we have seen, spreading the use of cash and concentrating elements of the dispersed population. Small towns came into being around trading posts—some of which, in Asian hands, had preceded colonial administration in the district.[33] Beside the main store sprang up others, attracting tailors and shoemakers to their stoeps for a wage or small rents. At first these craftsmen tended to be Asians, often poor or newly arrived kinsmen; later Swahili itinerants took their place, or local Africans, promoted perhaps from domestic porterage or work as nursemaids. Nearby the itinerant peanut seller with his tray would set up business in the shade of the tin-roofed stores. As more Asians moved in, fortresslike dwellings, their walls nearly touching, were constructed for their extended families, usually along one side of the road. Gasoline pumps, tearooms or hotels (serving non-African foods and beverages, as well as local African ones), and shops specializing in the sale of cloth, bicycle parts, tin basins, and cheap china began to cluster. Beneath a tree nearby, a wayside barber would set up his chair and mirror, and women traders would spread their cloth "counters" on the ground, on which to build their pyramids of peas and millet, a few bars of soap, small packets of tea, combs, and loose cigarettes. All these items were purchased in small amounts from Asian wholesalers, whose vans, or the bicycles of their African subdistributors, would begin to visit the small town regularly.

When the administration or the mission moved in on the small town it was usually at a short distance from the dukas, the state and the church racing, as it were, for the balmiest hill in the locality. If the boma were established before the trading center, as was sometimes the case, traders similarly set up their shops at a distance—a disquieting matter for early administrators, since, in their eyes, each step of the distance made control more difficult and the exploitation of the "innocent and gullible natives" more possible. Only later did town planners advocate, and with varying success enforce, the spatial segregation of Europeans, Asians, and Africans.

Gradually, as the population of the small town grew, the gap between the (European) boma and the (Asian) dukas was bridged by a ribbon of development along the road that linked them. Immigrant and local African carpenters, potmakers, bicycle repairers, tinsmiths, and sellers of medicine established workshops in their roadside homes to capture passing traffic. In time, hotels and lodg-

33. The following three paragraphs are taken from Vincent (1974a), pp. 263–264.

ing houses began to cluster on the roads at the edge of town at that point where Crown land under local African tenure met the township boundary (within which all building was government-controlled). These thatched huts or tin-roofed shacks, built on the land of indigenous entrepreneurs, were rented by the day, week, or month to single men, migrants, and travelers. A clear indicator of the transformation of the Teso economy was the "de-localisation of the individual" and the "government of migration."[34]

Throughout Teso, town growth was controlled by ordinances that regulated the siting and structure of housing and set out mandatory sanitary arrangements.[35] A request for Teso trading centers to be declared townships first occurred in June 1912, following complaints from residents about unsafe living conditions in Gondo.[36] At that time Kumi had a population of around 3,000 Africans (with 2 Europeans and 24 Asians) and Ngora 8,000 Africans (10 Europeans and 23 Asians), while Gondo's African residents numbered 5,000 (8 Europeans and 10 Asians).[37]

The establishment of district headquarters at Soroti in 1914 (along with the shift from water communication to rail that followed) brought about the decline of the small country towns and trading centers, except in the north, where the Asian commercial frontier advanced. By 1924, only four of the 1912 townships were still recognized as such: Kumi, Ngora, Gondo, and Soroti. Serere was gazetted a trade center, and no other localities were designated urban.[38] The populations of these five were, however, still increasing, significantly not with the expansion of commercial interests, but with what could be termed the laboring poor. Around 20 percent of the population, it will be recalled, were classified as laborers in the census of 1921. Restrictions on cotton marketing (discussed

34. The first term is taken from H. G. Wells, *Mankind in the Making* (1918), p. 379; the second from Heisler (1974).

35. See Thomas and Scott (1935), pp. 77–78, for a review of the Townships Ordinance, 1903, and the Township Rules, 1924.

36. TDA XMSN/1.31A. See also Vincent (1971), p. 42.

37. Communication, Sept. 26, 1912 (TDA XADM/10). There were in Soroti in 1912 no Europeans, 3 Asians, 4 Swahilis, and 4,000 Africans. None of these figures could, presumably, reflect residents within strictly defined town boundaries.

38. TDA VADM/1.

in the next chapter) and on African trading limited the urban opportunities of most of the population. Trading plots were allocated by
race and stalls were rented out at local markets. Crown land rent of
4 s. per annum was collected by township headmen from all artisans—cycle repairers, carpenters, fuel cutters, sellers of milk and
hides, peanut sellers, tailors, matmakers, butchers, potters, brick-
makers, cattle traders, drummers, ropemakers, and washermen. In
1927, trading plots remained unoccupied and African commercial
enterprise underdeveloped.[39]

Regional Differentiation and Underdevelopment

Even as the towns advanced at the expense of the countryside, so
different regions developed one at the expense of another. The years
from 1908 to 1917 witnessed the southern advantage; thereafter,
the economic frontier advanced in the north. Serere, throughout,
suffered relative deprivation.

The stimulus of rail communication upon production and trade[40]
and the mobility of individuals provided, as elsewhere in East Africa, a benchmark between the small-scale opportunities of the paro-
chially encapsulated and the transforming possibilities of those
whose horizons had been extended and whose future appeared
limitless. With the prospect of a railhead at Soroti, new possibilities
were envisaged for the northern counties: ranching and the export
of cattle, as well as the colonization of arable land by landless
families relocated from the south. The world depression of the
thirties and another world war were to intervene before the full
rejuvenation of the north came about; the decline of the west remained irreversible.

Under these conditions, then, differentiation within the population increased more sharply in the south than elsewhere. There
emerged a rural southern population made up of a class of increasingly wealthy landowners and an increasingly impoverished
peasantry. Both the terms "class" and "landowners" are used ad-

39. TDA VADM/5/2.
40. See, e.g., Anthony M. O'Connor, *Railways and Development in
Uganda* (1965), pp. 6–10, 18–19, 41–49.

visedly.[41] In the southern counties land came on the market, as it did not in Serere and the north, and with this family wealth became consolidated. Inequalities associated with the division of labor along with those stemming from the ownership of property began to generate inequalities "not only by the *inheritance* of great wealth but much more by the *accumulation* of modest wealth on the part of those in well rewarded occupations": the salariat.[42] In the south a full range of opportunities was seized for family advancement—partly because of its involvement in Mbale's commercial network, but also because of educational establishments not only on its doorstep but in the relatively close urban areas of Mbale, Tororo, and Jinja. Although the activity fields of an initial generation of southerners may have been essentially economic, over time a multiplicity of activities developed—social, religious and political. Gradually the more fortunate families became more and more closely involved with each other with corresponding incremental benefits to themselves and to their heirs.

Some of the features by which development in Teso might be measured in 1920 are shown in Table 8.[43] The greater population density (143 per square mile) of Kumi and Ngora counties became evident, as did, by 1920, the increasing nucleation around Soroti. Serere's population density of 73 persons per square mile was twice

41. The distinction between land "holders" and land "owners" made by Lloyd A. Fallers, "Social Stratification and Economic Processes" (1964), p. 120, parallels the distinction between "possessions" and "property." Not until land came on the market was the penetration of capital complete. A classic case study of this process is to be found in Frederick G. Bailey, *Caste and the Economic Frontier* (1957), esp. pp. 47–93. See also Vladimir I. Lenin, *The Agrarian Question and the "Critics of Marx"* (1954); "The Development of Capitalism in Agriculture" (1963); and *The Development of Capitalism in Russia* (1974), esp. pp. 71–142; and Bernard H. Slicher van Bath, *The Agrarian History of Western Europe, A.D. 500–1850* (1963), pp. 310–324.

42. Frank Parkin, *Class Inequality and Political Order* (1972), p. 24. Compare Mamdani (1976), pp. 10–11, 42–47, for Buganda.

43. The statistics used in Table 8 are taken from TDA VADM/5.2 and XADM/5.41. An extended analysis of the political implications of uneven regional development is to be found in Vincent (1977a). See also Anthony M. O'Connor, "Regional Inequalities in Economic Development in Uganda" (1963).

Table 8. *Measures of Development by County and Region, 1920*

		Population	Pop. Density	Poll Tax (Shillings)	Cotton Production (Tons)	No. of Bicycles
South	Kumi and Ngora	79,534	143	19,701	1,400	118
	Bukedea	30,477	85	–	–	54
West	Serere	36,659	73	10,622	600	93
North	Soroti	50,726	90	12,561	450	62
	Usuku and Amuria	45,674	35	9,316	350	35
Total		243,070		52,200	2,800	362

SOURCE: Annual Report, 1920. TDA. XADM/9; Provincial Annual Report, 1920. TDA. XADM/5.41; District Book, TDA. VADM/5/2.

that of the two northern counties, Usuku and Amuria. The population of each county in 1920 reflected, to some extent, its ability to support a locally born population and to attract newcomers (through town growth and expanding commercial and wage opportunities). Poll tax collected indicated not only the size of population but the efficiency of chiefs. While the poll tax collected from Serere and the southern counties was proportional to population, that for Soroti and the north was clearly below what might be expected. Cotton production figures and the number of bicycles (taxed) served as indicators of the relative wealth of each county. It will be seen from Table 8 that cotton production in Soroti and the north was considerably lower per capita than in Serere and the south; that of Usuku and Amuria was the lowest of all.

The number of bicycles was highest per capita in Serere in 1920, about half as high in Soroti and the south, and lowest, as could be expected, in the north. Although the figures are not sufficiently reliable to make the calculation of ratios worthwhile, differences between the three regions are, nevertheless, apparent. New hierarchical distinctions began to emerge both between and within divisions. Administrators began to rank the counties according to their development, and a county chief's advancement could be measured by his transfer from Serere to Soroti and thence to Kumi, just as his fall from grace was evidenced by his banishment to economically underdeveloped Usuku county.

Yet, the overwhelming character of Teso's development throughout was the dangerous narrowing of its economic base. A crisis was reached in 1917, and the following decade experienced a decline even in that single commodity, cotton, on which the government, the missions, and the traders pinned all their experience and hopes. Between 1920 and 1927, cotton production in Teso declined from 9.4 thousand tons to 7.8 thousand tons. Counterbalancing this statistic of peasant production is one from which we can infer an increase in wage labor: in 1920, 0.1 thousand acres and in 1927, 21.0 thousand acres are given over to the cultivation of cassava— the crop of the seasonal migrant and a famine crop par excellence.

The Famine of 1917–1919 and Its Aftermath

A final grim indicator of development in Teso lies in its epidemiology and mortality statistics at the end of the "development decade." The interest of the Department of Agriculture was centered primarily on the successful cultivation of cotton and only secondarily on food crops. Fortunately there was little experimentation by the department with indigenous grain seeds in these early years, and it may well be that respondents' pleasure in detailing the characteristics of each of several species of millet and sorghum reflected the incremental importance attached to the slightest differences in growing time, given short fallow and enforced planting dates.[44] Yet, as we now know, cultivation with short fallow tends to give rise to serious famines following upon recurring harvest disasters. This situation was accentuated by government insistence on early planting, which concentrated the total population's planting of grain within the same short span of weeks—an achievement abetted, as we have seen, by the increased availability of stronger iron hoes. Early planting both cut down on the time during which fallow was available for cattle pasturing and made more likely the wholesale failure of cereal crops (since all cereals

44. Respondents in 1966–67 made it clear that more varieties of food crop were grown "in earlier times," and that there was more exchange of seed between different areas.

have nearly the same growing season) if climatic conditions were bad.

But it would be misleading to attribute the famines of 1917–1919 in Teso to vagaries of the climate and deficiencies of agriculture alone. From the turn of the century, at least, the people had been less and less able to fall back upon hunting and gathering to supplement nutritional deficiencies when harvests failed. Prolonged drought had diminished supplies of groundwater and grasses for cattle; but, even more important, restrictions on population movement had prevented herd owners from moving from one pasture to another. Undernourished cattle were then more susceptible to endemic and epidemic diseases. Overgrazing destroyed the balance between arable and fallow, and a concentration of food crop consumers upset the ecological regime. At the same time, among humans, cerebrospinal meningitis became endemic; plague and smallpox were pervasive and venereal diseases on the increase.

Deaths from famine reported monthly to the district office by county chiefs are shown in Table 9. Their aggregation obscures the actual distribution of famine localities but it may be observed that nearly 44 percent of the 2,067 deaths occurred in the most densely populated southern counties of Kumi and Bukedea, those most involved in economic activity and urban living. Soroti, although the administrative headquarters of the district, was as yet only a small town and a mere 7 percent of the reported deaths occurred in Soroti county. Serere, which had experienced considerable concentrations of population as the infrastructure of economic development was established between the Lake Kyoga ports and the southern coun-

Table 9. *Deaths from Famine, January – June 1919*

	Jan. – Mar.	April	May	June	Total
Usuku	48	155	181	40	424
Soroti	30	52	62	--	144
Serere	104	319	168	--	591
Kumi	6	93	188	31	318
Bukedea	35	111	374	70	590
Total	223	730	973	141	2,067

SOURCE: Monthly Reports, 1918–1919, TDA. XADM/6. 18/18. Monthly Reports, 1919–1920, TDA. XADM/6. 34/19.

ties, suffered 26–28 percent of the mortalities according to these statistics. That this might be an underestimate is possible, given that the population of the county declined from 56,170 in 1911 to 36,454 in 1921. The remaining 20 percent of the famine deaths occurred in the north and, given the much larger populations of Usuku and Amuria (both underreported in 1911), the relative isolation of these counties clearly protected them, to some extent, from the epidemics that accompanied "progress." Mrs. Kitching of the CMS at Ngora and District Commissioner Paske-Smith were among the many victims.[45]

Particular events leading up to 1917 brought the crisis to a climax. Because of the war, large quantities of food crops had been planted in 1915, not for home consumption, but for export to the troops.[46] Cotton acreage was proportionately lower, which led the government to require more extensive cotton planting the following season. Excessively heavy rains in 1916 destroyed a large proportion of the standing crops, and output of both cotton and foodstuffs was small. But March 1917 saw an increase of 70 percent over the previous year's acreage (51,500 acres as compared with 34,000): finger millet decreased by 10,000 acres; sorghum by 15,000 acres; peanuts and sweet potatoes by 10,000 acres each. Two successive failures of the millet harvest, the first as a result of heavy floods in May and June 1917 and the second following prolonged drought from January to May 1918, brought widespread food shortages to the district. This left the population reliant almost solely on the October and November sorghum harvest in the north and sweet potatoes in the south. Famine conditions were recognized by January 1919. In the following six months, over two thousand persons died, proportionately more in Serere and Bukedea than elsewhere and more in the countryside than in the towns.

Several factors inhibited individual response to the worsening conditions. The low price offered for cotton in January 1918, a price "calculated to benefit all except the grower,"[47] led to there

45. Teso District Annual Report, 1914–15 (TDA XADM/9).
46. Ibid., 1917–18. "Shortage of Foodstuffs," 1914, 1916–18, 1919, 1919–24 (TDA XAGR/3, 270/14; 390/16; 14; 14/II).
47. Monthly Report by District Commissioner, January 1918 (TDA XADM/6.18/18).

being little cash flow for the purchase of foodstuffs. Asian shop-keepers (in Gondo, at least) hoarded grains to sell later at exploitative prices. The administration stepped in to organize the distribution of lily roots in distressed areas. Hoes were in short supply, and in July 1918 the agricultural officer arranged through P. E. Lord of the British East Africa Company (hereafter BEACo.) to have 10,000 cheap hoes imported. A few months later, Banyoro hoesmiths were again brought across by the administration in the hope that they could instruct local people in the craft; they sold 2,100 hoes at a price in Soroti 20 cents less than that of European imported hoes.[48] But the major contributory factor to the famine was the heavy demand for labor imposed upon adult males throughout the district. So significant is this that it provides the subject of detailed discussion in Chapter Ten. Voluntary labor was unavailable for the ginners, and the government began to supply 1,700 men per month to ginners, missionaries, and government departments on the ground that "all such work is of a public nature and helps forward the prosperity of the District."[49] Army recruiters rounded up over 17,000 men.

At the beginning of 1919 famine relief was undertaken: 300 tons of maize were imported into the district to be distributed by chiefs.[50] The Administration ordered that parish granaries be established, and all households were required to contribute part of their millet harvests in good years. Communally worked plots (*emono*) were established in 1920, and fines were levied on those who did not contribute voluntary labor.[51] Famine relief was also paid for by the people in increased taxes. The poll tax was raised from 5s. to 7.50s. in June 1918. Thus, in spite of the higher mortality and extensive labor service out of the district, revenue from the poll tax in these years rose from £350,560 in 1916–17 to £351,200 in 1917–18 to £344,340 in 1918–19 to £502,332 in 1920.[52] Not until 1924, however, was the district considered to have begun to fully

48. Ibid.
49. Teso District Annual Report, 1916.
50. "Shortage of Foodstuffs," 1919; Monthly Reports by District Commissioner, 1918–19 and 1919–20 (TDA XADM/6.21/17 and 6.18/18).
51. Teso District Annual Report, 1921.
52. Figures compiled from Teso District Annual Reports, 1916–1920.

recover from the famine; its population then was recorded as 213,941.[53] The district's "development" by 1915 had been achieved at the expense of the health and well-being of its laboring population.

Critical as conditions were in Teso at this period, a postscript should be added. We have seen the route of colonial penetration into the district from the south via first Busoga and then Bukedi. Deaths from famine in the Eastern Province during the worst six months were as follows:[54]

Bukedi	23,042
Busoga	5,717
Teso	2,131
Lango	337
	31,227

The creation of a peasantry carried heavy costs.

53. "District Notebooks and Instructions" (TDA XADM/10, 93/13). This was, of course, an estimate.

54. Monthly Reports by Provincial Commissioner, 1918 (TDA XADM/5, 41/18).

8. The Making of a Peasantry

Amid the fluctuations of policy, the colonial period consists, from the economic point of view, of one long attempt to bring [a region's] crops into the modern world, but not her peoples.

> Geertz 1963:48

The statistical correlation between cotton growing and poverty is startling.

> Zimmerman 1972:326

Cotton is, and must remain, a Black man's crop, not a white man's.

> Todd 1927:113

The diffidence of scholars over using the term "peasant" in African studies has a long history. Ken Post, in 1972, suggested that the reluctance of Anglo-Saxon scholars to use the term analytically might be related to their reluctance to use it in the metropolitan country.[1] But there was no reluctance to use the term on the part of British colonial administrators, agricultural officers, or Africans in Teso—the Luganda *bakopi* (peasants) was frequently on the lips of all. In 1927, for example, the district commissioner saw, for the first time since he had entered the country, women working on the roads. This, he thought, ought to be discouraged, citing an old regulation to that effect. At the same time, he observed: "This does not prohibit women from volunteering, as was the custom, to pick cotton or other crops at Government farms (near their homes and on daily pay) or to pick cotton at stores, provided they return home

1. Kenneth Post, "Peasantisation and Rural Political Movements in Western Africa" (1973), p. 223.

each day before dark. Peasant Women in England glean in the fields in the same way."[2]

It is today generally agreed, following Eric Wolf, that a peasantry is characterized by three sets of productive relations: those between the producer and the land; those between the producer and the market; and those between the producer and the state.[3] "It is precisely the characterization of the peasantry in terms of its position relative to other groups in the wider social system which has particularly important explanatory value in the analysis of development."[4]

The agrarian economy of Teso during these years was structured around the district's role as a dependent supplier of a primary agricultural product, cotton, within the modern world system. Since the government's overall concern was with a viable *Protectorate* economy, it is necessary to recognize the place of Teso's small-holding peasant production in this wider scheme of things. As the century passed, Uganda became divided into four economic regions. At the heart lay the developing industrial-commercial lakeshore of Buganda (and Busoga), where industry, plantations, sharecropping, and small-holding coexisted within a diversified economy importing wage labor. To the west lay the "market garden" kingdoms, where arable production for urban markets was accompanied by an outflow of migrant labor. The northwest and northern districts provided the labor force for much of the rest of the Protectorate; both cash crop cultivation and commercial cultivation were restricted by deliberate policy. Finally, to the east and northeast lay the districts (Bukedi, Teso, later Lango) in which the production of agricultural commodities for the export market—primarily cotton and coffee—created monocrop agrarian economies and stable, fairly homogeneous, agrarian societies.

With the decline of cotton production in Buganda—a decline attributed to tenant resistance to landlord expropriation[5]—the Teso peasant small-holding system was born. Its "performance was noted as far away as Westminster where Parliament remarked on

2. Teso District Book, 1927–31 (TDA VADM/5/3.85).
3. Eric Wolf, *Peasants* (1966b), pp. 4–17.
4. John S. Saul and Roger Woods, "African Peasantries" (1971), p. 100.
5. Mamdani (1975), p. 29.

Teso's striking economic success under British tutelage."[6] Statistics relating to Teso's production of cotton between 1909 and 1927 are shown in Table 10.

There are two principal ways of fostering cotton production: on plantations with a considerable outlay of imported capital (as in German East Africa) or on plots of land that remain in the ownership of the indigenous people. The Uganda Company was, apparently, the first to develop the latter system,[7] by which, without the costly purchase of land or capital investment in labor, seed and instruction were given free to growers who were then required to cultivate, harvest, and carry the product to market. The first, and perhaps dominant, feature of such a system is that through it no agrarian upper class develops. The land is owned by those who work it. There is, however, a substantial commercial and industrial class whose power and income is based on the control of processing machinery, storage facilities, transportation, and finance capital. The small-holder, then, can be considered as a worker in an agricultural system controlled by urban financial interests.[8] "The small-holding of the peasant is now only the pretext that allows the capitalist to draw profits, interest and rent from the soil, while leaving it to the tiller of the soil himself to see how he can extract his wages."[9] He is a laborer who happens to control a small piece of land from which he "extracts" his wages.[10] For the grower, the benefits of the system lie in his acquisition of cash for taxes (which saves him selling his cattle) and discretionary spending on "luxury" goods, hoes, plows, clothes (usually made of cotton), and bicycles (used for carrying the cotton to market) among them. This is the system that, in Uganda, has been termed "peasant cultivation."

The Land

It is generally believed that prior to colonization the Iteso practised "shifting cultivation," regularly breaking new land and leaving

6. C. C. Wrigley, "The Christian Revolution in Buganda" (1959b), p. 20.

7. Ehrlich (1953), p. 15.

8. See Teodor Shanin, "Defining Peasants" (paper, International Congress, 1978), p. 24.

9. Karl Marx, "The Eighteenth Brumaire of Louis Bonaparte" (1969), p. 174.

10. Jeffery C. Paige, *Agrarian Revolution* (1975), p. 13.

Table 10. *Statistics of Cotton Cultivation, Teso, 1909–1927*

	Cotton Acres	Raw Cotton Production (thousand tons)	Cotton Yield (lb./acre)	5-Year Average Yield (lb./acre)	Cotton Price to Grower (shillings/lb.)	Cotton Income (shillings)	Cotton Acres/ Total Acres	Total Cultivated Acres (in thousands)	Cumulative No. of Plows	New Plows
1909	—	.5	--	--	--	--	--	--	--	--
1910	5.0	1.1	--	--	--	--	--	--	3	--
1911	12.0	2.8	--	--	--	--	--	--	12	--
1912	14.1	3.0	477	--	--	--	--	--	--	--
1913	33.5	8.8	591	--	--	--	--	--	48	--
1914	35.4	5.7	363	421	--	--	--	--	--	--
1915	30.4	5.5	407	352	--	--	.12	244	100	--
1916	51.5	6.1	265	265	--	--	.24	212	--	--
1917	48.0	2.9	134	260	--	--	.23	208	--	--
1918	45.0	3.1	154	244	.20	24	.22	203	--	--
1919	38.3	5.8	340	214	.15	32	.21	186	210	100
1920	65.0	9.4	325	250	.08	26	.40	161	235	0
1921	47.0	2.4	116	280	.03	3	.21	228	240	25
1922	84.0	11.8	314	284	.30	126	.32	265	282	5
1923	68.0	9.4	307	277	.29	101	.28	245	734	42
1924	87.5	14.0	360	294	.25	120	.33	263	1,700	452
1925	97.5	12.1	287	281	.21	87	.34	291	2,700	420
1926	99.3	8.7	202	263	.15	44	.30	330	2,900	1,556
1927	69.7	7.8	250	259	.21	51	.27	260		231

SOURCE: Adapted from David J. Vail, *A History of Agricultural Innovation and Development in Teso District, Uganda* (1972), p. 146.

the old to revert to bush. Later practice, whereby an extended family or an individual owned a particular area of land and rotated cultivation within it is then attributed to population increase.[11] That this did not occur has already been demonstrated. The key factor in the shift to land as "territory" or "capital" was the monetization of the economy and the immobilization of taxpaying adults. Whether rotated cultivation occurred or whether fallowing became shorter or nonexistent depended upon inequities of landholding and demographic distributions deriving from precolonial (but not precapitalist) trade at the moment of contact. Everywhere, however, land was freely available to the cultivator through the articulation of kin or client ties.[12]

The first codification of Teso's customary land "laws" appears in 1957, prefaced by E. P. Engulu's judgment: "ememeete akiro arai ikisila luikamunitos nakalupo kotoma Teso" (there are no arrangements or laws concerning land in Teso).[13] All Teso became Crown land with its incorporation into the Protectorate in accordance with the Crown Land Ordinance of 1903. The occupation of so-called Crown land was, by customary usufruct title, nearly amounting to full ownership.[14] Title implied rights to cultivate, excavate, build, bury the dead, cut trees, lend, subdivide, and bequeath land or any part of it, but not the right to sell or rent it. A Land Transfer Ordinance (1906) prohibited the transfer of land from native to nonnative without the consent of the governor, and a Registration

11. This assumption lies implicitly behind Vail's discussion of the relationship between social organization and land use (Vail, 1972, pp. 32–38).

12. An account of land acquisition can be found in Vincent (1971), pp. 95–103. In 1921, population density per square mile was: in the north, 35; in Soroti, 90; Serere, 73; Kumi and Ngora, 143; Bukedea, 85. Not until the 1950s was a land shortage felt, and then only in the south.

13. Lawrance (1957), p. 241.

14. Ibid., p. 251; Parsons (1960), p. 25. The protecting government acknowledged "in the most binding terms, the paramountcy of the needs of the native populations. Land occupied and cultivated by natives will be as secure from alienation as if protected by title deeds, and only when the Protectorate Government can show that land can be disposed of without detriment to all reasonable future needs may it be alienated to nonnatives—and that by lease and not by free-hold" (Thomas and Scott, 1935, p. 102).

of Titles Ordinance was enacted in 1924. In Teso most transactions actions of Crown land related to township plots or sites for cotton ginneries and cotton-buying stores. The land of all townships remained the property of the government and was subject to strict control.

The indigenous system contained considerable disparity in the actual size of land endowments, related to whether the locality was heavily settled, to whether migrations might be undertaken to claim land from affines, and to phases within the development process of the domestic group.[15] Whether a Big Man was establishing himself through patronage and distribution; whether a man was a firstborn son; whether family land was to be divided between few or many sons were all factors in the man-land equation. Nevertheless, given these structural and situational contingencies, systematic variation on a regional basis can be discerned.

In the north, the size of the average landholding was greater but the range of differentiation within the population less; in Serere and the southern counties, the average amount of land held by an individual was less but the range of differentiation much greater. Thus, while the average family holding in the north was about 40 acres, that in Soroti 25, and that in Serere and the south 14, a large landholder might have 100–200 acres at his disposal.[16] The advent of colonial capitalism in Serere made of the small landowner a laborer but left the average and large landholder little changed. In the southern counties, on the other hand, the small landholder clung to his land, and over time to less and less land, as population

15. See Meyer Fortes, "Introduction," in Jack R. Goody (ed.), *The Development Cycle in Domestic Groups* (1958), pp. 1–14; and Goody (1971), pp. 21–38. Note, however, the need to escape from the closed system of the original formulation, and hence my use of the term "process" rather than "cycle." For the use of a similar model in peasant society, see A. R. Chayanov, *The Theory of Peasant Economy* (1966), pp. 118–194; Teodor Shanin, *The Awkward Class* (1972), pp. 63–80; and especially the essays of Robert Berkner, David Sabean, and Edward Thompson in Jack R. Goody, Joan Thirsk, and Edward P. Thompson (eds.), *Family and Inheritance* (1978), pp. 71–95, 96–111, 328–360.

16. These estimates are reconstructed from a manuscript entitled "Enquiry into Shifting Cultivation: Eastern Province Uganda, 1951," Appendix I, at the East African Institute of Social Research, Kampala.

pressure led to fragmentation. The large landholder meanwhile was able to capitalize on the market opportunities offered by the introduction of cotton and peanuts as cash crops; to enclose his land; to employ labor from localities outside of the south (especially from Serere, Karamoja, and Usuku); and to purchase land in order to avoid fragmentation. Thus, while the southern counties moved toward peasantization, Serere moved toward a proletarianization of its population. By the end of 1935 (when figures are first available) in Serere over half the adult males were in paid labor, in Ngora and Kumi one-fifth, and in the northern counties fewer than one in eight.

Land Use: Household Production

An overemphasis on land in agricultural production leads to a partial view of the dynamics of agrarian society. Ester Boserup, for example, neglects two aspects of tropical agrarian society that cannot be disregarded in Teso: first, that population growth (the major catalyst of agricultural growth) is *shaped* by colonial interference and, second, that agrarian society is made up only partially of agriculturalists.[17] Nevertheless, her emphasis on the frequency of cropping is important. When attention is focused on the frequency with which the different parts of the area belonging to a given holding is cropped, it becomes apparent that most of the land added to the sown area had previously been used as fallow land, pasture, or hunting ground. This was the case in Teso. The chief effect of agricultural innovation in Teso was encroachment on communal lands used for wood collecting and on hunting and herding lands.[18]

Between 1907 and 1927 agriculture shifted from bush-fallow cultivation to short-fallow cultivation throughout most of Teso district. According to whether primacy is placed on pastoralism or upon arable cultivation, so the shortening of the fallow period at the expense of pasturage variously affected the three zones. In the north, cattle dominated over cultivation; in the south, growing population led to increased arable and later cotton cultivation at the expense of herds. In forested and less populated Serere, where the

17. Ester Boserup, *The Conditions of Agricultural Growth* (1965), esp. pp. 11–36. See also Vincent (1977b), pp. 58–61.

18. The Teso annual hunt was abolished and hunting permitted only under European supervision.

plow was not as widely adopted, large herds were maintained alongside cultivation. With changes in the fallowing period, differences between the regions became more pronounced. Bush-fallow cultivation allows a fallow of six to ten years; short-fallow cultivation allows a fallow of only one to two years, so that the wasteland is invaded by nothing but wild grasses and no land has time to return to bush.

When long fallow is replaced by short fallow, "food consumption usually becomes concentrated on cereals which require a smaller input of labour, but also yield much less per hectare [than root crops] in terms of calories."[19] The main food crops grown in Teso were finger millet (*Eleusine coracana*), sorghum millet, peanuts, cowpeas, sweet peas, sweet potatoes, and sesame. The acreage devoted to each of these crops between 1909 and 1927 is shown in Table 11. The introduction of shorter fallow, the plow, and cotton (as well as constraints on crop exchange) encouraged the cultivation of millet at the expense of other food crops, halting the possible spread of sweet potatoes and peanuts from the south to the north. In a good year, these crops could have virtually eliminated "the hungry month" from the Teso calendar.

Cash demands that could only be satisfied by the growing of cotton increased tensions between cattle-keeping and cultivation.[20] The pastoral and arable economies were not integrated;[21] cattle were grazed on "waste" land on hill slopes or by swamps, where the soil was too eroded or too saline for cultivation. Fodder was not provided, so that cattle contested arable land. Early colonial administration was not sensitive to these interdependencies, and the agricultural practices of the indigenous economies were fractured by departmental edicts. Veterinary officials operated independently of agricultural officers and foresters separately from both. Their requirements were often in conflict to the extent that "improvement" measures were sanctioned by coercion and fines, and indigenous practices were, to a greater or lesser extent, rendered inoperable.

Within the constraints of this directed economy, indigenous re-

19. Boserup, (1965), p. 32.
20. For the reinforcement of this syndrome and its social effects, see Vincent (1971), pp. 179–180, 217.
21. With, e.g., the use of dung for manure or draught oxen for carts (cf. Slicher Van Bath, 1963, esp. pp. 9–17).

Table 11. *Statistics of Arable and Animal Husbandry, Teso, 1909–1927.*

	Total Cultivated Acres (thousands)	Peanuts, Acres (thousands)	Peanuts, Tons Sold	Finger Millet Acres (thousands)	Sorghum Acres (thousands)	Cassava Acres (thousands)	Sweet Potato Acres (thousands)	Sesame Acres (thousands)	Cowpea Acres (thousands)	Maize Acres (thousands)	Plantain Acres (thousands)	Rice Acres (thousands)	Goats (thousands)	Cattle (thousands)	Population (thousands)	Poll Tax (shillings)
1909																
1910																
1911													93	134		
1912													89	116	266	3.00
1913													85	120		3.00
1914													93	137		5.00
1915	244	30.0	85	60.0	45.0	3.0	30.0	3.0	35.0	2.0	6.0	.1	88	133		5.00
1916	212	20.0	182	50.0	30.0	3.0	20.0	3.0	25.0	2.0	7.0	.1	90	158		5.00
1917	208	10.0	48	50.0	25.0	3.0	30.0	3.0	28.0	3.0	8.0	.2	92	156		5.00
1918	203	10.0	45	50.0	25.0	3.0	30.0	3.0	25.0	3.0	8.0	.2	69	158		5.00
1919	186	7.0	57	50.0	25.0	4.0	36.0	1.0	20.0	3.5	.8	.1	69	156		5.00
1920	161	6.0	12	50.0	25.0	0.1	6.0	1.0	6.0	.1	1.5	0	92	172		7.50
1921	228	18.5	2	94.0	25.0	2.5	19.0	7.0	12.0	.7	1.5	.1	94	172		15.00
1922	265	17.5	500	93.0	21.0	3.0	23.0	8.0	15.0	.5	1.0	.1	94	178		15.00
1923	245	14.0	175	100.0	30.0	4.0	14.0	8.0	5.0	.6	1.0		94	202		15.00
1924	263	14.0	89	95.0	25.0	3.0	18.0	5.0	14.0	.5	1.0		56	200		15.00
1925	291	12.0	41	103.0	26.0	8.0	20.0	4.5	18.5	.8	1.2		58	242		15.00
1926	330	19.0	380	109.0	32.0	11.0	30.8	6.5	20.0	1.0	1.3	.1	84	244		15.00
1927	260	20.0	2	96.0	5.0	21.0	38.0	6.8	12.0	2.0	1.3	.5	88	277		15.00

SOURCE: Adapted from David J. Vail, *A History of Agricultural Innovation and Development in Teso District, Uganda,* (1972), p. 146.

sponses took several forms. Because the cultivation of cotton was required by statute of all individual adult males, increased demand led not simply to fragmentation of patrigroup (*ekek*), but to the colonization of new land as well. Both measures led to increasingly dispersed settlement along with recourse to communal work groups (*eitai*). This tended to increase differentiation between rich and poor.[22] Formerly, as one respondent after another stressed, twenty to forty persons had lived together in one large household, along with their livestock, ringed by a stockade of thornbushes. One of the most significant results of colonial rule, if reiteration be a guide, was the breaking up of the large household and the increased individuation of agricultural labor.[23] As the labor process took on different forms in the wider society, so the agricultural production unit changed from a tightly controlled extended household to a more tenuous integument of dependency-related households.

Land Use: Estate Production

Household production of cotton existed in Teso alongside estate production. By 1909 several hundred Baganda—county chiefs, mission workers, and other government agents—had cotton plots, and the first exposure of many Iteso to cotton cultivation was, as David Vail suggests, "undoubtedly on the estates of aliens." He overstates the case, however, when he continues: "The mistake of most students of Teso history is to reckon this a success of independent smallholding farmers when, in reality, it was largely the product of a master-serf relationship between aliens and Iteso."[24] Possibly this

22. Vincent (1971), pp. 191–208. This apparent interdependence—the production of a monocrop that is labor intensive at the same time as the main subsistence crop, with the corresponding labor bottleneck—goes some way toward accounting for the emergence of communal work groups in some regions (e.g., Teso, the Caribbean), but not in others (e.g., Brazil).

23. The increasing atomization of production at the level of the homestead is a clearly recognized part of the process of capitalist penetration. It is, however, necessary to recognize, at a certain phase, that the unit is not a localized corporate domestic group as, e.g., the models adopted by Immanuel Wallerstein, William G. Martin, and Torry Dickinson, *Household Structures and Production Processes* (1979) might lead one to expect, but a *network* of producer-consumers.

24. Vail, pp. 69–70. He produces no evidence to support his claim that more cotton was grown on estates than on small-holdings, and I know of

was what the provincial commissioner had in mind when he wrote of the desirability of sustaining "feudal" and "communal" systems and the need to discourage "individualism."[25] Already by 1913 (as Vail himself notes) the burst in both acreage and production in Teso reflects not only estate production at administrative centers but also substantial small-holder plantings in Serere and the south.[26]

Although the term "feudal" is really not appropriate, Boserup's analysis of agricultural growth is helpful:

> Feudal landlords may well use the labour services of hired labour to clear uncultivated land and set up "home farms" or manors. These may be regarded as a kind of government farm . . . It is pointless to ask whether these manors or these "chief's villages" belong to the landlord in his public or private capacity, since the very distinction between a public and a private sphere implied in this question is alien to the feudal society, at least in its early stages.[27]

In the beginning, compulsory quarter-acreages of cotton were certainly imposed on every household by agents and chiefs; these were, to some extent, the terms of their continued employment. Yet, since enforced cultivation by household units was not the most efficient means of expanding production, in 1913 cotton interests in Lancashire began to grow restless.[28] At the same time, however, S. Simpson and Frederick Spire and other local defenders of the

---

no records that would permit such an evaluation. He is wrong, moreover, in suggesting that this continued until the early 1920s (pp. 68–70).

25. Eastern Province Annual Report, 1912–13 (TDA XADM/5). His concern was more likely to have been with the hierarchical system of tax collection than with production, however, as is shown in the following chapter.

26. C. C. Wrigley (1959a), p. 20. Compare Vail, p. 69.

27. Boserup (1965), p. 84; cf. p. 83: "The salient features of communities with landlord tenure are best understood if the rights of the landlords and overlords are regarded as rights to tax the cultivators"; and Goody (1971), pp. 3–13, who argues strongly that in tropical Africa power rests on direct control over men, not on the appropriation of means of production, especially land.

28. British Cotton Growers Association (BCGA) Annual Report, 1913; Cyril Ehrlich "The Marketing of Cotton in Uganda, 1900–1950" (Ph.D. thesis, 1958), pp. 110–111. Compare the preface to Ehrlich (1953), where similar observations of economists are cited.

small-holder system of production began to discern the peasant's desire for cash as a cotton-growing incentive, an interest the administration did everything to encourage, even by entering the marketing arena. Vail's contention that small-holder predominance became established only in 1916 is based upon a decline in productivity after that date from around 460 pounds to 235 pounds an acre—a decline attributable much more, in fact, to the war and the increased demand for food crops for the troops, as well as to the dislocations in agrarian life discussed in the last chapter.

Not in cotton acreage and production figures but in the labor process lies the resolution of the issue of whether estate or household production was dominant. Whether cotton growing was an occupation (of a minimally prescribed acreage) largely enforced by chiefs or whether it was a voluntary, capitalist-inspired, agricultural enterprise by which a man of initiative could expand his land, acquire plows (and labor), and profit in the market will not necessarily be answered in the same manner for all localities in Teso district.

Cotton production required labor-intensive, sedentary agriculture, and throughout this period parish chiefs were called upon to spend a great deal of time restricting the movements of those resident in their parishes. Nevertheless, considerable variation was to be found in the composition of such parishes, both over time and over the geographical area of Teso. In Usuku, it is clear from the reports, a subchief's village (*mutala*, or parish) was made up of his followers. These, as already observed in the case of Ojotum's parishioners, were considered a corporate body and, for the most part, appeared to have acted as such. Chiefs spoke on behalf of "their people" and acted in their interest. When factionalism arose within a parish it might well be followed by emigration and possibly by prolonged feuding and bloodshed. Women and cattle were the spoils in the ensuing disputes, not land or residence rights—and certainly not plots of cotton.

In Serere and Kumi counties, matters were ordered differently. Although the southern chiefs were more likely to have jurisdiction over local followers than chiefs in Serere and therefore might be thought to have had greater altruistic regard for their welfare, all had around them demonstrations of the advantages to be gained from accumulating land and exploiting labor in the cultivation of cotton. Extensive cultivation and successful harvests at the Ngora mission plantations and at the Department of Agriculture farm in Kadunguru, as well as on the estates of former Baganda agents in these two counties, served as precept. Without any knowledge of how it was done—although we can hazard several guesses— southern and Serere chiefs were reported by 1916 to be *acquiring* land for the cultivation of cotton. By 1924, subcounty chiefs (and, as we have seen, it is significant that it is *this* group of chiefs) were said to earn £700 a year from cotton.[29] At prevailing prices and yields, that figure implies an estate of 100–200 acres and a considerable employment of labor power.

This, again, throws into doubt Vail's view of the process as a shift from estate production to small-holder cultivation. Whether the peasantry was embarking on similar expansion or whether most cotton growing was at this time still largely involuntary is not clear. For many cultivators, cotton would not have appeared to be the most lucrative form of investment—commercial possibilities, service, and crafts were more rewarding—but it would certainly have appeared preferable to the manual labor demanded so extensively. It is clearly necessary to consider whether the same options were open to the peasantry as to their chiefs.

Marketing

Because the cotton producing peasantry was so clearly a creation of the colonial state in Teso,[30] it comes as no surprise that the marketing of cotton involved competition between the state and various immigrant groups for the peasant surplus.[31] A full account

29. C. C. Wrigley (1959a), p. 49.

30. This situation was unlike that in Buganda and those regions of tropical Africa where state formation preceded colonial rule. Cf. Lloyd A. Fallers, "Are African Cultivators To Be Called Peasants?" (1961); Ranger (1978), pp. 102–128.

31. Gartrell (Ph.D., 1979), p. 205. "The new crop has to be produced by men who are, at least, during the early years, not always convinced of its advantages, particularly if it is not a food crop. Moreover, it has to be produced to a consistent standard of quality acceptable in world markets. The conversion to exchange production also involves the establishment of local markets, which not only absorb the new product, but also offer a range of consumption goods which will in turn encourage growers to desire

of the intricacies of the cotton pricing system cannot be given here, but suffice it to say that prices fluctuated enormously for the grower at different times and in different localities depending upon transportation costs and world market prices. The price for unstained cotton ranged from 0.03s. per pound (in 1920–21) to 0.30s. per pound (in 1921–22). The mean year-to-year fluctuation was 36 percent. The incipient crisis in the cotton industry in 1918 led the Protectorate government to intervene in cotton price fixing, and by ordinance establish a price ceiling. But this lasted only ten months, and after its repeal the government was obliged to step in as buyer of last resort. Bullish market conditions and buyers' competition returned in 1922. In 1926 a Cotton Ordinance was passed by which which a variable export tax was tagged to Liverpool lint prices, thus relieving the growers of the fluctuation in prices. Not until 1929, when the effects of the world depression were strongly felt in the industry, did the Protectorate government set up the first Commission of Enquiry into the Cotton Industry of Uganda. Marketing was among its chief concerns.[32]

From the earliest days, Asian middlemen were almost solely responsible for the purchase of cotton throughout Teso. Having bought the crops from African growers, they arranged for it to be transported to the ginneries on the heads of African porters. By 1913, throughout the Eastern Province as a whole, the head load system required half a million porters' loads per season. Demand was heaviest at those seasons when male labor was most needed for food crop production and, within a short time, the administration stepped in to control not only production, but marketing.

During the first cotton season after the establishment of district

---

cash and then continue to produce the cash crop. Hence the role of the trader becomes central to the process of development" (Ehrlich, Ph.D., 1958, p. 14). This development—the development of a home market—did not take place in Teso (see Anne Martin, *The Marketing of Minor Crops in Uganda*, 1963); hence analysis in terms of underdevelopment rather than development.

32. Uganda Protectorate, *Report of the Commission of Enquiry into the Cotton Industry* (1929). See also Edward A. Brett, *Colonialism and Underdevelopment in East Africa* (1973), pp. 237–265; Ehrlich (Ph.D., 1958), pp. 184–220; Vail, pp. 84–85.

headquarters at Kumi, markets were held from January to July.[33] After a three-month interval, buying again began in November, peaking in January and ending in March. During this five-month season cotton was purchased at Agora port, Kokolyo, Magoro, Gondo, Lale, and Sambwe, as well as at Kumi. In October 1911 buying began again at Kumi, the district officers traveled out in November to open markets at Agora, Gondo, and Sambwe. Sales peaked again between December and February, and the Gondo figures actually overtook those of Kumi. This time the buying season lasted well into July, although in the last two months the crop was purchased mainly from cotton growers in the outlying districts of Toroma and around the two ports of Lale and Gondo. After this ten-month buying season, a record crop of 9,814,037 pounds was harvested and sold.

The Kumi District Book records the purchase of cotton on January 27, 1910, by "Allidina" (actually Allidina Visram's agent in Kumi) and later that year by Hiralal, on behalf of the BEACo. Another Asian buyer was Tandu Ram. The agents of Max Klein and Banstead Bros. can also be presumed to be Asians, since most European buyers were mentioned by name: Lea Wilson of the Uganda Company, H. Wright, and Schultz and Postman of the German Ginning Company at Mbale. One entry refers to "Saidi," who bought nineteen loads of cotton at Rs.2.50 per frasila (i.e., 35 pounds) on March 7, 1910; he was possibly an Arab or Muganda trader. A great deal of selling and buying must have bypassed the district headquarters altogether, since many growers took their cotton directly to Asian dukas; others sold it to traders in Mbale, Jinja, and northern Busoga.

In 1911 the cotton output of the district was reported to be 2,800 tons, of which exactly half came from the two areas closest to headquarters, Kumi and Bukedea. Six hundred tons were purchased in Serere, 450 tons in Soroti, and 350 tons in Usuku. So abundantly was the cotton "simply pouring in" that buyers from Mbale and Jinja found themselves with too few rupees in their pockets. As a stopgap, the administration stored the cotton brought in by Chiefs Oumo, Ocheppa, and Kamasairi (for which they had been prepared

33. The account that follows was compiled from the Kumi Station Diary (TDA VADM/3/1).

to receive a payment of between Rs.3 and Rs.3.65 per frasila) until cash arrived in the district. On hearing this, the management of BEACo. sent a letter guaranteeing all cotton purchased by their agent, Hiralal, at Rs.5.50 per 100 pounds. The district officer wired a reply that this was of no use to the native who required cash. He also observed that the price offered was too low "at current Jinja rates" and wired the provincial commissioner at Jinja to request that transport be laid on to move the cotton to the market there. On February 16 all cotton buying stopped, since there was no more room to store it. Bukedea growers were instructed to take their cotton directly to Mbale. Nine days later, the market was opened at Gondo. Allidina Visram fared better in the cash shortage than Hiralal, for on February 18 the District Office received instructions from the Treasury at Kampala to pay him Rs.10,000 so that he could continue to purchase cotton in the district.[34] Visram was the biggest buyer in Teso for several years, storing cotton there and exporting it gradually. In September 1912 it was reported that he was beginning to ship the bulk of it from Gondo, to which port it had been carried the fifty miles from Kumi. Twenty thousand bags of cotton that he had purchased were, it was estimated, still stored at Kumi.[35]

The ad hoc arrangements to avert crises in 1911 led the administration toward greater control over marketing. As advocated by Hesketh Bell, "properly appointed markets" had been set up since 1909 at which cotton could be sold (and nowhere else). These markets were inspected by administrative officers, and at their discretion alone they were maintained. The cost of marketing was placed upon the growers, who were obliged to transport their cotton to these authorized marketplaces.[36] The considerable distances covered stimulated the sale of bicycles throughout the district: the 362 machines of 1911 rose to 1,000 (800 in the hands of natives) by 1913.[37]

34. The importance of specific Asian firms in the Protectorate's economy and their privileged position vis-à-vis the government has been suggested by Mamdani (1975) and (1976), pp. 65–119.

35. *Uganda Herald*, September 1912.

36. The account that follows relies heavily on Ehrlich (Ph.D., 1958), pp. 90–129; cf. R. R. Ramchandani, "Asian Contribution to the Uganda Cotton Industry" (paper, Makerere University College, Kampala, n. d.).

37. Teso District Annual Reports, 1911, 1913 (TDA XADM/9).

In 1913, fifteen centers were in operation: thirteen legally proclaimed market places and the BEACo. ginneries at Ngora and
Gondo. The markets were large enclosures containing stalls erected
by the buyers. No dues were charged, but all buyers had to be
licensed in order to erect stalls.[38] Later interpreted as a government
attack on free entry into the marketing side of the cotton industry,
licensing was not a deliberate first step. The administration's intent
was to protect the grower from exploitation by middlemen. It is
important, therefore, to discover who the purchasers of licenses
were and whether there existed, in fact if not in principle, restrictions that discouraged any of the population from believing
themselves eligible.

Teso district officers took upon themselves fairly stringent control
of markets because they felt that "there would be keen competition
among ginners and petty Indian and other buyers," and that
"speculative middlemen" would increase their difficulties.[39] They
therefore proposed restricting market days to one to three a week,
depending upon the size of the center. To make the most of the
limited staff available to them and to limit the numbers of buyers in
all markets they advocated a system of controlled auctions. When
the Department of Agriculture successfully opposed this suggestion,
the local officers maintained that the interests of the growers had
been sacrificed to those of the traders.

From this point on, the policies of the Teso administrators began
to clash with the agricultural policies of the Protectorate. The administrative officers saw themselves as guarantors of fair play for
the native. When their interference was questioned by the director
of agriculture in a letter to the provincial commissioner, the District
Office claimed that the communication was "tainted with inaccu-
rate statements and charges and animosity."[40] Especially resented
was the argument that district officers should have nothing to do
with the price at which cotton was sold, for the need for them to be
involved was, they felt, demonstrated daily. On one occasion, for
example, seventy-one buyers crowded a market center. The district

38. Various licenses (TDA XFIN/5.113). By 1927, market stalls were
had only at auction (TDA VADM/5.2).
39. Ehrlich (Ph.D., 1958), p. 106.
40. Monthly Report, August 1913 (TDA XADM/6.14). See also Ehrlich
(Ph.D., 1958), pp. 96–97.

officer, concerned at the "great amount of undetected fraud considering the class of buyer and class of seller," intervened. Three buyers were prosecuted for cheating.[41] The district officers regularly took it upon themselves to inform buyers of fluctuations in cotton prices reported from Kampala and to suggest to growers the minimum price they should accept. They attempted, in effect, to undermine the key principle upon which entrepreneurs in peripheral market areas could successfully operate. This early period of capitalist initiative required a diaspora of agents spinning a web of trade connections across widespread localities, using a knowledge of price differentials, a closed language, and skills in bookkeeping that were far in advance of the local peoples. In eastern Uganda, as elsewhere in East Africa, Asian traders excelled.[42]

Far from accepting any admonition for their behavior in controlling market prices, the administrative officers congratulated themselves upon their achievements. "It is evident from what the Director says that the natives have reason to congratulate themselves on a successful season . . . for they would not have obtained the good level prices which were realised had they not been assisted by the Administrative Officers."[43] More cotton than ever was grown the following season, and with the district officers holding the ropes, there was little that buyers could do but accept the restriction on profit.

The district officers voiced open dislike of middlemen while advocating the protection of both growers and ginners, particularly the local ginners—who "should be able to buy direct and pay *full prices* to the native growers without the intervention of any middlemen."[44] Since the ginners were, at this time, entirely European and the growers African, the attack appeared to be directed at the Asian entrepreneurs. Nevertheless, since buyers employed local Africans

41. Ehrlich (Ph.D., 1958), p. 96.

42. Compare Abner Cohen, *Custom and Politics in Urban Africa* (1969), pp. 1–22. See also Robert G. Gregory, *India and East Africa* (1971), Ramchandani (paper, n.d.).

43. Monthly Report (TDA XADM/6.14).

44. Ibid. The *Uganda Herald* of Mar. 14, 1914, reported that "any Indian with Rs. 100 to his name" could and did buy cotton, so that ginners were, that season, obliged to pay as much as Rs. 9 to obtain any cotton at all.

to drum up custom, African entrepreneurship was also stultified. Further, while apparently protecting the immediate interests of the cotton growers, the administrative crackdown on middlemen also served to close any possibility of higher prices being offered by ginners in Teso. It has been suggested that there were indications of an incipient combine between ginners and buyers in Teso as early as 1913. If this were so, it could be argued that, whereas individual peasants could not have held out against an illegal price-fixing combination, skilled middlemen might have been able to do so. Although "minimum prices were on occasion exceeded in competition on the spot . . . for the most part all buyers bought alike at one price which was the lowest the sellers would accept."[45]

The director of agriculture was himself subject to direct pressure from the governor (now Sir Frederick Jackson) and indirect pressure from vested interests at home in Britain. Almost immediately after the district officers' intervention in the market, the British Cotton Growers Association (hereafter, BCGA), which was linked to the BEACo. began to put pressure on the Colonial Office. The association's Annual Report of 1913 contains the passage:

> Representations have from time to time been made to the Association that Government officials were interfering in the local buying price for cotton, and also that unnecessary and harassing restrictions were being made as to markets, the number of buyers, etc. The Council fully recognise that these officials were actuated by the best of motives, but it was considered advisable to draw the attention of the Colonial Office to these allegations and also to point out that it was dangerous, and certainly very undesirable, that Government officials should interfere in what are mainly commercial matters. The main policy of the Association is that the native producer should be paid the highest possible price, and the Council are convinced that in Uganda there is sufficient competition to ensure this.[46]

At this point war intervened, and world cotton prices collapsed completely. For over six months growers found it practically impossible to sell their cotton. Being unable to store it effectively, they tended simply to neglect the crop, uproot it, and even burn it. Buying did not start again until February 1915, but heavy rains fell

45. Monthly Report.
46. Quoted in Ehrlich (Ph.D., 1958), p. 110.

in March before even a quarter of the crop had been marketed. Porters were drawn off for war service; food crops were grown for the war effort instead of cotton; and prices fell from Rs.9 to Rs.2.[47]

At this point, too, the BCGA entered into the buying and ginning of cotton in Teso on its own account, perhaps because of the increased flow of cotton to the Bombay mills as the result of the wartime dislocation of sea routes to Britain, and the increased interest of Indian companies in ginning in Uganda.[48] The existing marketing scheme with its multiplicity of market centers began to fold as the BCGA negotiated with two Teso firms, the Bukeddi Company and the German firm of Hansing and Company, to take over their companies.[49] Teso growers immediately felt a lack of markets in upcountry areas.

One of the few places where competition between ginner-buyers had always been highly localized was the Lake Kyoga port of Gondo, where both the Bukeddi Company and the BEACo. ran large gins. In 1915 the market opened on February 2, and during the first week only the Bukeddi Company bought, at a price of Rs.4 per 100 pounds, over 200,000 pounds of cotton. On February 15, BEACo. started buying at Rs.3 per 100 pounds, which was quickly raised to 3.50 to get a share of the cotton; the Bukeddi Company by the second week had dropped its price to 3.50. Buying began again on March 10. The BEACo. started at Rs.6 per 100 pounds but was quickly obliged to raise its price in the second week to Rs.6.50, the price offered by the Bukeddi Company.

Although the two companies were in minimal competition—the price as likely to be lowered by collusion as raised through competition—the Bukeddi Company turned to a different ploy. It began to distribute burlap bags along the roads so that growers could bag their cotton properly for transport to the ginneries. The BEACo. buyers then did the same. Rivalry was now manifested between the company porters, as they attempted to drum up custom en route to the ginnery. Fights broke out and (much more important in the eyes of the Department of Agriculture) cotton was soiled and

47. Vail, p. 146.
48. Mamdani (1975), p. 32.
49. Because the German company had been taken over by the government, this was a fairly straightforward matter.

wasted as it was transferred from the growers' bundles into the bags. Waysides were littered with dirty cotton and pieces of *byai* grass with which the bundles were tied. The agricultural officer stationed at Kadunguru spoke to the two managers, and the practice stopped.

During the 1918–19 season, competition was again rife at Gondo; the BCGA had by this time acquired the Bukeddi Company's ginnery. The BEACo. started buying at Rs.7, BCGA at Rs.10. The BEACo. then increased its price to Rs.12, and both ginneries bought at this price until the end of the month. At that time the BEACo. received instructions to reduce the price to Rs.7, which obliged it to drop out of the market until April, when the BCGA plant broke down.

By 1918, the BCGA controlled most of the cotton market in Uganda. At the end of the war, the Protectorate government proposed to undertake the purchase at a fixed price of all cotton grown. As prices recovered, however, the ginners rejected the government proposal and its marketing scheme dropped. But the government did intervene to promulgate an ordinance whereby it alone fixed the price to be paid to growers throughout the Protectorate. Local repercussions were felt, as middlemen made quick and easy profits by paying the government-controlled price to growers and then immediately selling at higher prices to the ginners. Rival buyers risked fines to entice growers with gifts of salt and cigarettes. The government stepped in again, this time restricting buying to ginners. Its goals were twofold: still to eliminate "undesirable elements" in the industry but also, now, to encourage the building of upcountry ginneries.[50] Not only did this further constrain Asian and African enterprise—the Asian members of the Uganda Cotton Ginners Association had protested the measure[51]—but, even more important, town growth in the district was immediately checked. In Gondo, for example, a pioneer industrial center with a sizable population (much of it alien to the district), systematic town planning had just

50. Ehrlich, (Ph.D., 1958), p. 126.
51. Asians "voiced the interests of the African growers and middlemen, and it was through the marketing side that the Africans could have developed that commercial sense to climb the next rung of the ladder and enter the ginning side" (Ramchandani, pp. 10–11).

begun when the new cotton promulgations were issued. Not only did the number of applications for plots of land at Gondo decrease, but many previous applications were withdrawn.

Cotton in Teso in no sense provided a basis for the emergence of a large stable middle class (as development theorists would put it) or for the acquisition of capital in more than a few hands, as did cocoa in the Gold Coast or coffee in Tanganyika. Throughout the world, cotton growing is associated with poverty. A black man's crop, not a white man's,[52] it is carrying parochialism too far to contend that "the parts of Uganda which are evidently the richest are those which have felt the impact of cotton."[53]

Cotton has long been one of the least rewarding cash crops for the peasant cultivator. Crawford Young has described cotton as one of the "lumbering oxen that draws Uganda's chariot of development";[54] yet, as far as Teso district is concerned, this particular lumbering ox has been stuck in the Teso mud for almost seven decades. The marketing of cotton as a cash crop brought the Teso farmer no further economic advancement after 1924. Profit did not lead him to increase his acreage, grow cotton more intensively, weed more thoroughly, or pick more opportunely. The nature of land tenure; soil erosion; poor marketing facilities; lack of investment capital for sprays, carts, weeders; banking conservatism; and rural insecurity—all contributed to this. Those who profited in Teso were those who invested their efforts in cattle trading, fishing, cash crops other than cotton, and, above all, education for their children. The range of goods stocked in the shops—shops that were few and far between in Teso—widened little after 1924. Any cash that was made from cotton and that was surplus to the bare necessities of life went for taxes, licenses, and, more rarely, school fees. Cotton as a cash crop for the peasant did little more than take care of that part of his divided world that related to the surplus or rent demanded of him by the urbanized political class of the country. Cattle provided

52. John A. Todd, *The Cotton World* (1927), p. 113.

53. Ehrlich (Ph.D., 1958), p. 1.

54. M. Crawford Young, "Agricultural Policy in Uganda: Capacity in Choice" (1971), p. 141. The argument that follows is taken from Joan Vincent, "Rural Competition and the Cooperative Monopoly" (1976), pp. 94–95.

a social and religious asset in the local arena, millet a social and political asset; but cotton was singularly a crop of governmental penetration, and one that was superimposed upon, not incorporated into, the Teso agricultural cycle. Cotton was the farmer's rent to government to be left alone.

Such would not have been the case, of course, if the profits from marketing Teso's cotton in the world market had been relayed down to its rural areas. As it was, the bulk of the profits went to overseas companies and to the electrification of Kampala.

9. Laboring Men: The Making of a Rural Proletariat

> I think that something in the nature of inducement, stimulus or pressure is absolutely necessary if you are to secure a result that is desirable in the interests of humanity and civilization.
>
> Joseph Chamberlain

> To separate labour from other activities of life and to subject it to the laws of the market was to annihilate all organic forms of existence and to replace them by a different type of organisation, an atomistic and individualistic one.
>
> Polanyi 1944:163

More crucial to the transformation of Teso than the introduction of cotton and its enforced cultivation was the effect of colonial administration upon the exchange of services and the allocation and distribution of labor. Contrary to first impressions, it was not the introduction of a cash crop that brought the Africans into the modern world system but the involvement of their labor. *The process required the creation of a rural proletariat.*

We have seen how "the labor problem" underlay the acquisition of the CMS industrial mission by the Uganda Company in 1904. The advantage of peasant cultivation of cotton rather than plantation agriculture lay in the hidden costs of labor.[1] From its beginnings, Teso's labor demands were always inordinately higher than elsewhere in the Protectorate. By 1910 they had already reached such a peak that missionaries hoping to hold open air services around Ngora were unable to get more than a few people together "owing to the constant occupation of the men, and women to some extent, in the cultivation of cotton, clearing of roads and other

1. Compare Vail (1972), p. 104.

Government work."[2] Touring the district in April, the government cotton inspector, A. R. Morgan, reported seeing "men as well as women work in the fields sunrise to sunset without ceasing."[3] This perhaps was not surprising at that time of the year. In April, the wettest month, finger millet, peanuts, and, in some places, sorghum and sesame were planted. For the cultivators Morgan saw in the fields, the compulsory planting of cotton, backed by fines and beatings, was a severe additional burden.

The severity of conditions in Teso led Bishop Tucker of the CMS to request the acting governor, A. G. Boyle, to look more closely at forced labor throughout the Protectorate. His first communication on the matter, of December 20, 1909, was prompted by a reading of the governor's report "The Cotton Industry of Uganda," wherein it was noted that not only was forced cultivation of cotton required in "the early days," but that cotton was still being grown under compulsion—and practically the whole crop in Bukeddi. "The fact is," the bishop asserted, "the feudal system is being run for all it is worth in the matter of labour in Uganda and the cultivation of cotton is no exception to this rule."[4]

Tucker itemizes seven forms of compulsory labor that he had observed in Teso:

1. Labor for traders
2. Labor for government work
3. Roadmaking
4. The bridging of swamps
5. The cultivation of cotton
6. The building of rest houses for government officers
7. The cultivation of large tracts of land at camping
   places for food.

Here spelled out is the human energy harnessed to Teso's development decade.

2. Arthur L. Kitching, Annual Letter, Nov. 10, 1910 (CMS Archives G3.A7/o, 1907–1915).

3. Agricultural general (TDA XAGR/1.G). For an account of his experiences in Teso as a cotton inspector, see A. R. Morgan, "Uganda's Cotton Industry—Fifty Years Back" (1958).

4. Bishop Tucker to Acting Governor, Dec. 20, 1909 (CMS Archives G3.A7/o); Hesketh Bell, "The Cotton Industry of Uganda," no. 62 of November 1909. It is not possible within the context of this study to

The bishop was given somewhat short shrift by the acting governor as far as forced cotton cultivation was concerned. Most of the other forms of compulsory labor were already causing official concern, and the worst of abuses were in the process of being removed. "With regard to the cultivation of cotton," Boyle replied,

> I think that the Government stands very largely *in loco parentis,* and just as primary education is obligatory in England, so I consider it is also our duty to educate the native in such agricultural pursuits as we consider will in the end enable him to improve his general condition and obtain those additional requirements which the march of civilisation demands. It is on that principle that I am of the opinion that it is still necessary in many parts of the Protectorate for the chiefs to continue to exercise their influence over their people in the way of getting them to cultivate cotton.[5]

The bishop and the governor, like most officialdom in the Protectorate at that time, assumed that chieftainship in Bukeddi was similar to that in the centralized kingdom of Buganda. They differed in that whereas Boyle desired to do away gradually with what he

---

provide a detailed account of the organization of the labor process, but such a study is forthcoming.

5. Boyle to Tucker, n.d., no. 144/09 (CMS Archives, G3.A7/o, 1907–1915). His position was, in a sense, defended even forty years later by that most liberal of colonial governors, Sir Philip E. Mitchell, who in his reminiscences, *African Afterthoughts* (1954), p. 98, recalled that

> The Governor [of Kenya] was persuaded to issue a circular instruction to the officers of the District Administration which told them in plain terms that they must not use compulsion to induce the natives to go and work on the farms of the new settlers, but that the natives must yield to persuasion and in fact go.
>
> The officers who received these and subsequent orders in the same sense naturally interpreted them to mean that they were required to use compulsion if necessary, but must not be found out. . . . They may well have held varying views as to whether compulsion in itself, openly used, was or was not justifiable in their own interests in the then condition of the mass of the people. After all, *the most severe and uncompromising compulsion had been used to get the first cotton planted in Uganda*; and who, looking at Uganda today, would say with assurance that it had not been in the long-term interests of the people? [Emphasis added.]

considered a feudal but indigenous and traditional system, Tucker felt that the evils of the system had been allowed too free a rein. His prime concern was the depopluation of the Protectorate, which he attributed to forced labor conditions.

Forced Labor for the Government

The poll tax placed upon the Teso native, whether of Rs.3 or double that amount, was the least of his taxation burdens: forced labor was a great deal more onerous during this early period. Two kinds of regular, unpaid labor were required of every adult male in the district. *Kasanvu* (a Luganda term meaning seven thousand) was introduced in Buganda in 1909 and thereafter adopted in other districts: it required one month's work from every able-bodied man every year and was in force in Teso from 1909 until 1922. Its introduction meant that for some fourteen years the labor market in Uganda was no longer open to the free play of supply and demand.[6] The second form of compulsory labor was known, again by a Luganda term, as *luwalo*. This involved an obligation to perform one month's unpaid labor for the local authority. Although it was unpaid, luwalo was regarded by the people as less burdensome than kasanvu because luwalo was usually performed near a man's home. He was also, it was suggested by respondents, working at something he understood; and it was supposedly a practice "sanctified by long tradition."[7] Although this may have been true of Buganda, it was not of Teso. Other factors might have accounted for a preference there, if in fact there were preferences. First was the chief's inability to sanction luwalo in certain parts of the district, especially in the early days. Related to this was the ability of astute men to cooperate with local chiefs when they were under immediate pressure from their superiors, a cooperation that could be used later in bargaining for personal advancement. Finally, and again related, as it was the more mature man who was able to bargain in this way, the fact that a villager pressed for luwalo labor could delegate part of his task to his wife (or wives) and sons—an impossibility in the case of kasanvu—meant that the indigenous hierarchy of work could be

6. Philip G. Powesland, *Economic Policy and Labour* (1957), p. 18.
7. *Uganda Notes*, July 1919, pp. 72–80.

brought into play for roadmaking as well as for agriculture.[8] (See Table 12.)

Nevertheless, luwalo was the system in which less accounting was done to higher authorities, and so consequently it was the system more open to abuse by agents and chiefs. In brokerage between government and people, the chief had a great deal of freedom of action. At no time during this period does one hear of chiefs representing the people or being loved by their people. Client chiefs had, after all, in their careers thus far exhibited considerable adroitness to survive and ambition to prosper. The introduction of luwalo into Teso society, where no man had such God-given rights over another, was for them a golden opportunity. The institution having been introduced, only the government agents and the district officers were in a position to affect how it was applied—apart from those who fled from it. Authority had of necessity to be delegated to chiefs, restrained by civil service rules. However flagrant their malpractice might be thought, without evidence action could not be taken against them. Practically, and realistically, given the newness of British administration, evidence was recognized as adequate grounds for fining or dismissing a chief for abuse of luwalo privileges only when there was much else to be dissatisfied about in his performance as well.

Table 12. *Distribution of* Luwalo *(compulsory unpaid labor) by County and Region, 1935*

	Total Luwalo Labor Force	Paid Labor Force	Population Not In Labor Force	Total Population
Kumi	13,426	3,047	3,258	19,731
Serere	3,733	4,928	339	9,000
Amuria	13,004	2,427	1,936	17,367
Soroti	7,657	3,378	2,020	13,055
Kasilo	3,452	2,812	118	6,382
Ngora	6,804	2,593	–	9,397
Usuku	9,266	961	1,508	11,735
Total	57,342	20,146	9,179	86,667

SOURCE: Luwalo labour, TDA. XLAB/2.65/33–35.

8. This practice was deplored by the District Commissioner even as late as 1920 (Monthly Reports, 1926–27, TDA XADM/6.107).

It is impossible to say, on the basis of either recorded testimony or oral history, how widespread abuses were. Evidence exists of forced labor being exploited by men of authority; there is also evidence of district officers taking action against exploiters. In April 1911, for example, the government agent at Malera, Sulimani, was discharged for conscripting twenty laborers from each subchief in his area and putting them to work on his own food and cotton plots. In his defense, he argued that he had intended to pay them later but, at the time, had no cash.[9] Although the Reverend Arthur Kitching commented favorably on agents as "go-betweens," doing good work, he noted that they were not highly paid. As a result, "a few have been unable to resist the temptation to get rich in a hurry and have combined with unscrupulous chiefs to practice extortion on peasants, who are too much afraid to make complaints to the British officials."[10] The extent to which chiefs could, in effect, check the activities of agents by reporting them to touring officers increased over time as more areas were brought under closer control. Possibilities for Baganda exploitation were comparatively short-lived except by those who remained from the freebooting days of Kakungulu and the last few who were retained after 1920. The latter were the most rigorously correct civil service employees in Teso at that time; only by such behavior would they have been retained in spite of growing opposition to the principle of employing agents at all. More blatant than the exploitation of labor by agents was that by chiefs, especially those at the lower levels of the hierarchy.

Construction Works

In indigenous Teso, where settlement was dispersed and the only commodity moved any distance from place to place was cattle, there were no roads. Tracks through the savanna grasses and passages through the sluggish waters of the sudd were adequate for the communication needs of interlocked communities. Conquest and exploitation brought roads to Teso, and as they served primarily military needs and only secondarily economic ends, the roads were

9. Kumi Station Diary, Apr. 7, 1911.
10. Arthur L. Kitching, *On the Backwaters of the Nile* (1912), p. 31.

straight and direct, unlike the caravan routes that explored the countryside through which they passed. Villages grew at regular intervals along the imperial roads, clearly located even today at the resting places of head porterage. Travel on foot or by hammocks slung from the shoulders of porters distributed the trade centers and aggregated a sector of the population.

The introduction of cotton brought modern transport to Teso. Although it was too little, as the district officers constantly pointed out, for the adequate development of a marketing system, such transport as there was nevertheless required good all-weather roads. In the first phase, the greatest mobilization of Teso labor was for head porterage. In the second phase, when *hamali* (porter-pulled) carts, bicycles, and later trucks were in use, public works on the roads—making them and maintaining them—was the major use to which labor, compulsory and "free", was put. The ubiquitous rivers and swamps, which required the construction of bridges and causeways at frequent intervals, and the diurnal rains, which flooded and washed away the road surface, involved labor gangs for most of the year and for many years. Roads and causeways began to link villages across swamps, but many were abandoned after a few years because they could not be maintained. The rains and the swamps, heavy and persistent, wiped the map clean. Although road building was needed to open up the country, keeping the country opened was much more difficult.

For a period of some twelve years, this task brought together in paid and unpaid service almost every Teso male as he reached adulthood. The shared experience of gang labor might well have created a class-consciousness such as that other routine aspect of life, peasant landholding, might never do. Conditions of labor service, therefore, bear inquiry.

The Kumi-Gondo road provides a case study.[11] Once the major caravan route passing from Mbale to Kabermaido and the country north of Lake Kyoga, it was inevitable with the creation of a new district out of the old Collectorate in 1909 and the location of its headquarters at Kumi that this trade route to the small port of Gondo would become the major artery of the developing district. An early administrative map of the district shows that this was so. Construction was begun on the stretch from Gondo to Serere in

11. The substantive data in the case that follows were taken from the Serere County Book (TDA VADM/13/1).

August 1915, since in that month—"the month of full stomachs"—
it was anticipated that food would be plentiful and there would be
no problems in maintaining the laborers. (As it was, rinderpest
broke out at Atira, Gondo, and Kadunguru in August and plague at
Gondo three months later.) By March 1916, 13.9 miles had been
completed, but not without repercussions in the surrounding countryside. On safari, District Officer E. D. Tongue discovered that the
population had been moving out of the country in considerable
numbers ever since. Most were adult males emigrating to Busoga
and Bunyoro; none of this had been reported by the chiefs. Mulangira, Gondo's chief, who had facilitated the work of pioneer
catechists in the area, was dismissed for inefficiency. (Mulangira [or
Oluga, to give him his Ateso name] had been gazetted in 1913 and
had been of considerable assistance to Coote on safari in 1909. In
Serere lore, he was one of the leaders responsible for "letting in the
Ganda." His dismissal was one of a number reflecting the changed
needs and expectations of the district's administration.)

In March 1916, 100 porters ordered to the Department of Public
Works fled after a few days into the neighboring counties. Chiefs
were ordered to arrest and punish them severely by impounding
their cattle. One of the runaways, Etidau, sought sanctuary at the
Mill Hill mission in Ngora—"following the not unusual custom of
the inhabitants of Serere County, he ran away and evidently came
to you," was the acerbic comment of the District Office, demanding
his return.[12]

The heavy rainfall of 1916 slowed up construction on the road
and also meant low food crop production and poor cotton for the
families of the construction workers. The poor health of Serere
residents came to the attention of the administration in this year
when 75 percent of Serere recruits for service with the King's African Rifles were rejected on medical grounds.[13] In September, a
European foreman was temporarily appointed to supervise the road
construction, and a few months later his infant son died of smallpox in Gondo—one of 239 fatalities. The road was completed that
year.

The metaling of trunk roads connecting chief centers with ports

12. "Education of the Natives, Missionary Work, 1913–15," Mar. 29,
1916 (TDA XEDU/3.109/13).
13. Eastern Province, Annual Report, 1916 (TDA XADM/5).

proceeded apace. The Kumi-Ngora-Agu road was completed and opened to the public, as was the Soroti-Lale road. Three miles of the Serere-Gondo road were metaled and a mile-long raised causeway built over the swamp at Kamod. A metaled road linked Kumi with Kapiri on Lake Bisina. Piers were completed at Agu, Gondo, and Lale. Those at Sambwe and Kagwara were left unfinished due to a lack of foremen.

Along what was now distinguished by the title of the Sambwe-Ngora Canal, recently surveyed by Lieutenant Buckler, Royal Navy, of the Busoga Railway Marine, side channels had been opened to Agule and Gogonyo in Pallisa county. Between two and three hundred men were employed each month to keep the canal open, enabling a ten-ton lighter to reach Ngora's port at Agu. Thirty tons of cotton were shipped a month, but this was a mere fraction of what was waiting in storage. The BEACo. used specially constructed punts; mission and administration canoes plied the canal. A large marine operation was mounted in February 1919 whereby a fleet of of canoes was organized to ferry *bigole* (water lily roots) from Lake Bisina to the shores of Serere county, where food shortages were extreme. Given the fact that much of the famine condition there was due to the excessive conscription of labor for roadworks, the irony of its relief lay in the alternative mode of transport by water.

Road haulage was not, however, superseded by the canal. Agu's facilities were quite inadequate for the needs of the cotton firms, and August and September regularly found 38,000 porters engaged in relay from center to center.[14] If the total population was, indeed, around 220,000 in 1911 (with an estimate of one in five as adult male) this figure suggests the mass mobilization of labor that cotton transportation involved—and the massive dislocation of agriculture, especially planting at the onset of the second rains in September. Under such conditions, women's field labor may well have increased. Since the month of full stomachs was usually a period of local feasting, visiting, and ritual commemorations of one kind and another, social life in the countryside must also have been severely disrupted.

14. Monthly Report by District Commissioner, September 1914 (TDA XADM/6.18/18).

The rate of pay of porters was fixed according to mileage. According to the district's annual report:

> the cheerfulness and rapidity with which [porters'] short stages are accomplished are the subject of favourable comment from all those who visit the District . . . the aversion of the Teso [sic] to this form of employment is rapidly diminishing. Even in the cotton season when the greatest strain occurs porters (whole distance ones) preferred to carry their loads to Gondo than to the nearer ports in order to obtain the additional money.[15]

The contradictions of head porterage and cotton cultivation were keenly expressed by Harper, the district agricultural officer. Thus, early in 1915 he deplored the fact that, in spite of cotton having been grown for five years, head porterage was still the main form of transport. Moreover, porterage was most in demand in the best cotton-growing areas, Serere, Kumi, and Bukedea.[16] Yet, when Serere was the only county not to achieve a satisfactory production, the causes were thought to lie not in labor demands, since "in cotton cultivation the whole family and not merely the able-bodied men work," but in the inadequacy of chiefs and the withdrawal of agents. Serere was adjudged "the county which has the chiefs of least influence . . . and the most unsatisfactory peasantry."[17] In spite of Harper's concern, the availability and low cost of labor discouraged firms from introducing other forms of transport, although ox wagons were introduced by the Uganda Company on four stretches of road (Kumi-Mbale; Gondo-Serere-Kyere; Kumi-Agu; and Lale-Soroti). The administration sourly noted the damage that wheeled vehicles did to the road surfaces and did nothing to encourage the innovation.

Organized resistance to forced labor in Teso led some chiefs to go

---

15. Teso District Annual Report, 1919 (TDA XADM/9). This seems hard to believe. Porters were paid 2 pence a day at a time when poll tax was 80 pence per annum and a cow cost 800 pence (i.e., £3.6.8).

16. Monthly Report by District Commissioner, June 1914 (TDA XADM/6.14), and again, Monthly Report by District Agricultural Officer, March 1915 (TDA XAGR/1.47).

17. Monthly Report by District Commissioner, April 1913 (TDA XADM/6.14).

in fear of their lives, but the usual recourse of the population was simply to move away.

Voluntary Labor for Private Enterprises

There are no accounts of working conditions at Teso's ginneries in the early modern period.[18]

Local respondents in Gondo found it difficult to divorce ginnery working conditions from those of the steamship company building the pier or the administration carrying out the infrastructure of the township. Where possible, those in the vicinity of these operations retreated into the bush and, as a result, labor had to be imported into the district.[19] The considerable discontent among laborers was easily quelled. As a contemporary observed: "Civilised countries need not think that they have the monopoly in labour disputes and strikes: for here among the semisavages of darkest Africa, such incidents are not uncommon. But here is a very simple remedy which, when threatened to be applied, often nips the strike in the bud: I refer to the *kiboko*"(a whip made of hippopotamus hide).[20]

It has been suggested that little purpose is served by distinguishing between labor for public works and labor for private employers in colonial possessions during this period. "Since other industries have been introduced with the sympathy, if not the assistance of the Government, official measures for obtaining labour do not discriminate between public and private employers."[21] Thus, in 1917, a draft of 1,700 men per month was raised by the administration to supply ginners, missionaries, and government departments. It was argued that "all such work is of a public nature and helps forward the prosperity of the District."[22] On the other hand, it must be observed that labor for public works was, superficially at least,

18. Inquiries into the cotton industry repeatedly stressed bad working conditions, housing, and food.

19. Vincent (1971), pp. 69–70.

20. *Uganda Herald*, Oct. 12, 1912. The communication came from J. Mackertich in Gondo.

21. Ida C. Greaves, *Modern Production among Backward Peoples* (1935), p. 112.

22. Teso District Annual Report, 1917–18.

under some form of administrative supervision, good and bad; private firms, like mission stations, while serving as redoubts from the oppressive measures of chiefs, were subject to their own forms of labor exploitation.

The Government of Migration

The small-holding agricultural system of Teso required the immobility of its population. As it was, not simply cotton production but tax collection and labor recruitment, too, suffered from population movement.[23] On his tour in 1913, the provincial commissioner (Frederick Spire) issued a directive:

1. It is the duty of the District Officers to discourage migrations.
2. A chief who encourages migrations is not fit for his post and will not long retain it after such conduct has come to the notice of this office.[24]

Barazas were held in Ngora, Soroti, and Gondo, and identical instructions were passed to both Teso and Lango districts. District commissioners must ensure that chiefs cooperated in the return of migrants: chiefs whose migrants were not returned were authorized to cross into the neighboring district to fetch them.

For chiefs this was a matter of some moment, since not only was promotion advanced by good performance in mobilizing labor, but income was derived from per capita taxation. Yet, in Teso society many sectors of the population were, by virtue of their primary occupations, very mobile. Pastoralism, trading, fishing, and, to a lesser extent, bush cultivation all required a certain amount of individual and group mobility. Bakenyi fishermen, for example, maintained networks of kin and affinal ties that extended around the eastern shores of Lake Kyoga and crossed numerous administrative boundaries. Banyoro and Basoga similarly came and went between western Teso and their lacustrine homelands, while Iteso pastoral

23. On the critical importance of population control, see Heisler (1974), esp. pp. 46–62 and 89–102. The following six paragraphs expand an argument presented in Vincent (1977a), pp. 146–147.
24. "Migration, 1913, 1915–24" (TDA XNAF/3.21/13, 15).

and inheritance patterns called for the movement of cattle and personnel over wide areas. The avoidance of taxation, cash-crop cultivation, and forced labor was thus readily articulated with existing migratory patterns. For certain periods of the year or in localities where heavy demands were made, young men were prone to "visit kin" elsewhere, returning months later when the hue and cry was over. This the administration had cause but not power to prevent. County touring books suggest the magnitude of the problem. Characteristic entries read as follows.

> A Musoga headman has been found in the district, collecting tax from Busoga removed from his country into this district. The removals are not of recent date and the practice is an objectionable one.
>
> . . .
>
> Some of the removals to Busoga have been traced by DC Busoga. 97 removed, of whom 24 were Ganda and Soga. The County Agent for Serere who is concerned with the collection of tax for non-natives of the district has been instructed to report and discourage immigration of Basoga.
>
> . . .
>
> May 1913. ADC Lango and DC Kumi agreed that chiefs should come to locate their men. The Kenyi emigrants in the Kelle region planted cotton so as not to be returned to Teso."[25]

Between May and October 1916, correspondence between the district commissioners of Busoga and Teso was related to fifty-seven Bakenyi and forty-two "Teso" emigrants pursued by their chiefs (twelve bore Ateso names; thirty appear to have been Basoga and Banyoro).[26] The Teso district commissioner attributed his problems to the greater effectiveness of his administration. "Border-hovering," he noted "continues to be a fairly popular pastime with the people and but little abatement can be looked for until administration on both sides of the boundary is approximately identical."[27] By October 1916 he was beginning to see the end of the road: "the

25. Extracts are taken from Monthly Reports by District Commissioner, 1912–13, 1915–16 (TDA XADM/6.14), and "Migration, 1913, 1915–24."

26. "Migration, 1915–24."

27. Annual Report by Provincial Commissioner, 1916 (TDA XADM/5.98).

fact that the Bakenyi are now being drawn for labour from all the four districts of the Province will be of great assistance in checking any further tendency to emigrate."[28] Not until the administration of Lango, northern Busoga, and eastern Bunyoro was as efficient could a concerted effort be made to prevent Teso's citizenry from leaving. The problem was aggravated for Teso by the fact that the neighboring regions were areas of marginal administrative returns. Hence no prompt action on the part of Lango and Busoga district officers could realistically be expected. A step toward conformity was taken in 1913, when a new poll tax ordinance was proposed that would bring the three districts into line—the tax in all being raised from Rs.3 to the level of Busoga's, which then stood at Rs.5 per annum.

Yet, by March 1916 the district's poll tax revenue had actually decreased, and a loss of Rs.13,079 was being attributed to emigration. Not until the following year was the stabilization of Teso's taxpaying population finally achieved, largely through the coercive efforts of local chiefs and the heavy penalties they were empowered to inflict. Chiefly powers at this time were enormously magnified, yet the men of Serere especially voted with their feet. They did not, however, join the labor forces of Buganda and Jinja; rather, they formed colonies in Bugerere, northern Buganda, Busoga, and Lango, where they could hold land with minimal interference and, as resident aliens, move easily to escape the tax collector's net.[29]

Taxation, though similar to forced labor in that it is an obligatory payment to a sovereign power, differs in one important respect. Taxation leaves some freedom of choice and initiative to the individual; labor drafts do not. Conquest societies, it is suggested, move inexorably to the imposition of poll taxes.[30] As a direct form of taxation, the poll tax tends to inhibit economic development and foster class exploitation. The poorest in the society have little recourse but to "withdraw from production into flight," vagabondage, brigandage, banditry—or to the anonymity of towns.[31] This impulsion, and the efforts to counteract it by the chiefs, was

28. "Migration, 1915–24."

29. Field notes, Serere, 1966.

30. M. J. Macleod, "The Sociological Theory of Taxation and the Peasant" (1975), p. 3. He is summarizing the argument of Gabriel Ardant, *Théorie Sociologique de l'Impôt* (1965).

31. Macleod, p. 5.

more advanced in Buganda and Busoga, where capitalism first entered, than in Teso; nevertheless, it created those wandering men of the Protectorate economy, many of whom ended up in Serere and the southern counties, further cheapening the cost of labor there.[32]

Migrant Wage Labor

Although no land in Teso was alienated for plantations, recruiters from other districts were able to enter the district. In May 1912, 400 men were taken to work on the Chiko estate in Busoga; the wage they were offered was Rs.3–4 per month. Others were employed at the Mabira Forest rubber plantation in Busoga.[33]

By 1913 kasanvu had been in operation sufficiently long, and sufficiently effectively, for several Teso natives to seek contract labor outside the district to escape it. In Teso, voluntary labor was hard to find. The arbitrary nature of a chief's powers at the local level may well have been a deciding factor for many young men. Since a similar trend was occurring in Busoga and Buganda, "a miniature boom" in plantation agriculture, due primarily to an influx of planters from England,[34] began to effect Teso. Competition for labor forced up the wage rate.

For those subject to the triple yoke of labor demands within Teso—forced cotton cultivation, a month's supply of labor for chiefs, a month's labor on public works for the government—to work on plantations in Buganda and Busoga might, indeed, appear relief. The Teso administration of course discouraged plantation recruitment, and where it occurred (a reflection of policy contradictions at the Protectorate level) it was strictly controlled.[35] Nevertheless, although permanent emigration was slight, seasonal or occasional migration slipped the record.

Military Conscription

A potentially more radical form of labor mobilization in these years was military conscription, which occurred first as frontier

32. See Hobsbawm (1964a) pp. 34–63; Vincent (1974a), pp. 268–272.
33. Miscellaneous correspondence with Provincial Commissioner, 1912 (TDA XADM/10.A)
34. Mamdani (1976), p. 53.
35. Miscellaneous correspondence with Provincial Commissioner, 1912.

expeditions within Uganda required porters[36] and subsequently as large-scale recruiting was instituted after Britain's entry into World War I. In September 1914, five hundred Teso porters were recruited and sent to Mombasa for military service in German East Africa. About 5 percent of them died. The balance returned in April 1915, after nearly eight months away.[37]

It was generally accepted by all colonial powers that some forced labor was necessary for military service. In Teso there were few volunteers, and the recruiters were prepared to take unorthodox measures to fill their quotas. An incident in April 1915 suggests that that there was little the young men could do to escape the draft, and those who intervened on their behalf were made to regret it.

On April 3, 1915, the S. S. *Stanley* arrived early in the morning at Gondo.[38] A noncommissioned officer was put ashore with instructions to look for Nubians and other likely recruits in Gondo while the steamer went on to Lale. He brought in four recruits, all Bakeddi ginnery porters. When Lt. E. A. G. Snell, the officer in command, returned with the ship to Gondo he was told that a Mr. Flesch, manager of the Bukeddi Company ginnery, had marched down to the lighter at two o'clock that afternoon with between a dozen and twenty porters armed with sticks. At that time they had taken no action, returning at five that evening with another white man and a *babu* (an Asian). They had then forcibly released the recruits, assaulting five of the steamer's crew in the process.

Flesch described the press-ganging. As the *Stanley's* crew came ashore, the ginnery porters had fled into the bush to avoid capture. Nevertheless, the four "recruits" had been struck down with sticks and tied together with a rope around their necks. The disruption of the afternoon's ginning had brought Flesch to the scene. All the bazaar had witnessed the action, and not for the first time. Some seven weeks previously, one of the ginnery clerks had been taken in a similar manner, with Europeans intervening to set him free and

36. Kumi Station Diary, Oct. 16, 1910.
37. Teso District Annual Report, 1914–15.
38. The account of this incident is taken from Secretariat Minute Reports (SMP) filed with correspondence in Native Affairs (Miscellaneous) (TDA XNAF/9); SMP 4429 (1915); Lt. E. A. G. Snell to Staff Officer, Bomba, Apr. 4, 1915; Mr. Flesch to District Commissioner, Soroti, Apr. 4, 1915; Flesch to Manager, BCGA, Jinja, Apr. 4, 1915; District Commissioner, Soroti, to Flesch, May 28, 1915.

being insulted by the recruiting gang as they did so. One of Mul-angira's men (he was still, then, chief at Gondo) had bribed the recruiters Rs.5 not to be taken; others had been less fortunate. To the manager of the BCGA at Jinja, Flesch gave more details. "There is no European control in Gondo," he complained, "so these Sou-danese [Nubians] are completely master of the place when they come here." In the April incident, forty porters had run away into the bush. Flesch was apparently less well equipped to deal with the recruiters than P. E. Lord, of the BEACo. ginnery, who, it was said, always carried a revolver and a knife in his belt.

Perhaps because it was wartime, the cotton industry was not in the forefront of the government's thoughts for the first time since the district was established: Flesch was court-martialed, charged with assault and interfering with troops in the execution of their duties. On May 28 he was found guilty and sentenced to a year's imprisonment with hard labor, a sentence commuted to a fine of Rs.400 or three month's imprisonment without hard labor.

A large-scale recruiting campaign was conducted at Soroti in October 1916. Every chief was instructed to send in to district headquarters 10 suitable men. There is no way of knowing, except on the basis of oral evidence, how the men were chosen, but a large number were rejected as medically unfit by the Military Labour Bureau and sent back on foot to their villages. The rest were drafted as porters to the front, since it was held that "Teso men were medically unfitted for Carrier Corps."[39] Another drive in May 1917 drafted 3,850 men, supplemented by monthly drafts of 1,100. Res-ident aliens did not escape: in July 1918 "twenty young Baganda for military service [were] collected in Serere County."[40] A total of 17,762 draftees were gathered from all counties of the district ex-cept Usuku. Of these, 13,321 (75 percent) were rejected as medi-cally unfit. The remaining 4,441 were sent to Mjanji in Kenya, but there a further 1,722 were rejected for medical reasons. In sum, 2,719 Teso men (15 percent of those rounded up locally) were sent to the front in Kenya and German East Africa. By May 1918 one-fifth had been either killed or repatriated.[41]

39. Monthly Report by District Commissioner, October 1916 (TDA XADM/6.14).

40. Monthly Report by District Commissioner, July 1918 (TDA XADM/6.18/18).

41. Teso District Annual Report, 1917–18.

This massive effort on the part of the administration aroused a violent reaction in all the affected counties. The wife of the chief at Kachumbala was murdered in May; and three months later an identical assault was carried out in Kumi, where Chief Oumo's wife was killed. The assassins were caught and executed publicly at the boma in Kumi.[42] Violence everywhere was immediate and direct, meted out quickly and forcibly by native and official alike. The final and most devastating result of the military drafts was the introduction into Teso of cerebral-spinal meningitis, brought by the returning carriers. By mid-1918, 674 deaths had been attributed to this disease. First reported at Gondo, and believed to be plague, it was diagnosed correctly in April 1917. By May there had been 29 deaths in Gondo alone, and further outbreaks developed. By March 1920, over 750 deaths had been attributed to it.

The return of a soldiery to the countryside often has radicalizing consequences. In Teso, the administration took precautions: it arranged that repatriates should be given jobs, many of them as askaris (watchmen) at ginneries, since "they could not be expected to return to their old status."[43] A somewhat self-serving proposition, this suited ginnery owners and government alike. Labor was still difficult to obtain and control in these years, and district officers might well have feared the impact of such men on disaffected rural areas. In ginneries they would be not only fully employed but continually under European or Asian supervision.

Conclusion

In this and the previous two chapters, an account has been given of transformations in Teso's economy until the year 1920. The development decade saw the introduction of cotton and the emasculation of precolonial arable, pastoral, and trade interdependencies. Labor was diverted from local and regional domestic economies to the world market system. The population declined; the colonial presence on the ground diminished.

42. Ibid.
43. Monthly Report by District Commissioner, April 1919 (TDA XADM/6.34/19). This recognition suggests that diversification of labor within the household was, possibly, well under way as a result of the diversion of males into wage labor. But there is as yet no field data to support this suggestion.

There would appear to have been in Teso between 1909 and 1920 conditions for the making of a rural proletariat. That this would have been more likely to emerge out of the labor process than out of production and marketing processes engenders a contradiction. The alienation of labor involved only one sector of the population. Thus, while males over the age of eighteen were obliged to maintain compulsory cotton acreages, to perform compulsory labor services, and to serve (many of them) out of the district in military drafts, the majority of the population—women and children—remain tied to small plots of land within a nonexpanding domestic economy.[44] The costs of reproduction within the capitalist economy were largely borne by these domestic households.[45]

The household remains geared in this economy of nascent capitalism to the petty capitalism of a cattle-bridewealth system.[46] To acquire a household, an adult male had to acquire a wife through the transfer of cattle from a group of his kinsmen to a group of hers. The main cog, as it were, in the economy of social reproduction thus remained an element virtually ignored by the cotton-centered capitalist economy that was transforming Teso. Reliable accounts of fluctuations in cattle transfer are lacking for this early period of Teso's history, but it is known from a later period that bridewealth became inflated to sixteen or twenty head of cattle, and that there was imminent danger of marriage being delayed for young men. Given the unrest that resulted, the government intervened to impose a mandatory bridewealth of five head of cattle in spite of the opposition of chiefs and local councillors.[47] The point I would make here, however, is that although the control of cattle and, ergo, of

44. Compare: "At first, capital subordinates labour on the basis of the technical conditions in which it historically finds it. It does not, therefore, change immediately the mode of production. The production of surplus-value—in the form hitherto considered by us—by means of simple extension of the working day, proved, therefore, to be independent of any change in the mode of production itself. It was not less active in the old-fashioned bakeries than in the modern cotton factories" (Karl Marx, *Capital*, 1967, vol. 1, p. 310).

45. See Burawoy (1977), esp. pp. 1050–1054.

46. For an account of bridewealth in Teso, see Vincent (1971), pp. 120–125.

47. Lawrance (1957), p. 202.

women and sons was in the hands of the older generation, and although there was strict government control over the movement of the rural population as a whole, there was little likelihood of the emergence of a discrete laboring class—or of laboring class consciousness. Not until there is some evidence that the laboring class has *reproduced* the conditions of existence of the system can one be more definitive.

It could further be argued that, until domestic units cut themselves free from the enveloping bonds of kinship, clientage, and communalism—themselves, by this time, shields against the pressures of capitalist development—the emergence of class was unlikely. That some, apparently, began to do so allows me to speak, in the next chapter, of nascent class. Elsewhere around the globe, the capitalist trajectory can be traced through the emergence of female-headed households; sibling households; lodgings for itinerant males; female domestic service; stem family inheritance; changed food consumption patterns, and so on. Data is lacking, until a later period, to document this in Teso. Nevertheless, as elsewhere, it is not only to the structural transformations of the poor, to the insulating adaptations of the common people, that we look for the emergence of class in capitalist society. Class formation requires the arbitrary closure of household units; the manipulation of family and inheritance; and the control of access to privilege. Here, this early period of Teso's history serves us better.

10. Nascent Class
in the World Economy

> Social potential has become the private power of the few. . . .
> The Labour of the many transforms itself into the *capital*
> of a privileged few.
>
> Rius, *Marx for Beginners*

> Sociologists who have stopped the time-machine, and, with a
> good deal of conceptual huffing and puffing, have gone
> down to the engine-room to look, tell us that nowhere at
> all have they been able to locate and classify a class. They can
> only find a multitude of people with different occupations,
> incomes, status-hierarchies, and the rest. Of course they are
> right, since class is not this or that part of the machine, but
> *the way the machine works* once it is set in motion—not
> this interest and that interest, but the *friction* of interests—the
> movement itself, the heat, the thundering noise. . . . Class
> itself is not a thing, it is a happening.
>
> E. P. Thompson, *The Poverty of Theory*, p. 85

> History is not order. It is disorder: a rational disorder.
> At the very moment when it maintains order, i.e., a structure,
> history is already on the way to undoing it.
>
> Sartre

This chapter attempts to address itself, head on, to two crucial issues in the transformation of Teso economy and society between 1890 and 1927: first, the emergence of class structures within the district and, second, the way in which class interests, within Teso society, themselves contributed to the shaping of development and underdevelopment. The discussion, therefore, is in terms of nascent class consciousness and class struggle, in spite of the short period with which this study is concerned and the small numbers involved.

In the larger framework it would certainly be possible to argue the class dimensions of the modern world capitalist economy, in which Africans, generally, as labor, confront European (and, in Teso, Asian) interests. Certainly the inculcation of ideologies (tribalism, racialism, even, perhaps, pastoralism) relates to aspects of consciousness along these lines. That the African people as a whole did, indeed, represent the laboring class within the imperial political economy has been clearly recognized by a succession of scholars. In 1929 Sydney Haldane, Lord Olivier distinguished three periods in colonial policy. The first was Trading—especially slave trading, which he called White Commercial Capitalism; the second was Colonization: Colonial Liberalism aiming at justice and humanity in relations with "colored" people. The third involved exploitation through the "development" of territories; this he called White Commercial Capitalism exploiting colored labour in Africa. He concludes, "practically the whole of our recent colonisation in Africa . . . has been essentially capitalist colonisation . . . financed by European syndicates and investors, and the active directing work of it done by men and women who go out as landowners or farmers or employers and organisers of labour . . . the labour of native black men."[1] Similarly, Ida Greaves noted that, generally, imperial relations with tropical countries did not take the form of colonization and settlement; rather, commercial interests brought indigenous populations under the imperial flag.[2] The African laboring class was clearly part of the European perspective.

The oppressive and exploitative features of the state lay not within the colonial territory but within a larger imperial system. Thus, agricultural production was interlocked between one colonial "estate" and another; troops from one area, India, were used to suppress revolt in another, Uganda. The system itself was embedded within a world political economy, as the African peoples' experience with cotton makes only too clear. A more useful approach, therefore, lies in what Fernando Cardoso has called "the movement of structures within the dependent country," the emergence of social formations. "Who are the classes and groups," he asks, "which, in the struggle for control of the reformulation of the existing order . . . are making a given structure of domination historically viable or are transforming it?"[3] In Teso the answer clearly is the chiefs, especially county and subcounty chiefs, comparatively few in number but outstanding in privilege. And yet, their role in the class

1. Olivier (1929), pp. 56–57.
2. Greaves (1935).
3. Fernando H. Cardoso, "The Consumption of Dependency Theory in the United States" (1977), p. 16.

struggle is far from unambiguous, and the outcome of the confrontations occurring in Teso between 1920 and 1927 cannot be simply explained in terms merely of productive and market forces.

The Material Condition of Teso Chiefs

The exploitative nature of the chiefly class that grew up in Teso between 1890 and 1927 is a matter of record.[4] Some idea of the gap that was opening between chiefs and the common people can be derived from the following figures. By 1929 the salary scale of chiefs (see Table 13) ranged from 560s. per year for a newly appointed (grade 9) subcounty chief to 22,000s. per year for the highest (grade 1) county chief.[5] With subcounty chiefs' remunerations, vast differences of wealth open up; those of lower chiefs were at the level of skilled employees. At this time, two sources of cash were available

Table 13. *Salary Scales of Teso Chiefs, 1929*

Chiefs	Pounds Sterling Per Annum
County	
Class 1	550 – 1,100
Class 2	480 – 970
Class 3	380 – 692
Class 4	300 – 415
Class 5	208
Subcounty	
Class 1	172
Class 9	28
Parish	
Class 1	28
Class 5	12
Village	
Class 1	16
Class 4	4

SOURCE: District Book, TDA. VADM/5/2.

4. An earlier version of this section appears in Vincent (1977a), pp. 150–153.
5. District Book, 1929 (TDA VADM/5/2).

to most peasants: the sale of cotton and the sale of labor power. The price of the former varied between 9.4s. and 20s. per 100 pounds between 1912 and 1927, so that from an average yearly production of 248 pounds a grower would receive about 38s.[6] The highest wage for unskilled labor during these years was 5s. per month, without food.[7] If such work was available throughout the year (it rarely was), an unskilled laborer might expect a cash income of 60s. per annum, that is 25 percent lower than that of the lowest-grade village chief.

In estimating relative costs for chiefs and commoners, it is useful to consider only school fees, taxes, and fines, which accounted for most of the cash expenditure in the agrarian economy. Education at Ngora High School cost a parent 60s. per annum, the total cash income of the unskilled laborer or one sixty-ninth of the annual income of a grade 5 county chief.[8] As we saw earlier, the poll tax increased during this period from 6s. in 1907 to 21s. in 1927.[9] Many chiefs not only neglected to pay tax, but also received rebates of 5–10 percent on tax collected, so that even in 1910 chiefs were already sharing among their number 39.8 percent of the district's total cash revenue.[10]

How far chiefly sanctions reached down into the security of the common man may be seen from the fines they were empowered to impose. For example, in 1927, a man could be fined 30s. for drunkenness—at the discretion of the chief; for bhang smoking a first offender was subject to a 20s. fine or twelve lashes; for moving cattle without a chief's permission, penalties of 50s., six months' imprisonment, and twelve lashes could be imposed. Labor defaulters were fined 5s. for each day's absenteeism, and of this, 3s.

6. Ibid., 1927 (TDA VADM/5/1). For cotton prices, see Vail, p. 175, or Table 10.

7. District Book, 1927.

8. Ibid., 1929.

9. "Native Poll Tax, 1911–19, 1923–24, 1926–28" (TDA VFIN/ 2/1–5).

10. "Chiefs proportionately fulfilled the poll tax obligations less than any other class of the community. The Saza [County] Chief of Soroti, for instance, had never bothered to pay tax in his life" (TDA XADM/9). This comment on Enosi Epaku was supplied by District Commissioner Philipps after Epaku's deportation.

went to the chief. A man wishing to commute his compulsory labor obligation to chiefs had to pay 10s. for each 24 days he did not work.[11]

Teso chiefs had early been able to corner much of the African share of the wealth generated in the district. They had also been able to ensure its future control by their kinsmen and clients, since their early advantages in disposing of labor, acquiring land, and educating those whom they chose to send to the mission schools were articulated with, and often reinforced by, strategic marriage alliances with those recognized as members of their cohort. They saw themselves as a privileged class, demanding a special ward for themselves and their families at Soroti Hospital and favored treatment at local dispensaries. A Muganda contemporary observed:

> previously there were no important chiefs above a man who possessed fifteen children. But now the man who some time back submitted to the Baganda is a real chief and rules about 5,000 people. Now the chiefs are important people, and they are marvelously rich. They dress themselves presentably; they have learnt Luganda, which they speak very well; they know how to judge law cases; they have bought many bicycles for themselves; and they understand the benefits of tax-collection![12]

The development of capitalism engenders, it is generally agreed, the emergence of class. As we have seen, however, economic development was not evenly distributed throughout Teso district. A combination of circumstances related to the location of missions and schools and a shift in communications gave to the south a certain advantage. Differentiation within the population increased more sharply in the south than elsewhere. There emerged a rural southern population made up of a class of increasingly wealthy landowners and an increasingly impoverished peasantry.

Among the advantages of the southern counties lay access to educational facilities, closer supervision by the administration—and hence greater ability to meet bureaucratic requirements—and the positive stimulus of estate management carried out by the Baganda colonists of Mbale. The retirement of Teso's Baganda agents placed

11. For a list of persons allowed to commute, see "Labour" (TDA VADM/5/2).

12. Soseni Kiza, "Teso, Bukedi" (1913), quoted by Twaddle (1967), pp. 275–276.

land on the market. This proved the ultimate factor in the chain of circumstances leading to the development of the south, the disadvantaging of Serere, and the underdevelopment of the North. The operation of a general law of uneven development, or combined and uneven development, as it is sometimes called (similar to that which we saw operating in Uganda as a whole) converted small operational differences into large structural disparities. These were reflected in intraclass struggle throughout the years that followed.

As Emwanu has pointed out, colonial rule was not received without resistance in Teso; and many of the indigenous leaders who lost out at its introduction, not being awarded chiefships, lived to see their sons' cohort challenging the established officeholders a generation later.[13] For the most part, the politics of the bourgeoisie that emerged involved competition for scarce resources, taking its most severe form a generation later, in 1957.

Education and Ideology

The Teso chiefs were a distinctive class, aggressive in defence of privileges. Their self-consciousness was wholly inculcated during the colonial regime—a component of estate management ideology, best expressed by lecturers at chiefs' training sessions at Serere that projected the African civil service chiefs as a classical English gentry. Elsewhere in Africa, the question of "colonial mentality" has arisen as scholars have attempted to understand the administrative successes of British colonialism and the failure of Africans to resist its burdens. In Teso, almost from the beginning, Iteso chiefs were taught that they were squires. Unquestioning of monarchical sovereignty, or of the centralized power immediately above them, they were taught the principles of the English class system in its agrarian dimension. When it was apparent that these were not indigenous rulers, and that principles of indirect rule were inapplicable, a combination of elite boarding school education and the periodic inculcation of the esprit de corps of a ruling class served instead.[14]

Although the Teso district commissioner in his 1912 report noted

13. Emwanu (1967), p. 179.
14. On the public school ethos of the ruling class, see Gartrell (Ph.D., 1979), pp. 96–119. See also Gale (1959), pp. 242–243.

that both the CMS Agricultural College and St. Joseph's School (Mill Hill mission) at Ngora contributed school leavers to the lower echelons of the administration, Protestant appointments predominated.[15] To some extent the reason for this lay in the type of education offered by each institution; more important, given the early establishment of a native clergy, the Church was a vehicle for upward mobility for the Catholic convert.

The CMS boarding school for chiefs' sons at Ngora had 65 pupils in 1911, 128 in 1914, and 120 by 1920. Its objective from the earliest days was to teach agriculture. The interplay of missionary and commercial activities that elsewhere in Uganda caused a public outcry, governmental criticism, and missionary embarrassment was, to Teso, part and parcel of an elitist educational strategy. The results of this involution did not become clear until a decade later, when the CMS tried to set its house in order.

A considerable advantage was enjoyed by the Roman Catholic mission in that it was encapsulated within a more tightly organized educational system than was the CMS station in Teso. In the same year that the Rev. (afterwards Archdeacon) T. R. Buckley was crying out for reinforcements, Bishop John Biermans, the Roman Catholic bishop of Gargara and vicar apostolic of the Upper Nile, had appointed a committee of four to consolidate the St. Joseph's Society's educational system. (The boarding school at Ngora was, indeed, an immediate outgrowth of this development[16]). Whereas the CMS provided three grades of school, Mill Hill provided only two. At the lower level, both missions had elementary schools attached to their churches. Elementary schooling was free, and, it was said, the schools were sufficiently numerous to enable education to be within the reach of every child. Boys and girls alike were taught to read Ateso and Luganda, although in the CMS only boys were taught elementary arithmetic and how to write Luganda. It was feared that, "were girls able to write, their time would be spent in writing affectionate letters to their male friends to the detriment of the morals of the community."[17]

15. Teso District Annual Report, 1912 (TDA VADM/4/1).

16. John Biermans, *A Short History of the Vicariate of the Upper Nile, Uganda* (1920), p. 32. See also Biermans to Wallis, May 26, 1914 (UNA SMP 1758/09).

17. District Commissioner to Provincial Commissioner, "Native Education," Oct. 25, 1923 (TDA XEDU/3).

Both missions also had boarding schools across the road from each other at Ngora, which took on political significance as successive generations of pupils were graduated. The Mill Hill mission later built a boys' boarding school at Madera near Soroti. Fees for the CMS school were 6os. per annum; those at Mill Hill were 3s. per annum. No concern was voiced about the divisiveness of the two systems within the district. Both missions believed that, in order to perpetuate the Church they were pioneering, a native Christian body had to be fostered from which a Christian elite would emerge as the leaders of a progressive people. At the same time, it was clearly recognized that, for such leadership to be acceptable and successful, the mass of the people had to know and acknowledge a lesser place. Thus, both the CMS and the Mill Hill mission were concerned that children in rural schools, taught by native catechists, should not be educated above their station in life. "Industry, perseverance and cleanliness" were the goals of village education.[18]

By 1920 the social implications of the CMS educational program at Ngora had become apparent: below the chiefly hierarchy imposed by the state, a skill hierarchy was developing. Whereas the Venerable Archdeacon Kitching had seen the contribution of education to Teso society in purely cultural terms—the influence of educated Christian Iteso over the tribe—the Reverend W. S. Syson in 1920 saw more acutely the possibilities of class cleavage in Teso. He urged that the elite principles underlying Protestant missionary education in Teso be cut away. "We must aid at including all classes within one Church . . . We are in the midst of a great Mass Movement in Teso with all its attendant joys and responsibilities. We are not only founding a new section of the Church of God but we are reforming a nation."[19]

A sharp distinction had, indeed, emerged between those pupils marked out for administration, those sent in for training in special trades, and those training as teachers at the missionary college. Whereas the first group of boys spent only two hours a day on agricultural work, devoting the rest to academic study, those acquiring industrial skills spent most of their time at the workbenches. Before 1919 the goals of most pupils—to become clerks and then

18. Education Scheme for Uganda, 1909 (TDA XEDU/2). See also Frank Carter, "Education in Uganda, 1894–1945" (Ph.D. thesis, 1967), p. 49.
19. W. S. Syson, Ngora, Annual Letter, 1919 (CMS Archives 63.A 7/0).

chiefs—could be reached; by introducing industrial training, an effort was made to equip all pupils, as Syson puts it, "to be something more than a 'mukopi' (peasant)".[20] By 1920, class consciousness was also apparent within the district at large. Teachers sent into the countryside were looked down upon by the chiefs and the high school educated, partly on account of their being peasants and partly on account of their lower standard of education.

A four-tier hierarchy was evolving. At the top were chiefs; next came (with missionary revisions in their educational strategies) teachers, then technicians; at the bottom of the heap lay, still, the unschooled peasantry. A formerly egalitarian society, in which rank and prestige could be gained by personal skill and prowess alone, was in the process of being transformed into one in which the class relationship dominated, rank was inherited, and privilege was reinforced.

The Southern Ascendancy:
Reciprocal and Residual Power

A significant phase in the development of society is reached, it is generally conceded (whether in the language of Marx, Weber, or Talcott Parsons), when the particularism of status gives way to individual contract based upon universal principles. In 1919 it was decided that the time was ripe to appoint subcounty chiefs outside of their own localities. The significance of the change was twofold: first, chiefs away from their own areas were able to operate comparatively free from the social restraints of kin and neighbors; second, given the uneven development of the missions' educational institutions, along with the more immediate and continuous involvement of the southern counties with their rulers, the majority of the chiefs given this new freedom were southerners. "Most of the talent at that time was to be found in Kumi . . . the exemplary county of the district."[21]

As the counties developed economically, opportunities for aggrandizement increased. Promoted for honesty and responsiveness to bureaucratic requirements (and it should be noted that the

20. Ibid.
21. Teso District Annual Report, 1920–21.

"failure rate" of Teso chiefs was extremely high), many a man was ultimately overwhelmed by the relative magnitude of the spoils of office at the county level, his bureaucratic downfall aided, in some cases, by those who coveted his power.[22]

While bureaucratic efficiency required the transfer of chiefs and limits to their self-indulgence, political and economic requirements tolerated some degree of consolidation, entrenchment and, eventually, accumulation of capital, political and economic. The client chiefs whom the Baganda appointed and whose retention the British were beginning to question by 1920 were of two kinds. First, those Big Men of the indigenous system who had received recognition after their cooperation with the Baganda; second, lesser men who, by virtue of armed force, had been able to set themselves up as Big Men and clients of the conquerors. I have argued the contingent similarity of the position of Baganda agents and Big Men in Teso; the agent's office takes on local coloring even as the Iteso chief is, in Michael Twaddle's term, Ganda-ized. In Bukedi district, to the south, the Baganda closely controlled the recruitment of local personnel. In Lango, Europeans made the selection; and of the thirty-three chiefs gazetted, not one had worked for the Baganda.

Given the infrastructure of the indigenous Iteso political economy and the development goals of the colonial power, continuity rather than chasm characterized power-holding in Teso. Although those who benefited most from 1897 to 1920 were, indeed, men who had acquired chieftainships under the Baganda and maintained them under the British, to perceive these alone as actors in the political arena would be to underestimate the networks of patronage and power that had existed. A third category of leader, of whose presence the administration was not fully aware until 1934, was composed of those who had neither succumbed to the Baganda nor been appointed formally to office, but whose local influence frequently underlay the success or failure of the government chief.[23]

22. Insights into the political intrigues involved in such situations were gained from interviews with prominent members of the Teso Teachers and Elders Association in Soroti and Serere counties. Several of these men were related to actors in the 1920–1927 political drama and were involved in the factionalism of the fifties.

23. For the basis of this comparison, see Tosh (1978a) pp. 181–218; Twaddle (Ph.D., 1967), p. 140ff, and (1969), pp. 197–206.

Shortly after 1912 many Baganda-instituted parishes and sub-counties had been amalgamated upon the deaths of their chiefs. Many appointments to office had not resulted in efficient administration. Where the imposition of alien rule had been by the selective use of force, the power and authority of those who were not Big Men in their own right had often crumbled when support was withdrawn. Many client chiefs had selectively accepted patronage without accepting its obligations, and, when such client chiefs were called upon to play more bureaucratic roles, some were able to make the transition while others were not. It was at this point that the Administration had begun to appoint *minor* chiefs from Kumi and Bukedea, and school leavers who had served as clerks in the District Office, as chiefs in the other counties. As early as 1913 they were transferred into Serere county, "where there are no men of ability fit for selection as sub-county chiefs, able men from the advanced counties of Kumi and Bukedea who can hardly hope for the promotion they deserve in their own counties".[24] The resentment caused by such appointments the Administration hoped to turn to advantage. "The whole of the administration of Teso seems to pivot on Kumi," the district commissioner reported. "The County Chief institution has already started the right sort of competition among counties, generally with a view to bettering Kumi."[25] The "sporting wars" of the nineteenth century had given way to the public school gamesmanship of the new era.

In 1919, then, the principle of appointing chiefs outside of their home areas was extended to subcounty chiefships—that very locus, as we have seen, of patronage and popular support, as well as of past and present resentments and hostilities. The itemwan, the subcounties, provided Teso's durable political arenas. There, deposed chiefs continued to operate behind the scenes many years after they had been discharged—serially incumbent as chief, parish councillor, clan elder, district councillor, and political party patron—through the pages of Teso's recorded history. Much of their power derived from personal networks of patronage established at the beginnings of their political careers, which they were able to operate regardless

24. Monthly Report (TDA XADM/6.14).
25. District Commissioner to Provincial Commissioner, Sept. 13, 1920 (TDA VADM/8/1).

of shifts in administrative recognition. Not until 1927, a not insignificant date, was a regulation introduced whereby dismissed chiefs had to move out of the areas of which they had been in charge "to prevent the constant case of intrigue in which dismissed chiefs endeavour to make the work and position of their successors as difficult as possible."[26]

In 1920, with its first appointment of Iteso county chiefs, the administration hoped to embark on a steady course of political development "with these young chiefs to provide the initiative and necessary impetus and a percentage of elders to maintain the ballast."[27] Within a few months, however, optimism dimmed. "The rapid progress of the District is not without its attendant dangers," the commissioner noted. "The Chiefs are for the most part young and inexperienced. Many of them have risen to positions of great responsibility in a very short time, and they need a great deal of guidance and assistance in carrying out their duties to prevent them losing sight of their obligations to the community in their desire for personal aggrandizement."[28] The ideology of squirearchy was wearing thin.

The county chiefs were building up, at the grassroots, a political machine based on patronage to subordinate chiefships. Thus, to their already existing control of one means of production—labor— and to their indirect control of another—the district's most vital product, cotton—they were beginning to add measures of closure and controlled access. Their increasingly corporate class interests were considerably underestimated by the administration. Combined with the covert political interest of the Mill Hill mission in getting rid of the stabilizing ballast (which tended to be largely Protestant), pressure was brought upon Echodu, the one remaining county chief of the old school. In 1926 he asked to be removed from Serere, where he could no longer "get on with" his young, progressive chiefs. That he was transferred to Usuku and retired there shortly afterward suggests the district commissioner's inability to sustain the ballast and keep the political vessel on the slow but

26. District Book, 1927–31 (TDA VADM/5/2).
27. Acting District Commissioner's Progress Report up to Oct. 31, 1920 (TDA XADM/9.29).
28. Annual Report, 1921 (TDA VADM/4/2).

steady course envisaged for it. Echodu's place was taken by Y. Opit, "young, clever and progressive but not altogether an ideal chief" in the eyes of one administrator.[29] Shortly afterward, Opit put himself forward under Enoka Epaku's auspices for appointment to Kumi, and in March 1925 Onaba, chief of Kumi, resigned, similarly expressing his "inability" to cope with the forces of change.[30]

The Politics of the Common Man

If the struggle of the salariat involved competition for spoils, that of the majority of the population was directed against the colonial system itself. Military and punitive expeditions were sent into the north to the Karamoja and Lango borders. Throughout the rest of the area, resistance took two forms: murder was directed against chiefs and their families and arson against government property. At a time when only chiefs were armed, guns were frequently reported stolen or mislaid. Recriminations were heavy and public executions carried out. A second more common form of resistance was simply to run away from the jurisdiction of a chief, as from labor requirements, enforced cultivation, and taxation.

Most notable, however, was the support of the Teso population, specifically those in the vicinity of small trading centers and townships, for the Malaki sect.[31] This was a movement that apparently started in Bunyoro around 1913 and was introduced into Teso from Mbale by none other than Semei Kakungulu. The timing of Teso's receptivity is not without significance; its growth paralleled the series of epidemics and disasters that struck the population during its development decade. "Any community that loses a substantial

29. Monthly Report (TDA XADM/6.40).

30. Ibid.

31. The sect was also known as the Society of the One Almighty God, Egibambo ebira mu Kitabu Ekitukuru (Raymond L. Buell, *The Native Problem in Africa*, 1928, vol. 1, p. 612). In terms of Bengdt G. M. Sundkler's distinction between "Ethiopian" and "Zionistic" independent churches, in *Bantu Prophets in South Africa* (1948), pp. 53–54, Malaki clearly falls into the first category. As far as I know, there has been no study of the Malakite movement. The movement was estimated to have 110,000 followers by 1921, after which it apparently collapsed, according to David R. Barrett, *Schism and Renewal in Africa* (1968), p. 29.

percentage of its young adults in a single epidemic finds it hard to maintain itself materially and spiritually. When an initial exposure to one civilised infection is swiftly followed by similarly destructive exposure to others, the structural cohesion of the community is almost certain to collapse."[32] A worldwide reaction to Spanish flu and its accompanying malaise was religious revival; in Teso this took the form of Malaki.

Yet the Malaki movement was also a clear expression of political dissent. Various components of colonial development were attacked, but especially those that concerned cattle, the land, and the condition of the people. Members of the movement refused to pay land tax, since part of the money went to support European mission doctors. Kakungulu himself went to prison for this offence. Unlike other parts of Africa, Teso roadside settlements and dense concentrations did not nurture witchcraft cults and counter movements.[33] Dissent focused directly on the practices of missionaries, doctors, and veterinary officers. The Malaki sect provided organized political opposition to European hegemony. The sect opposed cattle inoculation and monogamy, establishing its own churches and appointing its own ministers of religion to teach the true gospel of a non-European Christ. The movement's spread reflected the uneven development of the region. It was not a millenarian or utopian movement among the oppressed, deprived of the material advantages of "Western civilization," but an alternative form of political society mirroring in its sectarian aspect the fact that the authority of the colonial power rested, visibly, on the European missions. It flourished where land and marketing relations were most clearly seen as controlled by aliens (in towns, along trade routes, and near large estates), but its main thrust was against the state.

In Teso the sect first came to the attention of the District Office in August 1915. It will come as no surprise that Oumo of Kumi was first involved. Oumo, it will be recalled, owed his subcounty chiefship to Kakungulu after the defeat of Oloit of Kabata, in 1898. He

32. McNeill (1976), p. 69.

33. There were no witch-hunts or organized concern with sorcery in Teso as elsewhere in sub-Saharan Africa in response to epidemics and disease. See, e.g., Mary Douglas, "Witch Beliefs in Central Africa" (1967), and Victor Turner (1964).

had been gazetted by the British in 1913 and had been one of the first chiefs to bring in tax, cotton, and oxen for plow school. He was a reader with the CMS at Ngora, and it was the CMS who, in 1915, exerted pressure to have his Malaki reader returned to Kakungulu. Oumo's letter to Kakungulu describes his situation.[34]

August 3rd, 1915

To
    Chief Semei Kakungulu:
               How do you do, sir. Greetings. I inform you that the bearer, Aleni, I am sending back to you because I have already sixteen churches. Again, the European from Ngora called me the other day when the Bishop was present and asked me if I was reading. I said I was. They then told me that they heard I had another teacher in my country. I said that was so. They told me that if I preferred the new teacher they would recall theirs who was in my country. I am now sending back your teacher because the Europeans of Ngora are asking me many questions. The day they called me to Ngora the Chief of the Government was there.

For this reason I am returning your man.

Isaka Oumu
Chief, Kumi

Kakungulu immediately wrote to the district commissioner, W. G. Adams, asking for clarification because it was known that, in Buganda at least, the sect had government approval. There were, by this time, over two hundred Malaki adherents in Kumi and Kadunguru, where chiefs were being encouraged to build more chapels.[35] The Administration handled the matter carefully, with communications flowing throughout the hierarchy in both directions. The chief secretary finally approved barazas to be called throughout the district to make clear that the government was not concerned with religious beliefs or teachings, provided the people obeyed the laws of the land. On the other hand, the district commis-

34. Oumo to Kakungulu, Aug. 3, 1915; sect of Malaki, extension of 1915–16 (TDA XEDU/3.372).
35. Kakungulu to Adams, Aug. 11, 1915 (ibid.).

sioner was asked to submit either monthly or special reports on "the progress of the movement."[36] Only one chief, Oriudda, appears to have stepped out of line, mobilizing forced labor to build a Malaki church at Kamuda. The Soroti county council was instructed to start an inquiry. Proceedings were instituted against Oriudda, who was found guilty and fined Rs.25. No further action was taken, "as this might be construed by certain adherents of this sect into a form of persecution."[37]

Organized resistance in the guise of religious movements was not uncommon in sub-Saharan Africa. Unique, surely, however, is Kakungulu's influence in Teso—not as a conqueror, administrator or subimperialist, but as a political entrepreneur in a global environment. Isaka Oumo was retired from government service in 1920, along with several other long-established Chiefs. Oriudda was transferred in 1918 to Mukura, in Soroti County, where he served under a "new man," Enoka Epaku. Together they were to be dismissed eight years later, when the challenge to colonial rule moved out from behind the skirts of sectarianism to open political confrontation.

The Cotton Boycott of 1920

There had clearly emerged in Teso by 1920 a powerful, nominally Christian, salaried group of southern chiefs whose increasingly joint interests brought into opposition those who had not been able to enter the political arena until later, when much of the southern power had been both consolidated and spread. Because the logistics of Protestant penetration into Teso had encouraged a working alliance between the administration and the CMS at Ngora, northern chiefs seeking European patrons sought the support of Roman Catholic fathers who had established schools in Usuku county as well as in the south. The Mill Hill mission, having long chafed at the

36. District Commissioner to Provincial Commissioner, Eastern Province, Aug. 14, 1915; Provincial Commissioner, Jinja, to Chief Secretary, Entebbe, Aug. 19, 1945; Provincial Commissioner, Eastern Province, to District Commissioner, Teso, Aug. 30, 1915; District Commissioner, Teso, to Provincial Commissioner, Eastern Province, Sept. 7, 1915 (ibid.).

37. District Commissioner, Teso, to Provincial Commissioner, Eastern Province, Jan. 8, 1916 (ibid.).

overrepresentation of Protestant converts among the chiefs, appears to have cooperated.[38]

The specific event that provoked the mobilization of the northerners and Catholics was the appointment of the first independent Iteso county chief in June 1920. For the British officers this was, as the District Commissioner put it, "a most significant event in the History of Teso indicating that the local native is now considered to have reached the stage beyond the necessity of outside tuition and help in his internal affairs."[39] They were dispensing at last with supervisory Baganda agents. The Iteso chiefs, however, looked on this as an invitation to take a more active role in government, advancing the district along lines that would enhance their own autonomy, power, and class interests.

The first Iteso county chief in May 1920 was Nasanairi Ipokiret, a CMS-educated Christian who had been subchief at Ngora, where he had succeeded Ijala when that relict of pre-Baganda politics finally retired in December 1918 after a productive career. Three months later, Isaka Onaba was appointed to Soroti County, Enoka Epaku to Serere, and Eria Ochum to Usuku. Three of the four had gone directly from school to become interpreters at the district headquarters. "This," the district commissioner noted in a progress report, "has proved a successful method of preparing them for their future responsibilities. It gives them a knowledge of our administrative customs in dealing with all manner of work and also gives them broad insight into the 'pros and cons' of all the chiefs etc. throughout the district."[40] Inevitably, this experience at the center of administrative intelligence served the chiefs well in establishing popular careers. The insight they gained into the workings of their masters perhaps contributed to the dismissal of two of them within the decade.

Ipokiret's death in November 1920 of septicemia entailed the promotion of Onaba to Kumi and Epaku to Soroti. Ochum continued in Usuku until 1924, when he was elevated to his home county of Kumi. His transfer, a promotion, was bitterly resented in

38. District Book (TDA VADM/5/2).
39. Monthly Report (TDA XADM/6.11).
40. Annual Report (TDA XADM/9.29).

the north.[41] Ochum, a southerner, was held responsible for the dismissal of several northern chiefs first gazetted in 1913, among them Okurut of Kapujan, Ojenatum, Ochoppo of Abela, and Obukwi of Kokolyo; but it is likely that, in fact, these retirements were part of the Administration's restructuring of the postwar district. To what extent his own dismissal less than a year later was due to the machinations of Epaku and the northern chiefs is not clear; it coincided with the arrival of a new district commissioner, J. E. T. Philipps, who had a reputation for putting houses in order ("he made a habit of exposing abuses").[42] Ochum's place was taken by Nasanairi Esunyet, a thirty-five-year-old Southerner but a Roman Catholic.

The Iteso "new men" began flexing their muscles immediately, filling the wartime vacuum that had preceded their appointment. Distinct from their predecessors, Teso's district officers after 1919 were part of a new breed of colonial recruit—commissioned army officers discharged from the war. In Teso they retained their titles: Capt. A. E. O. Black; Capt. C. S. Nason; Capt. A. B. Trewin; and, most important of all in the events that follow, Capt. J. E. T. Philipps. Apart from the two months when Rubie returned to serve in the district and the fourteen months when E. A. Temple-Perkins (later to become provincial commissioner, Eastern Province) served there, new (young) men shared—or competed for—the helm of district management in Teso.

The chiefs began by confronting the district officers with a show

41. This resentment lingered well into the 1950s, surfacing in a factional dispute that brought about the temporary dissolution of the district council in 1957.

42. His predecessor, A. E. O. Black, had expressed regret that increasing red tape permitted only occasional short safaris into Teso's villages. "One therefore sits in Soroti with an uneasy feeling that one can only see what the chiefs wish one to see" (District Commissioner's conference, 1921 (TDA XADM/1.21)). A short account of Philipps' career appears in Tosh (1978a), pp. 219–224. Teso material would seem to confirm Tosh's assessment, but final judgment must await further research. One might hypothesize, indeed, that J. E. T. Philipps was the Max Havelaar of the Ugandan civil service, and that such characterizations of him as exist are stereotypes of one who "rocks the boat" (see Multatuli [pseud.], *Max Havelaar*, 1967).

of strength in the one area of strategic resources to which they had the closest access and over which they had the most direct control: the cotton crop and the men who produced it.

In 1918 (when the poll tax was raised from 5s. to 7s.) the cotton price stood at 20 cents a pound. By 1919 it had fallen to 15 cents and by 1920 to 8 cents, until it finally reached an all-time low of 3 cents a pound. At this point the chiefs stepped in, calling upon the peasants to withold their crop from the market. Up until this time administrators had had nothing but praise for the caliber of the county chiefs, remarking upon their popularity with the peasantry and their ability to win cooperation. Especially praiseworthy was their ability to maintain discipline. In the cotton boycott these talents were put to popular use. "The chiefs were controlling the situation, the *Bakopi* (peasants), with few exceptions. . . taking their lead from the chiefs."[43] The county chiefs were feeling their power, and, although one report suggested that beatings and intimidation occurred, in most places the chiefs' powers of persuasion were sufficient for growers not to sell until the price was higher.[44] Everywhere preparations were made to store cotton rather than sell it. The northern chiefs held out longer against District Office orders to desist than did those of Kumi. Tension occurred when the assistant superintendent of police threatened an assembly of county and subcounty chiefs at Toromo in Usuku with criminal prosecution, but eventually an agreement was reached—after late-night sessions between the district commissioner and Epaku, the county chief of Soroti.

Epaku issued a letter authorizing the settlement, pledging that there would be no further delay in cotton reaching the market. This was communicated by the District Office to the ginners. It is not surprising that one historian, writing of resistance to alien rule in Teso, singles out Epaku's career for special attention; but it is necessary to qualify his conclusions. Epaku was the leader, not of a nationalist revolution, but of a reform commodity movement typical of a small-holding agricultural system. Thus:

> A combination of noncultivators dependent on income from commercial capital and cultivators dependent on income from land leads to a *reform*

43. Monthly Report, January 1921 (TDA XADM/7.4.21).
44. Ibid.

commodity movement. Such a combination of income sources is typical of small holding systems. *The reform commodity movement is concerned with the control of the market in agricultural commodities.* It demands neither the redistribution of property nor the seizure of state power. The typical tactic of such movements is a limited economic protest. The greater the sensitivity to markets in small holding systems, the greater the probability of a reform commodity movement (emphasis added).[45]

The Purge of the Chiefs

Revolutionary leader or not, Enoka Epaku, county chief of Soroti, was deported from Teso in 1927 following several months of political crisis. What happened is still not clear; the affair remains politically controversial, and existing records are obscure. There was apparently no trial of the accused, or civil service or public inquiry. Although provisions existed whereby the governor of Uganda was required to report details of deportation orders to the secretary of state in London under the Uganda Deportation Ordinance (Number 15 of 1908) of the Uganda Protectorate Laws, no such communication has been found.

It is not clear to this day exactly what Epaku—along with Opit, county chief of Serere, and, significantly, a Mill Hill mission priest—did to bring about their deportation. An administrator himself, J. C. D. Lawrance accepts and downplays the Teso administration's stated reasons for Epaku's dismissal, namely corruption and inefficiency, noting that "it was not always the gravity of the offence which dictated whether or not a dismissed chief was deported, but the degree of his standing and the effect which his continued presence would have on the maintenance of good order in the district."[46] Certainly the provisions of the Uganda Deportation Ordinance were sufficiently broad to make this possible:

> Any person [who is] conducting himself so as to be dangerous to peace and good order in any part of the Protectorate or is endeavouring to excite enmity between the people of the Protectorate and His Majesty, or

45. Paige (1975), p. 70.
46. Emwanu (1967), p. 181, n. 55. The editors of the *Uganda Journal* had invited J. C. D. Lawrance, a former Teso district commissioner, to comment upon Emwanu's essay.

is intriguing against His Majesty's power authority in the Protectorate [may] be deported from any part of the Protectorate to any other part of the Protectorate.[47]

Emwanu, historian of Teso's populism, reports a battery of recollections from local informants:

Epaku was so strongly opposed to forced labour that he became the champion of the underdog by openly speaking against it . . . the British Administration wanted to introduce a system of land tenure that would allow individual freehold which Epaku opposed . . . Epaku had become so popular that the people wanted to make him "Kabaka" of Teso, a proposition which the administration would not allow.[48]

All these commentaries upon the Epaku affair tell us more about those who make them than about the event or its political meaning.

The purge of the chiefs in 1927 is presented in the historical narrative of Teso as a confrontation between the chiefs and the newly appointed district commissioner, Capt. J. E. T. Philipps. An experienced administrator who had served in Bahr-El-Ghazal Province before his transfer to Uganda, Philipps, according to John Tosh, "made a habit of exposing abuses."[49] As Tosh notes, Philipps was commended at the highest level for his actions in Teso but in November 1927 was transferred out of the district. Perhaps he was, indeed, "more adept at uncovering abuses than at suggesting how they should be checked."[50] After short service in Lango, where he

47. Uganda Protectorate Laws: Uganda Deportation Ordinance, no. 15, 1908.

48. Emwanu, p. 179.

49. Tosh (1978a), p. 223.

50. Ibid. This episode is discussed in Emwanu, pp. 178–179. It also figured among the grievances of northerners in the 1950s. Teso had become renowned as one of the most progressive districts of Uganda—the first, indeed, to have a democratically elected district council. Government consternation was considerable, therefore, when, within a very short time, that council broke down. Even more perplexing to the Commission of Inquiry was the claim of the Iseera faction that the deportation of Epaku thirty years earlier was one of the origins of ill-feeling and rivalry between north and south. The opening speech of the inquiry, by Enosi Ejoku, M. B. E., a northerner who had been appointed sub-county chief of Adachal in 1927 in the reshuffle following Epaku's dismissal, and who was successively county chief of Napak, Usuku, Amuria, and Kumi before becoming chair-

also exposed abuses, Philipps was retired, protesting, from the Colonial Service.

Rather than explore Chief Epaku's protestations over Protectorate policies or District Commissioner Philipps' "self-appointed role as scourge of the wicked,"[51] let us instead follow the trail of events leading up to the confrontation of the two men in 1927. If the confrontation of 1921 revolved around the chiefs' control of the peasantry and, through them, the marketing of cotton, the political crisis of 1927 involved an even more fundamental class interest: the production and exploitation of labor.

Six months after taking office in April 1926, Philipps set out to codify the labor requirements of Teso district. His belief that "the labour situation is the thing which, beyond general native administration, I have felt to be the most important in this District," was comfortingly in accordance with "two things which home and the Governor are now insisting on," the reduction of all labor known as "forced and unpaid."[52]

More important even than this codification (aimed at reducing luwalo and checking the abusive labor powers of chiefs[53]) was the

---

man of the council in 1949, accused both past and present southern chiefs of nepotism and of unjustly getting rid of their northern rivals. He also accused the District Office of greatly favoring the people of the south against the north. One of the main northern complaints was that over the years the southerners had had an undue share of chiefships of all grades, and that when transferred they had taken junior chiefs and clerks with them.

Once again, in 1955, as in 1926, hostility and envy were directed not only across the Agu divide but against the Protectorate government. On this occasion, northern councillors attempted to stir up the peasantry against the introduction of graduated tax and against the government's land tenure proposals. Closer analysis reveals a connection between careers as civil service chiefs and election to the council, as well as retention of power by the very same men who had been cadet combatants in the political arena of the 1920s.

51. Tosh (1978a), p. 220.

52. Quarterly Report (TDA XADM/7.106).

53. The codification (Labour, District Office, Oct. 13, 1926 (TDA VADM/5/1)) ran as follows:
    1. Every Teso peasant who is a taxpayer is liable for labour as follows:
        a. 3 days in every month for *Luwalo Labour* (roads, bridges, etc.).

appointment of a labor inspector, whose task it was to tour regularly and to spot-check labor gangs at work. Critically, the appointment was made from outside the Teso political system, thus rendering the officer immune from the pressures of the local patronage system. Moreover, the inspector's rank was comparable with that of the senior county chief of Teso, with equivalent pay.

In December 1926 Chief Benedicto Dake, previously political agent and chief of the largest county in Kigezi, was appointed for a five-year term of office. Philipps made it clear that he trusted Dake implicitly because the latter would not be in a position to "receive any of the 'perks' which in the opinion of the native (and in reality) constitute the principal value of the position of County Chief." Furthermore, Dake had traveled widely with Philipps in West Africa, Spain, Portugal, and England (in what capacity it is not clear) and so had "been enabled to see at close quarters a considerable amount of those things which enable a man to acquire a sense of proportion and of the power of the Empire."[54]

As a result of the inspector's efforts, it was clear by the end of March 1927 that within the district there were "numbers of favoured individuals whose wealth or relationship has previously obtained for them a sheltered life." The inspector's efforts "have been as unpopular with the Chiefs concerned," Philipps notes, "as they are popular with the people, who work with increasing cheerfulness

---

      b. 1 day in every month for *Chief's Labour*, and 6/- p.a. payment as "Chief's labour commutation fee" (or 4 days in every month in lieu of payment).

2. The labour unit is the *muluka* [parish], 4 per *gombolola* [county]. Each muluka has a week of the month allotted to it for free labour.

3. In their week, the men of that muluka then work on the Tuesday, Wednesday, and Thursday for Luwalo, and on Saturday for the Chief. Exemption tickets for native shop owners, fundis, etc., cost 25/- p.a.

4. Native holders of labour tickets who are (a) regular in their attendance (shown on tickets), (b) in possession of genuine chits giving them leave of absence (with dates), are excused Luwalo and Chief's Labour *while thus employed*.

5. All others (with a few defined exceptions) are liable to be taken by Chiefs for "lukiko labour."

54. District Book (TDA VADM/5/3).

as the reign of privilege and favouritism is gradually suppressed."[55]

In May 1927 an inquiry instigated by the District Office increased the now mounting hostility between the Administration and the chiefs. Philipps invited the opinions of ginnery owners and European and Asian traders concerning the performance of chiefs during the 1926–27 cotton season. Among the colorful responses to his circular appear phrases such as "selfish, incompetent and grabbing"; "a bad example in that they indulge too freely in drink, especially when on Safari"; "their main object is to get rich as quickly as possible"; "do not have the interests of their people at heart"; "understand the value of money and have no interest in their people"; and so on.[56]

What is at issue here is not management views of chiefs but the fact that chiefs knew of the inquiry and resented it. No longer could they harbor a belief that they were simply the lower and middle echelons of an autonomous imperial system of authority that reached through them to the district officers, the district commissioner, the provincial commissioner, and the governor to the king himself, as they and their predecessors had been given to believe on attaining office. Made manifest was their role as shop stewards in a production enterprise geared to the interest of alien cotton ginners and an expatriate British officialdom.

This combination of interests—capital and colonial—loomed ominously in another domain, too. From 1920 on, there had been in Teso growing fears of European alienation of land in the Kenya fashion. By 1926 several alien estates had been registered, notably those of J. Mackertich (now in the hands of Mrs. Mackertich) at

55. Quarterly Report. It may be of interest to note that Philipps, while speaking out against the use of women's labor on road works, opposed the use of luwalo labor for the building of a maternity home on the grounds that he was trying to reduce impositions on the peasantry. He observed: "It is, I believe, accepted that the more hardy and uncivilised races, like the Teso, whose women moreover undergo no circumcision and are fairly free of V.D., are less in need of advanced maternity treatment than the 'softer' peoples who have been longer in touch with civilization and whose women do not enjoy such physical advantages" (District Book, 1927 (TDA VADM/5/3)).

56. Native affairs, general (TDA XNAF/9.91, circular no. 5 of 1927, with responses).

Kabos in Bugondo, 76 acres; the Foster Brothers' ginnery land and residential site near Kamod in Serere, 6 acres; the Bombay Uganda Company's agricultural plantation of 12,858 acres at Arapai in Soroti; and the latter company's estate of 296 acres and an agricultural plantation of 99.9 acres, at Achwa in Soroti.[57] In the southern counties, land had been alienated only to the missions at Ngora. When land subsequently came on the market, it was bought up by the salariat so they could develop estates in the Ganda manner. By 1926 it appeared that the northern chiefs were to be denied the same opportunities in their region.

There are grounds in all these proposed and impending changes for a confrontation between chiefs and the District Office. We do not know the form it took; we do not know of the encouragement it appears to have received from members of the Mill Hill mission. On record, however, are the events of June 12, 1927, when the provincial commissioner addressed a large public baraza in Soroti and, after attacking the corruption and self-interest of chiefs in general, publicly dismissed Chiefs Enoka Epaku of Soroti and Yeremiah Opit of Serere. The provincial commissioner threatened others with dismissal, too, if they did not disengage from activities in certain unnamed political organizations. His allusion, and it was no more, was probably to "the League for obtaining for Roman Catholics a greater share in the Administration of the country," founded by Father J. Kiggen of the Mill Hill mission. The commissioner reminded the assembled chiefs of their client status: "It was the Government who introduced the position of County Chiefs into Teso where it had never existed before," yet "the machinations of a few . . . had produced maladministration and unrest." He spoke of individuals who had "exploited the peasantry and made themselves rich by the sweat of *their* brow and at *their* expense." He spoke further of excessive attention paid to fashionable clothing and motorcars and, more pointedly, of nepotism, bribery, and cliques in power.[58]

57. District Book (TDA VADM/5.51).
58. In spite of these severe measures, Philipps, fewer than three months later, saw the unrest continuing, "old allies of certain ex-chiefs continuing a desultory and restless intrigue" against the District Office, abetted by "a certain Advocate [who] appears still to be interesting himself in native policies. He is alleged to work through native touts and to be kept informed by a local religious agency. He visits dismissed chiefs and other natives by

In October 1927, after the mass dismissals of leading chiefs and subchiefs, Baganda agents were back in office. Temeteo Musaka was appointed agent for Kumi, Ngora, and Usuku, and Eria Gya-

---

night" (Quarterly Report). Philipps' successor, H. A. Mackenzie, described this man as "a fanatical and anti-Government Sinn Fein Lawyer who desires the Catholic Church to have temporal and spiritual power in Teso. The Catholic Mission resent the fact that the Government has to maintain good order and discipline and wish to be responsible for them. Their actions are being curbed" (Annual Report, 1927–28, TDA XADM/9).

A fragment found in the TDA, unconfirmed by research in the Mill Hill mission archives, concerns the Kumi county chief, Nathaniel Esungett, and refers back to a confidential report of June 13, 1927. Three charges are made aginst Esungett, and they add to our knowledge of missionary endeavors in the political field of Teso.

Resentful of the number of Protestant-trained Iteso in administration, Father Kiggen, the priest in charge at Ngora, organized a "League for the obtaining for Roman Catholics a greater [share] in the Administration of the Country." Esungett accepted appointment as president of the league without consulting the district commissioner. It would appear that the district commissioner learned of his political activities from the Muganda native adviser, Temeteo Musaka, who reported in May 1927 that Esungett had become the "tool of the Mill Hill Mission at Ngora." In this letter, the district commissioner comments that the actual word used by the adviser, *bamukyamya* (literally, they are making him crooked), is not without significance. Father Kiggen is reported to have told Esungett that he owed his appointment as county chief to the political influence of the mission, and this does, indeed, appear to have been the case. The district commissioner's predecessor, Capt. C. S. Nason, had refused to recommend Esungett, whereupon Father Kiggen had written to the Chief Secretary of Uganda and the decision was reversed.

Esungett was clearly behaving in a manner that Philipps found embarrassing. He was "strongly suspected of habitually divulging contents of Government correspondence to the Mill Hill Mission," and of handing over official information concerning details of lukiko monies to an advocate to support a complaint against the district commissioner—which, it was intended, should be forwarded to the central government in Entebbe.

The actual memorandum found in the archives is fragmentary—it seems likely that it was just this sort of document that was destroyed with the handing-over of power in 1963—but it seems reasonable to believe that the provincial commissioner's subsequent baraza in Soroti was a result partly of this information about political dealings of the Catholic Church with the administration.

genda for Soroti, Serere, and Amuria; Abdullah Makabire was assistant for Usuku. The novel grouping of the counties across the
north-south divide provides a first intimation, perhaps, of the administration's belated recognition of the deepseated hostilities in the
District.

The reintroduction of Baganda agents, wrote the district commissioner, "may appear paradoxical to our Western ideas of self-
determination and democracy. In Teso, thank goodness, we are not
yet troubled with either of these false premises. The peasantry have
suffered so heavily from the contempt and exploitation by their
black coated compatriots that they frankly welcome a protective
shock-absorber above them."[59]

What then are we to conclude from this episode? Although
records no longer exist from which to judge the extent to which the
commissioner operated under a conspiracy theory in order to ra-
tionalize growing unrest at his own authoritarianism, the newly
appointed county chiefs of the second decade were clearly too ambitious in their political goals. Yet, that these goals were to benefit
the peasantry, rather than to profit an emergent class, seems questionable. Emwanu has suggested that County Chief Epaku was
deported because of the "immense popularity which he enjoyed
among his own people . . . He was especially concerned with the
welfare of the people of Teso as a whole."[60] A class analysis of this
situation, in which administrators and civil service chiefs alike
claimed to be the defenders of the Teso peasantry, might recall that:

> each new class which puts itself in the place of the one ruling before it
> is compelled, merely in order to carry through its aim, to represent its
> interests as the common interest of all the members of society . . . The
> class making a revolution appears from the very start, merely because it
> is opposed to a class, not as a *class* but as the representative of the whole
> society; it appears as the whole mass of society confronting the one
> ruling class. It can do this because, to start with, its interest really is more
> connected with the common interest of all non-ruling classes, because
> under the pressure of conditions its interest has not yet been able to
> develop as the particular interest of a particular class.[61]

59. Philipps to Provincial Commissioners, no. 106/105 (TDA
XADM/9).
60. Emwanu, p. 179.
61. Karl Marx and Friedrich Engels, *The German Ideology* (1977),
pp. 65–66.

It is necessary also to look behind the event to perceive that its timing coincided with a rising threat to the success of specific world market interests in Teso, as elsewhere in Uganda. "Certainly the peasants of Uganda," C. C. Wrigley notes, had no heartier champions in this period than the spokesmen of the European commercial community, who lost no opportunity of drawing attention to the exactions of land-owners and chiefs."[62] In Teso, indeed, as we have seen, the district commissioner actually went out of his way to invite the comments of the peasantry on local chiefs in a questionnaire inquiry he instigated in May 1927. In the long run, however, explanation lies, at least partly, with the market interests of the world economic system; "the peasants, if given the chance, would buy Manchester fabrics, Birmingham hardware, Coventry cycles, whereas wealthy chiefs spend their money on American cars."[63]

Our argument has, indeed, come full circle.

Conclusion

Here lies the irony of the colonial system in Teso that makes an anticipation of class struggle in the European sense difficult. The emergence of the common people in England predated England's involvement in the *modern* world economic system. The making of the *English* working class in eighteenth-century England was, in a world systemic sense, the crystallization of consciousness among a labor aristocracy—the privileged and protected English workers within an imperial system where colonial labor provided the economic underclass. It is in contradistinction both to the ruling, exploiting class above them and to the inferior, exploited class below them (most visibly the Irish) that the English artisan and shopkeeper gained his sense of self.

What, then, stopped the common people of Teso from attaining class consciousness? Most significantly, it may be suggested, colonial control channeled and limited, to an enormous extent, communications; controlled individuals in movement; and advanced an idealized sense of locality and parochial identification such as much of Africa had not known before. Development economists never cease to deplore the poor communications systems of East African

62. C. C. Wrigley (1959a), p. 51.
63. Ibid.

territories, and yet their geopolitical function was well served. Lines of road and rail were for the carriage of commodities, not persons; their orientation and poor quality inhibited the movement of persons in any but the colonially desired direction. As a result, entire shifts in economic production and marketing fields occurred, rendering the agricultural population infinitely more susceptible to the vagaries of season and climate than ever it was before. More than this, taxation and local bureaucracy pinned down the laboring man; Margery Perham's metaphor of the "iron grid of colonialism" is indeed apt.

At this point, too, it is necessary to introduce that other factor of nineteenth- and twentieth-century Teso political economy which made its human condition so very different from that of Europe. In Teso the political economy was established by conquest, and domination was maintained by the introduction of aliens at crucial points in the development economy. Possibly it is, indeed, to the smallness of the artisan and shopkeeper sector that the lack of political consciousness in Teso agrarian society can be attributed. Throughout its colonial history, commerce and trade were largely in the hands of Asians and other non-Iteso: Somalis, Arabs, Nubians. The grievances of the peasantry were thus often deflected onto resentment of aliens. Nevertheless, given that small-holder economies are not characterized by the considerable indebtedness that marks plantations, haciendas, and sharecropping regions (although certainly some existed), this potential for violence did not take on major proportions. Since many of Teso's alien traders were Muslims with African wives, racialist antagonisms were muted. Indeed, since the administration saw its role, specifically, as one of protecting the interests of the natives against alien, racialist exploitation, abuses deriving from antagonistic producer-marketing relations tended to occur at the grassroots, between Africans.

Nor, as elsewhere in Africa, can returning soldiers or returning migrants be looked upon as instigators of political movements. The former were easily assimilated into ginnery employment as guards and night watchmen, a program that had the joint approval of both ginners and the administration. The latter were very few. Nor were women active in Teso politics in the early modern era—a fact that might be accounted for by the new demands placed upon them by subsistence cultivation, for some had played a role earlier. To this day, most farm work is done with hoes alone, and transportation is lacking. Moreover, as in many small-holder economies, whereas marketing arrangements for the agricultural commodity to be exported were excellent, arrangements for the marketing of food crops were abysmal, so that heavy reliance on the domestic unit and localized exchange had to develop.

Once again, it is necessary to stress destruction of the previously more diversified economy; the de-skilling of the Teso peasantry, the heavy labor tax and cultivation demands placed on the men, and the burdens of reproduction placed on the women. It is common to find that such populations, suffering constant food shortages and riddled with disease, are anything but politically active except where survival is at risk. Above all, however, coercive measures immediately came into play when any organized political movements were initiated from below. Nevertheless, such social movements as did develop in Teso, if apparently apolitical, were actually directed, if not against the oppressive, then accurately against the extractive forces in their society.

It is out of the contradictions in the ensemble of social relations in East Africa—contradictions engendered by an objective position as labor in a transnational capitalist economic system and a subjective position as "subaltern groups" (to use Eric Hobsbawm's expression) in a colonial political system—that Teso's laboring poor emerged. Although the closure of a dominant class was well under way in East Africa, and the class consciousness of that group was apparent, the system as a whole remained one of no-classness; conflict was not expressed as class struggle. In cases such as this, Hobsbawm suggests,

> the unity felt by the subaltern groups will be so global as to go beyond class and state. There will not be peasants, but "people" or "countrymen"; there will not be workers, but an indiscriminate "common people" or "labouring poor", distinguished from the rich merely by poverty, from the idle (whether rich or poor) by the compulsion to live by the sweat of their brow, and from the powerful by the unspoken or explicit corollary of weakness and helplessness.[64]

Hobsbawm sees this as a precapitalist societal condition; more accurately, it bespeaks a nonstate phenomenon—a transnational cap-

64. Eric J. Hobsbawm, "Class consciousness in history" (1971), p. 10.

italism. Thus, in Teso, one finds a global politics at the local level, its consciousness engendered by the bourgeoisie, accompanying an intraclass struggle for power within the territory.

Today, perhaps, one would conclude that the specific form of capitalism that imbued colonial Teso in its early days with the seeds of privilege and self-aggrandizement led to the events narrated here. The checks and balances of the indigenous system were undermined not simply by a lack of understanding on the part of colonial bureaucracy but by conquest, famine, and disease—and a disregard for their consequences, provided these consequences were selectively distributed.

The cruel irony for Teso, perhaps, was that those in charge in the years after 1927 looked to the loss of the past and not to the present around them for explanations and solutions. "Among the peasantry," Philipps' successor noted two months after his arrival in the district,

> orders were disobeyed with impunity. Debt is appalling, all are improvident. It is stated that there are no hereditary chiefs in Teso. I fail to understand how a tribe of 225,000 would have kept their country unless they had leaders before the British Government took over the Country. I am searching for the sons of the old leaders as they may be worth promoting to office, and have authority which the present chief now holding office does not.[65]

The dramas of history are, indeed, played first as tragedy and then, again, as farce.

65. Monthly Report, December 1930. (TDA XADM/6.108).

Glossary

abakungulu	Luganda	men of Kakungulu, Kakungulu's followers
Amerikani	Swahili	cotton cloth, originally imported from the United States
amuron (pl. amurok)	Ateso	a woman seer, prophetess
arionga	Ateso	a time of origins and journeys
askari	Swahili	soldier, watchman
asonya	Ateso	(adv.) very long ago
ayah	Hindi/Swahili	children's nursemaid
baraza	Swahili	an assembly
boma	Swahili	enclosure or fortification; later used for an administrative headquarters
duka	Swahili	shop
ebeli	Ateso	famine
eitai	Ateso	communal work group
eitela (pl. itela)	Ateso	administrative parish; cf. *mutala*
ekek	Ateso	patrigroup
emono	Ateso	communally worked plots of land
etem (pl. itemwan)	Ateso	administrative sub-county; lit. 'hearth'

emuron (pl. imurok)	Ateso	a male seer, prophet
hamali	Swahili	porter; hence *hamali* cart, a cart pulled by men
kanzu	Swahili	a white cotton robe, usually worn by Muslims
katikiro	Luganda	Prime Minister
kazanvu	Luganda	a month's obligatory unpaid labor
lukiko	Swahili	council, formal gathering of chiefs
luwalo	Luganda	compulsory unpaid labor for local chiefs
magendo	Swahili	black market
manyatta	Masai	young warriors' lodge; wrongly used by colonial officers for any village of grass huts.
matoke (pl.)	Swahili	lit. 'sweet bananas'; used in Uganda for any kind of banana
mukopi (pl. bakopi)	Luganda	peasant
mutala	Luganda	administrative parish; cf. *eitela*

Bibliography

A. *Unpublished Sources*

1. *Archives*

Public Record Office, London (PRO): Until 1905 Uganda was the responsibility of the Foreign Office, and between 1905 and 1927 of the Colonial Office. Military and administrative records relating to Bukeddi and Teso are covered in the series "Uganda: Foreign Office Correspondence, 1892–1905, FO/403 (Confidential Prints)"; and in Colonial Office records (CO/536).

Uganda National Archives, Entebbe (UNA): Administrative documents after 1906 are arranged in Secretariat Minute Papers (SMP). After 1919, John Tosh has noted (1978a, p. 276), it was difficult to get clearance for any documents apart from quarterly and annual reports. Indirect use has been made of this source through the unpublished notes of Sir John M. Gray (n.d.), who first went to Uganda as an assistant district officer in 1920, and was resident magistrate in Soroti in 1958. The Uganda National Archives also hold what is left of the former Eastern Province Archives (EPMP).

Teso District Archives, Soroti: These archives (TDA) have been called by John Tosh "the best organized archives in Uganda" (1978a, p. 227). They contain over 300 volumes and 2,700 files. Between April 1959 and February 1960, early files (1912–1948) were integrated with current volumes under a comprehensive subject index. Those used in this study were Administration (ADM), Agriculture (AGR), Census and Statistics (CST), Education (EDU), Finance (FIN), Labor (LAB), Miscellaneous (MIS), Missions (MSN), Native Affairs (NAF). The prefix X indicates files prior to 1948, the prefix V is used for those after 1948.

Church Missionary Society Archives, 157 Waterloo Road, London: These archives (CMS Archives) contain the annual letters and reports of missionaries in Uganda from 1877. These are filed separately by writer under the general CA6 category from 1877–1880, and thereafter filed together in chronological order under a G3.A7/O heading from 1907–1927. Correspondence between Kampala and London, 1907–1925, falls under G3.A7/O, and there is a most valuable and comprehensive index to this in three files: G3.A7/P1 (–1906); G3.A7/P2 (1907–1915); G3.A7/P3 (1915–1927). The archives also contain missionary diaries and private papers. These, along with bound volumes of CMS periodicals and journals (i.e., *Church Missionary Society Gazette; Church Missionary Society Gleaner; Church Missionary Intelligencer, and Church Missionary Review*), are listed separately below under various authors of published works.

Mill Hill Mission Archives, St. Joseph's College, Mill Hill, London: These archives contain the diary of the Budaka mission, 1901–1919 (DBM). This series of notebooks contains a brief account of daily events, visits to other missions, etc., written by various members of the mission including Father Gregorius Kestens and Father Christopher J. Kirk. Ten notebooks cover the period of this study: Book I, Sept. 10, 1901–Apr. 26, 1903; Book II, Apr. 27, 1900–Jan. 31, 1904; Book III, Feb. 14, 1904–May 24, 1905; Book IV, May 1, 1907–Mar. 31, 1909; Book V, Apr. 1, 1909–May 13, 1912; [Books VI and VII were missing]; Book VIII, Sept. 1, 1913–Dec. 31, 1919; Book IX, Jan. 1, 1920–Dec. 31, 1923; Book X, Jan. 1, 1924–Dec. 31, 1928. These archives also contain private papers such as those of Rev. E. Grimshaw listed below; I follow Hubert Gale (1959, p. 321) in distinguishing the original manuscript notebook (Grimshaw, n.d., orig.) from the abbreviated typescript based upon it (Grimshaw, n.d.).

The library of St. Joseph's College contains volumes of Mill Hill mission periodicals such as *St. Joseph's Advocate* (in which appeared, at intervals, the Status Animarum for the Upper Nile Vicariate) and *St. Joseph's Advocate (Ireland)*.

East African Institute of Social and Economic Research Archives, Nsubuga Block, Makerere University College, Kampala: These archives (EAISR) contain research notes and documentation deposited by fellows of the institute since its inception in 1948. This documentation includes copies of early administrative and agricultural reports relating to Teso; these are listed separately below under various authors of private papers.

2. *Private Papers, Diaries, Reports*

Anon.
1951 "Enquiry into Shifting Cultivation: Eastern Province, Uganda." Typescript. East African Institute of Social and Economic Research, Kampala.

Bell, William D.
1906 Copy of a letter in the District Office, Mbale, relating the activities of Swahili cattle raiders. MSS. Afr.s.1010. Rhodes House, Oxford.

Bishop, A.M., and D. Ruffell
n.d. "A History of the Upper Nile Diocese." Church Missionary Society Library, London.

Blackhurst, I.
1965 "The Forts of Kakungulu." Final report on the Imperial College Uganda Expedition. Typescript. Library of the Royal Geographical Society, London.

Coote, J.M.
1909 Diary, Bukeddi District, Uganda, "A Tour in the Teso Country." MSS. Afr.s.1383. Rhodes House, Oxford.

Gray, Sir John M.
n.d. Notes relating to Kakungulu. Uncatalogued box file. Cambridge University Library, Cambridge, England.
1924 "Report on the Claims of Semei B. Kakunguru against the Government of the Uganda Protectorate, including a sketch of Kakunguru's career, 1888–1904." Royal Commonwealth Society, London.

Grimshaw, E.
n.d., orig. "Some Notes on the Apostolic Vicariate of the Upper Nile, 1895–1945." A handwritten book of 164 pages with maps and photographs. UNV 11a. St. Joseph's College, Mill Hill, London.
n.d. "Some Notes on the Apostolic Vicariate of the Upper Nile, 1895–1945, by Father E. Grimshaw, based on his own memoirs and the notes of Father Thomas Mathews." Typescript. UNV 11a. St. Joseph's College, Mill Hill, London.

Hughes, J. E. M.
1953 Fieldwork notes of District Forestry Officer to District Officer, Soroti, 15 June 1953. Fieldwork notes cabinet, African Studies.

East African Institute of Social and Economic Research, Kampala.

Johnstone, R. H.
1921   "Past Times in Uganda." MSS. Afr.s.376. Rhodes House, Oxford.

Kagwa, Temeo
n.d.   "The History of Bukeddi." MSS. Makerere University College library (Africana section), Kampala.

Nagashima, N.
1968   "Historical Relations among the Central Nilo-Hamites." Social Science Conference paper. Makerere University, Kampala.

Ormsby, Stanley W.
1897–1908 Letters home from Uganda. MSS. Afr.s.105. Rhodes House, Oxford.

Perryman, P. W.
1922   Diary of a safari from Entebbe across Elgon to the Suk Hills, February to March 1922. MSS. Rhodes House, Oxford.

Ramchandani, R. R.
n.d.   "Asian Contribution to the Uganda Cotton Industry." Rural Development Research Seminar paper. Makerere University College, Kampala.

Shanin, Teodor
1978   "Defining Peasants: Conceptualisations and Deconceptualisations, Old and New, in a Marxist Debate." Paper presented at the International Congress of Anthropological and Ethnological Sciences Post-Plenary Conference on the Social Anthropology of Peasantry, Lucknow, India.

Snowden, J. D.
1913–15 Diaries, an Agricultural Officer, of tours of inspection in Uganda. 2 vols., with associated reports and notes. MSS. Afr.s.921. Rhodes House, Oxford.

Temple-Perkins, E.A.
1946   Drafts for reminiscences of service in the Uganda Administration. MSS. Afr.s.1512. Rhodes House, Oxford.

Tothill, John D.
1935   "Ploughing as a Factor in Native Agriculture in Uganda." Typescript. East African Institute of Social and Economic Research, Kampala.

Twaddle, Michael J.
1968/69 "Bakungu Chiefs of Buganda under British Colonial Rule, 1900–1930." Social Science Research Council Conference paper. University of East Africa, Nairobi.

1969   "Segmentary Violence and Political Change in Early Colonial
        Uganda." Social Science Research Council Conference paper.
        University of East Africa, Nairobi.
Uganda Company
1903–48 Minute Books. 7 vols. Rhodes House, Oxford.
1914–33 Journal. 3 vols. Rhodes House, Oxford.
Uzoigwe, G. N.
1968/69 "Kabalega's Abarusura: The Military Factor in Bunyoro." So-
        cial Science Research Council Conference paper. University of
        East Africa, Nairobi.
Van Zwanenberg, Roger
1972   "Anti-slavery, the Ideology of Nineteenth-Century Imperialism
        in East Africa." Conference paper. Historical Association of
        Kenya, Nairobi.
Waswa, Simion
n.d.   "Kakungulu." MSS. Notebook. East African Institute of Social
        Research, Kampala.

3. Dissertations

Battle, Vincent
1974   "Education in Uganda." Ph.D. Teachers College, Columbia
        University, New York.
Carter, Frank
1967   "Education in Uganda, 1894–1945." Ph.D. University of Lon-
        London.
De Kiewet, Marie
1955   "The Imperial British East Africa Company, 1875–1895."
        Ph.D. University of London.
Ehrlich, Cyril
1958   "The Marketing of Cotton in Uganda, 1900–1950: A Case
        Study of Colonial Government Economic Policy." Ph.D. Uni-
        versity of London.
Gartrell, Beverly
1979   "The Ruling Ideas of a Ruling Elite: British Colonial Officials
        in Uganda, 1944–1952." Ph.D. City University of New York.
King, John W.
1964   "Nile Transport in Uganda." Ph.D. Northwestern University,
        Evanston, Ill.
Pasteur, D.
1968   "The expansion of the Church of Uganda (NAC) from Bugan-
        da: Partnership or Conflict." Ph.D. University of Birmingham,
        England.

Pirouet, M. Louise
  1968   "The Expansion of the Church of Uganda (NAC) from Bugan-
          da into Northern and Western Uganda between 1891 and
          1914, with special reference to work of African teachers and
          evangelists." Ph.D. University of East Africa, Nairobi.
Rowe, John
  1966   "Revolution in Buganda, 1856–1900." Ph.D. University of
          Wisconsin, Madison.
Sheriff, Abdul M. H.
  1971   "The Rise of a Commercial Empire: An Aspect of the Eco-
          nomic History of Zanzibar, 1770–1873." Ph.D. University of
          London.
Tosh, John A.
  1973   "Political Authority among the Langi of Northern Uganda,
          1800–1939." Ph.D. University of London.
Twaddle, Michael J.
  1967   "Politics in Bukeddi, 1900–1939: An historical Study of Ad-
          ministrative Change among the Segmentary Peoples of Eastern
          Uganda under the Impact of British Colonial Rule." Ph.D. Uni-
          versity of London.
Van Zwanenberg, Roger M.A.
  1971   "Primitive Capital Accumulation in Kenya, 1919–1939: A
          Study of the Processes and Determinants in the Development of
          a Wage Labour Force." Ph.D. University of Sussex.

B. *Published Works*

Abrams, Philip
  1978   "Towns and Economic Growth." In Philip Abrams and Ed-
          ward A. Wrigley (eds.), *Towns and Societies: Essays in Eco-
          nomic History and Historical Sociology*. Cambridge: Cam-
          bridge University Press.
Ajayi, J. F. Ade
  1970   "The Continuity of African Institutions under Colonialism." In
          Lewis Gann and Peter Duignan (eds.), *Colonialism in Africa*,
          1870–1960, vol. 1, pp. 497–509. London: Cambridge Univer-
          sity Press.
Alavi, H.
  1973   "Peasant Classes and Primordial Loyalties." *Journal of Peasant
          Studies* 1(1):23–62.
Allen, William
  1965   *The African Husbandman*. New York: Barnes & Noble.

Alpers, Edward A.
 1973 "Rethinking African Economic History: A Contribution to the Discussion of the Roots of Underdevelopment." *Ufahamu* 3(3): 97–129.
 1975a "Eastern Africa." In Richard Gray (ed.), *The Cambridge History of Africa*, vol. 4. *1600–1790*, pp. 478–481. Cambridge: Cambridge University Press.
 1975b *Ivory and Slaves: Changing Pattern of International Trade in East Central Africa to the Later Nineteenth Century*. Berkeley and Los Angeles: University of California Press.
Amin, Samir
 1976 *Unequal Development: An Essay on the Social Formation of Peripheral Capitalism*. New York: Monthly Review Press.
Ansorge, William J.
 1899 *Under the African Sun*. London: W. Heinemann.
Apthorpe, Raymond
 1968 "Does Tribalism Really Matter?" *Transition* 7:18–22.
Ardant, Gabriel
 1965 *Théorie Sociologique de l'Impôt*. 2 vols. Paris: Imprimerie Nationale.
Arrighi, Giovanni, and John S. Saul
 1973 *Essays on the Political Economy of Africa*. New York: Monthly Review Press.
Ashe, Robert F.
 1889 *Two Kings of Uganda*. London: S. Low, Marston, Searle & Rivington.
 1895 *Chronicles of Uganda*. New York: Randolph.
Atieno–Odhiambo, E. S.
 1972 "The Rise and Decline of the Kenya Peasantry, 1888–1922." *East African Journal* 9(5). (Reprinted in Peter C. W. Gutkind and Peter Waterman [eds.], *African Social Studies: A Radical Reader*, pp. 233–240. New York: Monthly Review Press, 1977.)
Austin, Herbert H.
 1903 *With Macdonald in Uganda*. London: Edward Arnold.
Bailey, Frederick G.
 1957 *Caste and the Economic Frontier*. Manchester, Eng.: Manchester University Press.
Baker, Sir Samuel White
 1874 *Ismailia*. London: Macmillan.
Barber, James P.
 1964 "The Macdonald Expedition to the Nile, 1887–99." *Uganda Journal* 28(1):1–14.

1968   *Imperial Frontier: A Study of Relations between the British and the Pastoral Tribes of North-East Uganda*. Nairobi: East African Publishing House.

Barrett, David R.
1968   *Schism and Renewal in Africa*. Nairobi: Oxford University Press.

Beachey, R. W.
1962   "The Arms Trade in East Africa in the Late Nineteenth Century." *Journal of African History* 3(3):451–467.
1967a   "The East African Ivory Trade in the Nineteenth Century." *Journal of African History* 8(2):269–290.
1967b   "Macdonald's Expedition and the Uganda Mutiny, 1887–1898." *Historical Journal* 10:237–254.

Beadle, L. C., and E. M. Lind
1960   "Research on the Swamps of Uganda." *Uganda Journal* 24(1):84–96.

Beattie, John
1971   *The Nyoro State*. Oxford: Clarendon Press.

Bell, Sir Henry Hesketh
1946   *Glimpses of a Governor's Life*. London: S. Low, Marston & Co.

Bell, W. D. M.
1949   *Karamoja Safari*. London: Gollancz.

Bernstein, Henry, editor
1978   "Notes on Capital and Peasantry." *Review of African Political Economy* 10:60–73.

Biebuyck, Daniel P., editor
1963   *African Agrarian Systems*. London: Oxford University Press.

Biermans, John
1920   *A Short History of the Vicariate of the Upper Nile, Uganda*. London: Mill Hill Fathers.

Black-Michaud, Jacob
1975   *Cohesive Force: Feud in the Mediterranean and the Middle East*. New York: St. Martin's Press.

Blackledge, G. R.
1900   "Correspondence." *Church Missionary Intelligencer* (July): 157.

Bond, George C.
1967   *The Politics of Change in a Zambian Community*. Chicago: University of Chicago Press.

Boserup, Ester
1965   *The Conditions of Agricultural Growth*. Chicago: Aldine.

1970   *Woman's Role in Economic Development*. New York: St. Martin's Press.

Boyle, J.
1904   "Cotton Growing in British Possessions." *United States Consular Reports* 74(281):241–250.

Braudel, Fernand
1972   "History and the Social Sciences." In Peter Burke (comp.), *Economy and Society in Early Modern Europe*. New York: Harper & Row.
1973   *Capitalism and Material Life, 1400–1800*. New York: Harper & Row.

Brenner, Robert
1977   "The Origins of Capitalist Development: A Critique of Neo-Smithian Marxism." *New Left Review* 104:27–59.

Brett, Edward A.
1973   *Colonialism and Underdevelopment in East Africa*. London: Heinemann Educational Books.

Bridges, R. C.
1970   "John Hanning Speke: Negotiating a Way to the Nile." In Robert I. Rotberg (ed.), *Africa and Its Explorers*, pp. 95–138. Cambridge, Mass.: Harvard University Press.

Buckley, T. R.
1902   "Correspondence." *Church Missionary Intelligencer* (March):191.

Buell, Raymond L.
1928   *The Native Problem in Africa*, vol. 1. New York: Macmillan.

Burawoy, Michael
1977   "The Functions and Reproduction of Migrant Labor: Comparative Material from Southern Africa and the United States." *American Journal of Sociology* 81(5):1050–1087.

Burke, Fred G.
1964   *Local Government and Politics in Uganda*. Syracuse, N.Y.: Syracuse University Press.

Cardoso, Fernando H.
1972   "Dependency and Development in Latin America." *New Left Review* 74:83–95.
1977   "The Consumption of Dependency Theory in the United States." *Latin American Research Review* 12(3):7–24.

Caulk, R.A.
1972   "Firearms and Princely Power in Ethiopia in the Nineteenth Century." *Journal of African History* 13(4):609–630.

Chapman, Stanley D.
1972   *The Cotton Industry in the Industrial Revolution*. London: Macmillan.
Chayanov, A. R.
1966   *Organizatsiya Krest' yanskogo khozyaistra*. Translated as *The Theory of Peasant Economy*; D. Thorner, R. E. F. Smith, and B. Kerblay, eds. New York: Irwin.
Childe, Vere G.
1952   *What Happened in History*. Harmondsworth, Middlesex: Penguin Books.
Clark, Colin, and Margaret Haswell
1966   *The Economics of Subsistence Agriculture*. London: Macmillan.
Clendenen, Clarence, Robert O. Collins, and Peter J. Duignan
1966   *Americans in Africa, 1865–1900*. Stanford, Calif.: Stanford University Press.
Cliffe, Lionel
1977   "Rural Class Formation in East Africa." *Journal of Political Studies* 4(2):195–224.
Cohen, Abner
1969   *Custom and Politics in Urban Africa*. London: Routledge & Kegan Paul.
1974   *Two-dimensional Man: An Essay on the Anthropology of Power and Symbolism in Complex Society*. Berkeley and Los Angeles: University of California Press.
Cohen, David W.
1972   *The Historical Tradition of Busoga, Mukama, and Kintu*. Oxford: Clarendon Press.
1974   "Pre-Colonial History as the History of the 'Society.'" *African Studies Review* 17:139–174.
Collins, Robert O.
1970   "Samuel White Baker: Prospero in Purgatory." In Robert I. Rotberg (ed.), *Africa and Its Explorers*, pp. 139–174. Cambridge, Mass.: Harvard University Press.
Collins, Robert O., editor
1968   *Problems in African History*. Englewood Cliffs, N.J.: Prentice-Hall.
Colson, Elizabeth F.
1951   "The Plateau Tonga of Northern Rhodesia." In Elizabeth F. Colson and Max Gluckman (eds.), *Seven Tribes of British Central Africa*. London: Oxford University Press.
1970   "African Society at the Time of the Scramble." In Lewis H.

Gann and Peter J. Duignan (eds.), *Colonialism in Africa, 1870–1960*, vol. 1, pp. 27–65. London: Cambridge University Press.

1971 "The Impact of the Colonial Period on the Definition of Land Rights." In Victor Turner (ed.), *Colonialism in Africa, 1870–1960*, vol. 3. London: Cambridge University Press.

Cook, Sir Albert R.

1945 *Uganda Memories, 1897–1940*. Kampala: Uganda Society.

Coquery-Vidrovitch, Catherine

1977 "Research on an African Model of Production." In Peter C. W. Gutkind and Peter Waterman (eds.), *African Social Studies: A Radical Reader*, pp. 77–92. New York: Monthly Review Press.

Crabtree, William

1901 "Openings Beyond Uganda: An Appeal for Bukeddi." *Church Missionary Intelligencer* (May):369–370.

1902 "Correspondence." *Church Missionary Intelligencer* (June):2.

Crazzolara, J. Pasquale

1950–54 *The Lwoo*. 3 vols. Verona: Instituto Missioni Africane.

1960 "Notes on the Lango-Omiru and the Labwor and Nyakwai." *Anthropos* 55:174–214.

Cummings, Robert

1973 "A Note on the History of Caravan Porters in East Africa." *Kenya Historical Review* 1(21):109–138.

Cutler, Anthony, Barry Hindness, Paul Hurst, and Athar Hussain

1977 *Marx's "Capital" and Capitalism Today*. 2 vols. London: Routledge & Kegan Paul.

Dak, O.

1968 *A Geographical Analysis of the Distribution of Migrants in Uganda*. Kampala: Department of Geography, Makerere University College.

Douglas, Mary

1967 "Witch Beliefs in Central Africa." *Africa* 37(1):72–80.

Dunbar, A. R.

1965 *A History of Bunyoro-Kitara*. East African Institute of Social Research. Kampala: Oxford University Press.

DuPlessis, Johannes

1930 *The Evangelisation of Pagan Africa*. Cape Town and Johannesburg: J. C. Juta & Co.

Durkheim, Emile, and Marcel Mauss

1967 *Primitive Classification*. Chicago: University of Chicago Press.

Dyson-Hudson, Neville

1962 "Factors Inhibiting Change in an African Pastoral Society."

Transactions of the New York Academy of Science 24:771–801.

1966   *Karimojong Politics*. Oxford: Clarendon Press.

Edel, May

1965   "African Tribalism—Some Reflections on Uganda." *Political Science Quarterly* 80(3):357–372.

Egimu-Okuda, N.

1973   "The Occupation of Amuria and the Rise of Omiat." In John B. Webster (ed.), *The Iteso during the Asonya*. Nairobi: East African Publishing House.

Ehrlich, Cyril

1953   *The Uganda Company, Limited: The First Fifty Years*. Kampala: Uganda Co.

Elkan, Walter

1960   *Migrants and Proletarians*. London: Oxford University Press.

Emudong, C. P.

1973   "The Settlement and Organisation of Kumi during the Asonya." In John B. Webster (ed.) *The Iteso during the Asonya*. Nairobi: East African Publishing House.

Emwanu, G.

1967   "The Reception of Alien Rule in Teso, 1896–1927." *Uganda Journal* 31(2):171–182.

Ennew, Judith

1977   "Peasantry as an Economic Category." *Journal of Peasant Studies* 4(4):295–322.

Fallers, Lloyd A.

1961   "Are African Cultivators To Be Called Peasants?" *Current Anthropology* 2(2):108–110.

1964   "Social Stratification and Economic Processes." In Melville J. Herskovits (ed.), *Economic Transition in Africa*. Evanston, Ill.: Northwestern University Press.

Fearn, Hugh

1956   "Cotton Production in the Nyanza Province of Kenya Colony, 1908–54." *Empire Cotton Growing Review* 33:123–136.

1961   *An African Economy: A Study of the Economic Development of the Nyanza Province of Kenya, 1903–1953*. London: Oxford University Press.

Feis, Herbert

1930   *Europe, the World's Banker, 1870–1914*. New Haven: Yale University Press.

Fieldhouse, D. K.

1961   "Imperialism: An Historiographical Revision." *Economic History Review* 14(2):187–209.

Fishbourne, C. E.
1909   "Lake Kyoga (Ibrahim) Exploration Survey." *Geographical Journal* 33:192–195.
Ford, John
1971   *The Role of Trypanosomiases in African Ecology: A Study of the Tsetse Fly Problem*. Oxford: Clarendon Press.
Fortes, Meyer
1937   "Culture Contact as a Dynamic Process." *Africa* 9:24–55.
1958   "Introduction." In Jack Goody (ed.), *The Development Cycle in Domestic Groups*, pp. 1–14. Cambridge: Cambridge University Press.
Fried, Morton H.
1975   *The Notion of the Tribe*. Menlo Park, Calif.: Cummings.
Funnell, D. C.
1972   *Service Centres in Teso*. Kampala: Department of Geography, Makerere University College.
Gale, Hubert P.
1959   *Uganda and the Mill Hill Fathers*. London: Macmillan.
Gann, Lewis H., and Peter J. Duignan, editors
1970   *Colonialism in Africa, 1870–1960*, vols. 1 and 2. London: Cambridge University Press.
Geertz, Clifford
1963   *Agricultural Involution*. Berkeley and Los Angeles: University of California Press.
1968   *Islam Observed: Religious Development in Morocco and Indonesia*. New Haven: Yale University Press.
Good, Charles M.
1970   *Rural Markets and Trade in East Africa*. Chicago: Department of Geography, University of Chicago.
1972   "Salt, Trade, and Disease: Aspects of Development in Africa's Northern Great Lakes Region." *International Journal of History* 5:43–86.
Goody, Jack R.
1971   *Technology, Tradition, and the State in Africa*. London: Oxford University Press.
1976   *Production and Reproduction: A Comparative Study of the Domestic Domain*. Cambridge: Cambridge University Press.
Goody, Jack R., editor
1958   *The Development Cycle in Domestic Groups*. London: Cambridge University Press.
Goody, Jack R., Joan Thirsk, and Edward P. Thompson, editors
1978   *Family and Inheritance: Rural Society in Western Europe, 1200–1800*. Cambridge: Cambridge University Press.

Gray, Sir John M.
1963   "Kakunguru in Bukeddi." *Uganda Journal* 27:31–59.
Gray, Richard, and David Birmingham, editors
1970   *Pre-Colonial Trade in Africa*. London: Oxford University Press.
Greaves, Ida C.
1935   *Modern Production among Backward Peoples*. London: Allen & Unwin.
Gregory, Robert G.
1962   *Sidney Webb and East Africa: Labour's Experiment with the Doctrine of Native Paramountcy*. Berkeley and Los Angeles: University of California Press.
1971   *India and East Africa*. Oxford: Clarendon Press.
Grove, D.
1961   "Population Densities and Agriculture in Northern Nigeria." In Kenneth Barbour and R. M. Prothero (eds.), *Essays on African Population*. London: Routledge & Kegan Paul.
Groves, Charles Pelham
1970   "Missionary and Humanitarian Aspects of Imperialism from 1870 to 1914." In Lewis H. Gann and Peter J. Duignan (eds.), *Colonialism in Africa, 1870–1960*, vol. 1, pp. 462–496. London: Cambridge University Press.
Gukiina, Peter M.
1972   *Uganda: A Case Study in African Political Development*. Notre Dame, Ind.: University of Notre Dame Press.
Gulliver, Philip H.
1951   *A Preliminary Survey of the Turkana*. Cape Town: University of Cape Town.
1952   "The Karamojong Cluster." *Africa* 22(1):1–22.
1955a   "The Teso and the Karamojong Cluster." *Uganda Journal* 20(2):213–215.
1955b   *The Family Herds*. London: Routledge & Kegan Paul.
1969   *Tradition and Transition in East Africa: Studies of the Tribal Element in the Modern Era*. Berkeley and Los Angeles: University of California Press.
Gulliver, Philip H. and Pamela Gulliver
1953   *The Central Nilo-Hamites*. London: International African Institute.
Gutkind, Peter C. W.
1969   "The Small Town in African Urban Studies." *African Urban Notes* 3(1):5–10.

Gutkind, Peter C. W., and Immanuel Wallerstein, editors
1976   *The Political Economy of Contemporary Africa*. Beverly Hills, Calif.: Sage Publications.
Gutkind, Peter C. W., and Peter Waterman, editors
1977   *African Social Studies: A Radical Reader*. New York: Monthly Review Press.
Habakkuk, H. J., and P. Deane
1965   "The Take-off in Britain." In Walt W. Rostow (ed.), *The Economics of Take-off into Sustained Growth*. London: Macmillan.
Hall, A. R., editor
1968   *The Export of Capital from Britain, 1870–1914*. London: Methuen.
Hancock, William K.
1940   *Survey of British Commonwealth Affairs*, vol. 2. London: Oxford University Press.
Hansen, Holger B.
1977   *Ethnicity and Military Rule in Uganda*. Uppsala: Scandinavian Institute of African Studies.
Hartwig, G. W.
1970   "The Victoria Nyanza as a Trade Route in the Nineteenth Century." *Journal of African History* 11:335–352.
Heisler, Helmuth
1974   *Urbanisation and the Government of Migration: The Interrelation of Urban and Rural Life in Africa*. London: C. Hurst & Co.
Herring, R. S.
1973   "Centralisation, Stratification, and Incorporation: Case Studies from North-Eastern Uganda." *Canadian Journal of African Studies* 7:497–514.
Hjort, Anders
1979   *Savanna Town: Rural Ties and Urban Opportunities in Northern Kenya*. Stockholm: Department of Anthropology, University of Stockholm.
Hobsbawm, Eric J.
1964a   *The Labouring Men*. London: Weidenfeld & Nicolson.
1964b   "Introduction." In *Precapitalist Economic Formations*. New York: International Publishers.
1968   *Industry and Empire: An Economic History of Britain since 1750*. Harmondsworth, Middlesex: Penguin Books.
1971   "Class Consciousness in History." In Istvan Mezzaros (ed.), *Aspects of History and Class Consciousness*, pp. 5–21. London: Herder and Herder.

1973   "Peasants and Politics." *Journal of Peasant Studies* 1(1):3–22.
        1(1):3–22.
Hobson, John A.
1902   *Imperialism: A Study.* London: Nisbet.
Hodgkin, T.
1972   "Some African and Third World Theories of Imperialism." In
        Roger Owen and Brian Sutcliffe (eds.), *Studies in the Theory of
        Imperialism.* London: Longmans.
Hyam, Ronald
1964   "Review of Africa and the Victorians." *Historical Journal*
        7:154–169.
Jackson, Sir Frederick J.
1930   *Early Days in East Africa.* London: Arnold. (Reprinted 1969.)
Jameson, J. D., editor
1970   *Agriculture in Uganda.* Oxford: Oxford University Press.
Jeffries, Sir Charles J.
1972   *Whitehall and the Colonial Service.* London: Athlone Press.
Jenkins, A. O.
1939   "A Note on the Saza of Bugerere, Buganda Kingdom." *Uganda
        Journal* 6(4):204–206.
Johnson, Alex
1929   *The Life and Letters of Sir Harry Johnston.* London: Jonathan
        Cape.
Johnson, Marion
1974   "Cotton Imperialism in West Africa." *African Affairs*
        73:178–187.
Johnston, Sir Harry H.
1902   *The Uganda Protectorate.* 2 vols. New York: Dodd, Mead.
1923   *The Story of My Life.* London: Chatto.
Jones, E.
1960   *Agriculture in Eastern Province, Uganda.* Entebbe: Uganda
        Government Press.
Jones, Gareth S.
1971   *Outcast London: A Study in the Relationship between Classes
        in Victorian Society.* Oxford: Clarendon Press.
Jones, Herbert G.
1926   *Uganda in Transformation, 1876–1926.* London: Church Mis-
        sionary Society.
Jones, Thomas J.
1925   *Education in East Africa.* New York: Phelps-Stokes Fund.
Kagola, B. M.
1955   "Tribal Names and Customs in Teso District." *Uganda Journal*
        19:41–48.

Kasfir, Nelson
1976   *The Shrinking Political Arena*. Berkeley and Los Angeles: University of California Press.
Keltie, Sir John Scott
1893   *The Partition of Africa*. London: E. Stanford.
Kennedy, F. R.
1937   "Teso Clans." *Uganda Journal* 5(2):137–139.
Kessler, Clive S.
1978   *Islam and Politics in a Malay State: Kelantan, 1838–1969*. Ithaca, N.Y.: Cornell University Press.
King, T. W.
1966   "Nile Transport in Uganda." *East African Geographical Review* 4:25–26.
Kirk, Rev. C. J.
1903   "Correspondence." *St. Joseph's Advocate* 41:248–249.
Kitching, Arthur L.
1912   *On the Backwaters of the Nile*. London: T. Fisher Unwin.
1913   "Correspondence." *Uganda Notes* (November):154.
1935   *From Darkness to Light: A Study of Pioneer Missionary Work in the Diocese of the Upper Nile*. London: Society for the Promotion of Christian Knowledge.
Kiwanuka, M. S. M. Semakula
1968a   *Empire of Bunyoro-Kitara: Myth or Reality?* Kampala: Longmans.
1968b   "Bunyoro and the British: A Reappraisal of the Causes for the Decline and Fall of an African Kingdom." *Journal of African History* 9(4):603–619.
1972   *A History of Buganda: From the Foundation of the Kingdom to 1900*. New York: Africana Publishing Corp.
1975   "The Emergence of Buganda as a Dominant Power in the Interlacustrine Region of East Africa, 1600–1900." *Makerere History Journal* 1(1):19–31.
Kiza, Soseni
1913   "Teso, Bukedi." *Ebifa mu Buganda* (July).
Kjekshus, Helge
1977   *Ecology Control and Economic Development in East African History: The Case of Tanganyika, 1850–1950*. Berkeley and Los Angeles: University of California Press.
Kottack, Conrad P.
1972   "Ecological Variables in the Origin and Evolution of African States: The Buganda Example." *Comparative Studies in Society and History* 14:351–380.

282 *Bibliography*

Kuczynski, Robert R.
  1937   *Colonial Population*. London: Oxford University Press.
  1948   *Demographic Survey of the British Colonial Empire*. London: Oxford University Press.
Laclau, Ernest
  1971   "Capitalism and Feudalism in Latin America." *New Left Review* 67:19–38.
Lamphear, John
  1976   *The Traditional History of the Jie of Uganda*. Oxford: Oxford University Press.
Landes, David S.
  1958   *Bankers and Pashas: International Finance and Economic Imperialism in Egypt*. Cambridge, Mass.: Harvard University Press.
Langdale-Brown, I., H. A. Osmaston, and J. G. Wilson
  1962   *The Vegetation of Eastern Province, Uganda*. Entebbe: Uganda Government Press.
Langlands, Brian W.
  1962   "Concepts of the Nile." *Uganda Journal* 26(1):1–22.
  1966   "The Banana in Uganda, 1860–1920." *Uganda Journal* 30(1): 30(1): 39–63.
  1968   "Teso District, East Uganda: A Study in Regional Economic Development." In Herfried Berger (ed.), *Ostafrikanische Studien*, pp. 199–210. Nürnberg: Im Selbstrerlag des Wirtschafts- und Sozial-geographischen Instituts der Friedrich-Alexander Universitat.
  1971   *The Population Geography of Teso District*. Occasional paper no. 36. Kampala: Department of Geography, Makerere University College.
Langlands, Brian W., and G. Namirembe
  1967   *Studies on the Geography of Religion in Uganda*. Kampala: Department of Geography, Makerere University College.
Lawrance, J. C. D.
  1953   "Rock Paintings in Teso." *Uganda Journal* 17(1):8–13.
  1955   "A History of Teso to 1937." *Uganda Journal* 19(1):7–40.
  1957   *The Iteso*. London: Oxford University Press.
Lenin, Vladimir I.
  1924   *Imperialism: The Highest Stage of Capitalism*. Detroit, Mich.: Marxian Educational Society.
  1954   *The Agrarian Question and the "Critics of Marx."* Moscow: Progress Publishers.
  1963   "The Development of Capitalism in Agriculture." *Collected Works*, vol. 12, pp. 190–282. Moscow: Foreign Languages Publishing House.

1974   *The Development of Capitalism in Russia*. Moscow: Progress Publishers.

Leys, Colin
1974   *Underdevelopment in Kenya: The Political Economy of Neo-Colonialism*. Berkeley and Los Angeles: University of California Press.

Low, Donald A.
1956   *Religion and Society in Buganda, 1875 –1900* . Kampala: East African Institute of Social Research.
1964   "The Northern Interior, 1840–1884." In J. D. Fage and Roland A. Oliver (eds.), *The Cambridge History of Africa*. London: Cambridge University Press.
1965   "Uganda: The Establishment of the Protectorate, 1894–1910." In Vincent T. Harlow and Elizabeth M. Chilver (eds.), *History of East Africa*, vol. 2, pp. 57–120. Oxford: Oxford University Press.
1973   *Lion Rampant: Essays in the Study of British Imperialism*. London: Cass.
1974–75 "Warbands and Ground-Level Imperialism in Uganda, 1870–1900." *Historical Studies* 16:584–597.

Low, David A., and R. Cranford Pratt
1960   *Buganda and British Overrule, 1900 –1955* . London: Oxford University Press.

Lugard, Sir Frederick J. D.
1893   *The Rise of Our East African Empire*, vol. 2. Edinburgh: W. Blackwood & Sons.
1922   *The Dual Mandate in Tropical Africa*. Edinburgh: W. Blackwood & Sons.

Luxemburg, Rosa
1972   *The Accumulation of Capital*. New York: Monthly Review Press.

Macdonald, John R. L.
1897   *Soldiering and Surveying in British East Africa*. London: Edward Arnold.

Macfarlane, Alan
1977   *Reconstructing Historical Communities*. London: Cambridge University Press.

McGough, Joseph
1956   "The Late Father Christopher J. Kirk, O.B.E." *St. Joseph's Missionary Advocate (Ireland)* 8(1):14–17.

McHenry, George
1863   *The Cotton Trade*. London: Sanders, Otley & Co.

Macleod, M. J.

1975　"The Sociological Theory of Taxation and the Peasant." *Peasant Studies Newsletter* 4(3):2–6.

McMaster, David N.

1962　*A Subsistence Crop Geography of Uganda*. London: Geographical Publications.

McNeill, William H.

1976　*Plagues and People*. New York: Doubleday-Anchor.

Mafeje, A.

1971　"The Ideology of Tribalism." *Journal of Modern African Studies* 9(2):253:261.

Mamdani, Mahmood

1975　"Class Struggle in Uganda." *Review of African Political Economy* 4:26–61.

1976　*Politics and Class Formation in Uganda*. New York: Monthly Review Press.

Manghezi, Alpheus

1976　*Class, Elite, and Community in African Development*. Uppsala: Scandinavian Institute of African Studies.

Martin, Anne

1963　*The Marketing of Minor Crops in Uganda*. London: Her Majesty's Stationery Office.

Marx, Karl

1967　*Capital*. 3 vols. New York: International Publishers.

1969　"The Eighteenth Brumaire of Louis Bonaparte." In Karl Marx and Friedrich Engels, *Selected Works*, pp. 95–180. New York: International Publishers.

1973　*Grundrisse: Introduction to the Critique of Political Economy*. Harmondsworth, Middlesex: Penguin Books.

Marx, Karl, and Friedrich Engels

1977　*The German Ideology*. New York: International Publishers.

Masefield, Geoffrey B.

1972　*A History of the Colonial Agricultural Service*. Oxford: Clarendon Press.

Matson, A. T.

1965　"Macdonald's Expedition to the Nile." *Uganda Journal* 29(1):98–103.

1966　"A Note on F. Spire." *Uganda Journal* 30(2):281.

1968a　"Macdonald's Manuscript History of the Events of 1897 to 1899." *Uganda Journal* 32(2):217–219.

1968b　"Baganda Merchant Venturers." *Uganda Journal* 32(1):1–15. 32(1):1–15.

1969　"A Further Note on the Macdonald Expedition, 1897–1899." *Historical Journal* 12:155–157.

1971 "Bibliography of the Works of Sir John Gray." *Uganda Journal* 35(2):161–174.
1973 "Introduction." In reprint of Herbert H. Austin, *With Macdonald in Uganda (1903)* , pp. v–xxiii. London: Edward Arnold.
Mazrui, Ali.
1967 "Tanzaphilia." *Transition* 6:20–26.
Meillassoux, Claude
1960 "Essai d'interpretation du phenomène economique dans les sociétés traditionelles d'auto-subsistance." *Cahiers d'Etudes Africaines* 1:38–67.
1971 *The Development of Indigenous Trade and Markets in West Africa*. London: Oxford University Press.
1972 "From Reproduction to Production." *Economy and Society* 1(1):93–105.
1973 "The Social Organisation of the Peasantry." *Journal of Peasant Studies* 1(1):89–90.
Merrill, Michael
1977 "Cash Is Good to Eat: Self-Sufficiency and Exchange in the Rural Economy of the United States." *Radical History Review* (Winter):42–71.
Miller, Charles
1974 *Battle for the Bundu: The First World War in East Africa*. London: Macmillan and Jane's.
Mintz, Sidney
1973 "A Note on the Definition of Peasantries." *Journal of Peasant Studies* 1(1):91–106.
1974 "A Rural Proletariat and the Problem of Rural Proletarian Consciousness." *Journal of Peasant Studies* 1(3):291–325.
Mitchell, Sir Philip E.
1954 *African Afterthoughts*. London: Hutchinson.
Moore, Ernest D.
1931 *Ivory, Scourge of Africa*. New York: Harper.
Morgan, A. R.
1958 "Uganda's Cotton Industry—Fifty Years Back." *Uganda Journal* 22:107–112.
Morris, H. Stephen
1968 *The Indians in Uganda*. Chicago: University of Chicago Press.
Moyse-Bartlett, Hubert
1956 *The King's African Rifles*. Aldershot, Eng.: Gale and Polden.
Multatuli (pseudonym)
1967 *Max Havelaar, or the Coffee Auctions of the Dutch Trading Company*. Leyden: Sijthoff; London: Heinemann; New York: London House & Maxwell.

Mutibwa, P. M.
1976   "White Settlers in Uganda: The Era of Hopes and Disillusionment, 1905–1923." *Transafrican Journal of History* 5(2):112–122.
Neill, Stephen C.
1964   *Christian Missions*. Harmondsworth, Middlesex: Penguin Books.
1966   *Colonialism and Christian Missions*. London: Lutterworth Press.
Nurkse, Ragnar
1962   *Patterns of Trade Development*. Oxford: Basil Blackwell.
Nyakatura, John W.
1973   *Anatomy of an African Kingdom: A History of Bunyoro-Kitara*. New York: Doubleday-Anchor.
Ochieng, W. R.
1972   "Colonial African Chiefs." In Bethwell A. Ogot (ed.), *War and Society in Africa*. London: Frank Cass.
O'Connor, Anthony M.
1963   "Regional Inequalities in Economic Development in Uganda." *East African Economic Review* 1:33–42.
1965   *Railways and Development in Uganda*. Nairobi: Oxford University Press.
1966   *An Economic Geography of East Africa*. New York: Praeger.
O'Connor, J.
1970   "The Meaning of Economic Imperialism." In Robert I. Rhodes (ed.), *Imperialism and Underdevelopment: A Reader*, pp. 101–150. New York: Monthly Review Press.
Ogot, Bethwell A.
1967   *History of the Southern Luo*. Nairobi: East African Publishing House.
Ogot, Bethwell A., editor
1972   *War and Society in Africa*. London: Frank Cass.
Ogot, Bethwell A., and J. A. Kiernan, editors
1968   *Zamani: A Survey of East African History*. Nairobi: East African Publishing House.
Okalany, D. H.
1973   "Mukongoro during the Asonya." In John B. Webster (ed.) *The Iteso during the Asonya*. Nairobi: East African Publishing House.
Oliver, Roland A.
1952   The Missionary Factor in East Africa. London: Longmans.

1957 *Sir Harry Johnston and the Scramble for Africa*. London: Chatto & Windus.

Olivier, Sir Sydney H.
1929 *White Capital and Coloured Labour*. London: L. and V. Woolf.

Orde-Brown, Granville St. John.
1933 *The African Labourer*. London: Oxford University Press.

Owen, Edward R. J.
1969 *Cotton and the Egyptian Economy, 1820 –1914: A Study in Trade and Development*. Oxford: Clarendon Press.

Owen, Roger, and Brian Sutcliffe, editors
1972 *Studies in the Theory of Imperialism*. London: Longmans.

Owen, W. E.
1921 "The Missionary in Politics." *Church Missionary Review* 72: 135–144.

Paige, Jeffery G.
1975 *Agrarian Revolution: Social Movements and Export Agriculture in the Underdeveloped World*. New York: Free Press.

Palmer, Robin, and Neil Parsons, editors
1977 *The Roots of Rural Poverty in Central and Southern Africa*. Berkeley and Los Angeles: University of California Press.

Parkin, David, editor
1975 *Town and Country in Central and Eastern Africa*. London: Oxford University Press.

Parkin, Frank
1972 *Class Inequality and Political Order*. New York: Praeger.

Parsons, D. J.
1960 *The Systems of Agriculture Practised in Uganda: The Teso System*. Entebbe: Uganda Government Press.

Perham, Margery
1962 *Colonial Reckoning*. New York: Knopf.

Peters, Karl
1891 *New Light on Dark Africa*. London: Ward, Lock & Co.

Philipps, J. E. T.
1922 "The Tide of Colour." *Journal of the African Society* 21:129–135, 309–315.

Phimister, I. R.
1974 "Peasant Production and Underdevelopment in Southern Rhodesia, 1890–1914." *African Affairs* 73:217–228.

Polanyi, Karl
1944 *The Great Transformation*. Boston: Beacon Press.

Post, Kenneth
  1973   "Peasantisation and Rural Political Movements in Western Africa." *European Journal of Sociology* 13(2):223–254.
Postlethwaite, John P.
  1947   *I Look Back*. London: Boardman.
Powesland, Philip G.
  1957   *Economic Policy and Labour*. Kampala: East African Institute of Social Research.
Pratt, R. Cranford
  1965   "Administration and Politics in Uganda, 1919–1945." In Vincent T. Harlow and Elizabeth M. Chilver (eds.), *History of East Africa*, vol. 2, pp. 477–483. London: Oxford University Press.
Price, T.
  1963   "The Church as a Land-holder in Eastern Africa." *Bulletin of the Society for African Church History* 1:1–11.
Purvis, John B.
  1909   *Through Uganda to Mount Elgon*. London: T. Fisher Unwin.
Ranger, Terence O.
  1968   "Connections between 'Primary Resistance' Movements and Modern Mass Nationalism in East and Central Africa." *Journal of African History* 9(3):437–453; 9(4):631–641.
  1970   "African Reactions to the Imposition of Colonial Rule in East and Central Africa." In Lewis Gann and Peter Duignan (eds.), *Colonialism in Africa 1870 –1960* , vol. 1, pp. 293–324. London: Cambridge University Press.
  1978   "Growing from the Roots: Reflections on Peasant Research in Central and Southern Africa." *Journal of Southern African Studies* 5(1):99–133.
Ranger, Terence O., editor
  1965   *Emerging Themes in African History*. London: Heinemann Educational Books.
Rayne, Henry A.
  1923   *The Ivory Raiders*. London: W. Heinemann.
Richards, Audrey I.
  1939   *Land, Labour, and Diet in Northern Rhodesia: An Economic Study of the Bemba Tribe*. London: Oxford University Press.
  1960   *Economic Development and Tribal Change*. Nairobi: Oxford University Press.
Richards, A. R.
  1977   "Primitive Accumulation in Egypt, 1790–1882." *Review* 1(2): 1(2): 30–49.
Rigby, Peter
  1969   *Cattle and Kinship among the Gogo*. Ithaca, N.Y.: Cornell University Press.

Rius (pseudonym)
1976   *Marx for Beginners*. New York: Two Continents Publishing
        Group.
Roberts, A. D.
1962   "The Sub-Imperialism of the Baganda." *Journal of African His-
        tory* 3(3):435–450.
1963   "The Evolution of the Uganda Protectorate." *Uganda Journal*
        27(1):95–106.
Robinson, Ronald E., and John Gallagher, with Alice Denny
1961   *Africa and the Victorians: The Official Mind of Imperialism*.
        London: Macmillan.
Roscoe, John
1901   "Among the Wild Bakeddi." *Church Missionary Gleaner*
        (May):66–68.
1915   *The Northern Bantu*. Cambridge: Cambridge University Press.
1969   *Twenty-five Years in East Africa*. New York: Negro Univer-
        sities Press.
Rostow, Walt W.
1960   *The Stages of Economic Growth*. Cambridge: Cambridge Uni-
        versity Press.
Rotberg, Robert I., editor
1970   *Africa and Its Explorers: Motives, Methods, and Impact*. Cam-
        bridge, Mass.: Harvard University Press.
Rowe, John A.
1964   "Land and Politics in Buganda, 1875–1955." *Makerere Jour-
        nal* 1:1–13.
Sanderson, G. N.
1965   *England, Europe, and the Upper Nile, 1882–1899: A Study in
        the Partition of Africa*. Edinburgh: Edinburgh University Press.
1974   "The European Partition of Africa: Coincidence or Conjunc-
        ture?" *Journal of Imperial and Commonwealth History*
        3:1–54.
Saul, John S., and Roger Woods
1971   "African Peasantries." In Teodor Shanin (ed.), *Peasants and
        Peasant Societies*, pp. 103–114. Harmondsworth, Middlesex:
        Penguin Books.
Scherer, James A. B.
1916   *Cotton as A World Power*. New York: Frederick A. Stokes.
Semmel, Bernard
1960   *Imperialism and Social Reform, 1895 –1914* . Cambridge,
        Mass.: Harvard University Press.
Shanin, Teodor, editor
1971   *Peasants and Peasant Societies*. Harmondsworth, Middlesex:
        Penguin Books.
1972   *The Awkward Class*. Oxford: Clarendon Press.

Slicher van Bath, Bernard H.
 1963   *The Agrarian History of Western Europe, A.D. 500 –1850* .
         New York: St. Martin's Press.
Smalldone, J. P.
 1972   "Firearms in the Central Sudan: A Revaluation." *Journal of
         African History* 13(4):591–607.
Southall, Aidan
 1970   "The Illusion of the Tribe." *Journal of Asian and African Stud-
         ies* 5:1–12.
 1975   "From Segmentary Lineage to Ethnic Organisation." In Max-
         well Owusu (ed.), *Colonialism and Choice: Essays Presented to
         Lucy Mair*, pp. 203–230. The Hague: Mouton.
Speke, John H.
 1863   *Journal of the Discovery of the Source of the Nile*. Edinburgh:
         W. Blackwood.
Stahl, Kathleen M.
 1951   *The Metropolitan Organisation of British Colonial Trade: Four
         Regional Studies*. London: Faber and Faber.
Starrett, Henry P.
 1917   *East African Markets for Hardware and Agricultural Imple-
         ments*. (Special Consular Report to the Department of Com-
         merce, United States Government, no. 78.) Washington, D.C.:
         Government Printing Office.
Stock, Eugene
 1899   *The History of the Church Missionary Society*. 3 vols. London:
         Church Missionary Society.
Strayer, Robert W.
 1978   *The Making of Mission Communities in East Africa: Anglicans
         and Africans in Colonial Kenya, 1875 –1935* . Albany: State
         University of New York Press.
Sundkler, Bengdt G. M.
 1948   *Bantu Prophets in South Africa*. London: Oxford University
         Press.
Sundström, Lars
 1974   *The Exchange Economy of Pre-Colonial Tropical Africa*. New
         York: St. Martin's Press.
Sutton, John E. G.
 1973   *Early Trade in Eastern Africa*. Nairobi: Historical Association
         of Tanzania.
 1968   "The Settlement of East Africa." In Bethwell A. Ogot and J. A.
         Kiernan (eds.), *Zamani: A Survey of East African History*.
         Nairobi: East African Publishing House.

Ternan, Trevor P. B.
1930   *Some Experiences of an Old Bromsgrovian*. Birmingham, Eng.: Cornish Brothers.
Thiel, E. P.
1962   "Frederick Spire, S. M. B." *Uganda Journal* 26(1):89–101.
Thomas, Harold B.
1939   "Capax Imperii: The Story of Semei Kakunguru." *Uganda Journal* 6(2):125–136.
Thomas, Harold B., and R. F. Lindrell
1956   "Early Ascents of Mount Elgon." *Uganda Journal* 20(2):113–128.
Thomas, Harold B., and Robert Scott
1935   *Uganda*. London: Oxford University Press.
Thomas, Harold B., and A. E. Spencer
1938   *A History of Uganda Land and Surveys*. Entebbe: Uganda Government Press.
Thompson, Edward P.
1963   *The Making of the English Working Class*. London: Gollancz.
1967   "Time, Work-Discipline, and Industrial Capitalism." *Past and Present* 38:56–97.
1978a   "Eighteenth-Century English Society: Class Struggle without Class?" *Social History* 3(2):133–165.
1978b   *The Poverty of Theory and Other Essays*. New York: Monthly Review Press.
Thornton, Archibald P.
1959   *The Imperial Idea and Its Enemies*. London: Macmillan.
Thruston, Arthur B.
1900   *African Incidents*. London: J. Murray.
Todd, John A.
1923   *The World's Cotton Crops*. London: Macmillan.
1927   *The Cotton World*. London: Pitman.
Tosh, John
1970   "The Northern Interlacustrine Region." In Richard Gray and David Birmingham (eds.), *Pre-Colonial Trade in Africa*, pp. 103–118. London: Oxford University Press.
1978a   *Clan Leaders and Colonial Chiefs in Lango: The Political History of an East African Stateless Society circa 1890-1939* . Oxford: Clarendon Press.
1978b   "Lango Agriculture during the Early Colonial Period: Land and Labour in a Cash-Crop Economy." *Journal of African History* 19:415–439.

Tothill, John D., editor
1940   *Agriculture in Uganda*. Oxford: Oxford University Press.
Trowell, Kathleen M., and K. P. Wachsmann
1953   *Tribal Crafts of Uganda*. London: Oxford University Press.
Tucker, Alfred R.
1896   "Correspondence." *Church Missionary Society Gleaner* 23:155.
1904   "A Journey to Mt. Elgon and the Bukeddi Country." *Church Missionary Intelligencer* (April):261–262.
1908   *Eighteen Years in Uganda and East Africa*. London: Edward Arnold.
Tucker, Archibald N.
1956   *The Non-Bantu Languages of North Eastern Africa*. London: Oxford University Press.
Turner, Victor M.
1964   "Witchcraft and Sorcery: Taxonomy versus Dynamics." *Africa* 34:314–324.
Twaddle, Michael J.
1966   "The Founding of Mbale." *Uganda Journal* 30(1):25–38.
1969   "Tribalism in Eastern Uganda." In Philip H. Gulliver (ed.), *Tradition and Transition in East Africa*, pp. 193–208. Berkeley and Los Angeles: University of California Press.
1972   "The Muslim Revolution in Buganda." *African Affairs* 71:54–72.
Uchendu, Victor
1969   *Field Study of Agricultural Change*. Nairobi: East African Literature Bureau.
Uchendu, Victor, and K. R. M. Anthony
1975   *Agricultural Change in Teso District, Uganda*. Nairobi: East African Literature Bureau.
Uganda Government
1962   *Atlas of Uganda*. Kampala: Uganda Government Press.
Uganda Protectorate
1921   *Uganda Protectorate Census of 1921* . Entebbe: Uganda Government Press.
1929   *Report of the Commission of Enquiry into the Cotton Industry of Uganda*. Entebbe: Uganda Government Press.
1958   *Report of the Commission of Enquiry into the Management of the Teso District Council*. Entebbe: Uganda Government Press.
Uzoigwe, G. N.
1972   "Pre-Colonial Markets in Bunyoro-Kitara." *Comparative Studies in Society and History* 41:422–455.
1974   *Britain and the Conquest of Africa: The Age of Salisbury*. Ann Arbor: University of Michigan Press.

1976   "The Victorians of East Africa, 1882–1900: The Robinson and and Gallagher Thesis Revisited." *Transafrican Journal of History* 52:32–65.

Vail, David J.
1972   *A History of Agricultural Innovation and Development in Teso District, Uganda.* Syracuse, N.Y.: Syracuse University Press.

Vandeleur, Seymour
1898   *Campaigning on the Upper Nile and Niger.* London: Methuen & Co.

Van den Bergh, J.
1901   "Correspondence." *St. Joseph's Advocate* 4:53–54.

Van Velsen, Jaap
1974   "Social Research and Social Relevances: Suggestions for a Research Policy and Some Research Priorities for the Institute of African Studies." *African Social Research* 17:517–553.

Van Zwanenberg, Roger, with Anne King
1975   *An Economic History of Kenya and Uganda, 1800–1970.* London: Macmillan.

Vere-Hodge, Edward R.
1960   *Imperial British East Africa Company.* London: Macmillan.

Vincent, Joan
1971   *African Elite: The Big Men of a Small Town.* New York: Columbia University Press.

1974a   "The Changing Role of Small Towns in the Agrarian Structure of East Africa." *Journal of Commonwealth and Comparative Politics* 12:261–275.

1974b   "Visibility and Vulnerability: The Politics of Pacemakers." *Africa* 44:222–234.

1976   "Rural Competition and the Cooperative Monopoly: A Ugandan Case Study." In June Nash, J. Dandler, and N. Hopkins (eds.), *Popular Participation in Social Change: Cooperatives, Collectives, and Nationalized Industry.* The Hague: Mouton.

1977a   "Colonial Chiefs and the Making of Class: A Case Study from Teso, Uganda." *Africa* 47(2):140–159.

1977b   "Agrarian Society and Organised Flow: Processes of Development Past and Present." *Peasant Studies* 4(2):53–65.

1978   "Teso in Transformation: Colonial Penetration in Teso District, Eastern Uganda, and its Contemporary Significance." In Lionel Cliffe, James S. Coleman, and Martin Doornbos (eds.), *Government and Rural Development in East Africa: Essays on Political Penetration.* The Hague: Martinus Nijhof.

Wadsworth, Alfred P., and Julia de Lacy Mann
1931   *The Cotton Trade and Industrial Lancashire, 1600–1780.*

Manchester, Eng.: Manchester University Press.
Wallace, Anthony F. C.
1978   *Rockdale: The Growth of an American Village in the Early Industrial Revolution*. New York: Knopf.
Wallerstein, Immanuel M.
1970   "The Colonial Era in Africa: Changes in the Social Structure." In Lewis H. Gann and Peter J. Duignan (eds.), *Colonialism in Africa, 1870–1960*, vol. 2, pp. 399–421. London: Cambridge University Press.
1974   *The Modern World System*. New York: Academic Press.
Wallerstein, Immanuel M., William G. Martin, and Torry Dickinson
1979   *Household Structures and Production Processes: Theoretical Concerns, Plus Data from Southern Africa and Nineteenth-Century United States*. Binghamton, N.Y.: Fernand Braudel Center for the Study of Economies, Historical Systems, and Civilizations.
Wallis, H. R.
1920   *Handbook of Uganda*. London: Crown Agents for the Colonies.
Watson, William
1964   "Social Mobility and Social Class in Industrial Communities." In Max Gluckman (ed.), *Closed Systems and Open Minds*. Manchester, Eng.: Manchester University Press.
Webster, John B.
1970   "Research Methods in Teso." *East African Journal* 7(2):30–38.
1972   "The Civil War in Usuku." In Bethwell A. Ogot (ed.), *War and Society in Africa*. London: Frank Cass.
Webster, John B., editor
1973   *The Iteso during the Asonya*. Nairobi: East African Publishing House.
Wells, H. G.
1918   *Mankind in the Making*. New York: Scribner.
Were, Gideon S.
1967   *A History of the Abaluyia of Western Kenya, 1500–1930*. Nairobi: East African Publishing House.
Williams, F. L.
1937   "Teso Clans." *Uganda Journal* 4(2):174–176.
Willis, John J.
1925   *An African Church in the Building*. London: Church Missionary Society.
Wilson, Godfrey
1941   *An Essay on the Economics of Detribalisation in Northern Rhodesia*. Lusaka: Rhodes-Livingstone Institute.

Wolf, Eric
1966a "Kinship, Friendship, and Patron–Client Relations in Complex Societies." In Michael Banton (ed.), *The Social Anthropology of Complex Societies*. New York: Praeger.
1966b *Peasants*. Englewood Cliffs, N.J.: Prentice-Hall.
Wolff, Richard D.
1974 *The Economics of Colonialism: Britain and Kenya, 1870–1939*. New Haven: Yale University Press.
Wood, J. G.
1868 *The Natural History of Man, Being an Account of the Manners and Customs of the Uncivilised Races of Men: Africa*. London: Routledge.
Wood, L. J.
1974 *Market Origins and Development in East Africa*. Kampala: Department of Geography, Makerere University.
Woolf, Leonard S.
1920 *Empire and Commerce in Africa: A Study in Economic Imperialism*. London: Allen & Unwin.
Wright, A. C. A.
1942 "Notes on the Iteso Social Organisation." *Uganda Journal* 9(2):57–80.
1958 "Review of the Iteso." *Uganda Journal* 22(1):89–91.
Wrigley, C. C.
1957 "Buganda: An Outline Economic History." *Economic History Review* 10(1):69–80.
1959a *Crops and Wealth in Uganda: A Short Agrarian History*. Kampala: East African Institute of Social Research.
1959b "The Christian Revolution in Buganda." *Comparative Studies in Society and History* 2:33–48.
1971 "Historicism in Africa: Slavery and State Formation." *African Affairs* 70:113–124.
Wrigley, Edward A.
1972 *Nineteenth-Century Society: Essays in the Use of Quantitative Methods for the Study of Social Data*. Cambridge: Cambridge University Press.
Young, M. Crawford
1971 "Agricultural Policy in Uganda: Capacity in Choice." In Michael F. Lofchie (ed.), *The State of the Nations: Constraints on Development in Independent Africa*. Berkeley and Los Angeles: University of California Press.
Zimmerman, Erich W.
1972 *World Resources and Industries*. New York: Harper & Row.

Index

Abonya of Angodingodi, 84, 85
Acholi, 23, 62, 73, 146, 147
Adams, W. G., 153, 246
Administration, 68, 102, 123,
124; compartmentalization of,
196, 205, 206; and cotton
activity, 203–207 passim;
effect of war on, 167;
Kakungulu's position in, 50,
59, 60, 98–99, 108, 114,
116–117; military, 39, 41, 44,
249; policy towards missions,
136–137, 247; transfers
within, 183–184
Agents: Baganda, 36, 101, 115n,
125, 126, 128, 130, 131, 165,
177, 201, 224, 236–237, 241;
and cotton production, 170,
198–201 passim; exploitation
of labor, 215, 216, 217;
restoration of, 257, 258; tax
rebates of, 150–151;
withdrawal of, 166, 167, 248
Age sets, 89, 95, 103–104
Agi of Mukongoro, 103
Agriculture, 64–65, 195–201;
arable cultivation, 195–196;
effect of iron hoes on, 173,
184; effect of plows on,
173–176; on government
farms, 189, 209; implements,
66, 174, 175; industrialization
of, 149, 158, 196; mission
instruction in, 109, 164, 178,
238; pre-colonial, 66n, 68, 79
Agu, 69, 101, 220; swamp, 63,
70, 163, 165, 167
Akokoroi River, 82, 83, 85
Alpers, Edward A., 4

America, 2, 14, 174n, 174, 175,
259
Amin, Idi, 13
Amin, Samir, 6, 112n
Amodan of Nyero, 89, 92, 94,
102, 103
Amuge of Kelim, 128, 129, 130
Amuria, 63, 74, 79, 81, 82, 140,
145, 152, 258
Arabs, 25, 37, 45, 57, 71, 72, 73,
177, 203, 260
Arms, 22, 59, 74, 131; allocation
to chiefs, 102–104 passim;
Kakungulu's, 47, 50, 58, 88;
Mutesa's, 25, 26; smuggling
of 35, 36; theft of, 244; trade
in, 2, 9, 26, 28, 72, 73, 75
Artisans, 7, 69–70, 145, 147,
158, 179, 181, 259, 260
Ashe, Rev. Robert, 35, 45
Asians, 154–156; as cotton
ginners, 209, 227; as
middlemen, 202; and middle
sector, 158; movement of,
167, 180; religious differences
among, 155; traders, 73, 119,
154–155, 178–179; troops,
53, 56

Bachopi. See Ipagero
Badama, 147
Baganda: agents, 36, 101, 115n,
125, 126, 128, 130, 131, 165,
177, 201, 224, 236–237, 241;
characteristics of, 32–33; in
Teso, 86, 88, 95–101 passim,
104–105, 125, 144, 149;
troops, 39, 47, 48n, 61, 114.
See also Estates

Designer: Al Burkhardt
Compositor: Interactive Composition Corp.
Printer: Braun-Brumfield, Inc.
Binder: Braun-Brumfield, Inc.
Text: 10/12 Sabon
Display: 16/18 Sabon